Fretboard Logic

Volume III

Bill Edwards

Bill Edwards Publishing
17329 Emerald Chase Dr
Tampa FL 33647

Dedication

For Annalee with the faraway eyes, and Evelyn who is so far away.

Special thanks to David Carlisle, Eric Statham and John Hudzietz.

Teachers who wish to use this method may purchase it at a special discount by contacting us directly. We maintain an online database for the purpose of referring both teachers and students who are using Fretboard Logic in their area.
For a listing in our registry please contact us at:

Bill Edwards Publishing Corp.
17329 Emerald Chase Dr
Tampa FL 33647-3516
(813) 985-2689 Phone
(813) 615-0123 Phone
(813) 971-9222 Fax
mail@billedwards.com Email
billedwards.com Website

Printed in the United States of America

Contents

Our destination is never a place but rather
a new way of looking at things.

Henry Miller

Preface

In the film "The Karate Kid," an old master has been persuaded to take on a young boy as a student. But first the boy must prove his desire to learn and his ability to take instruction. Before they can begin the lessons, the inscrutable one asks for help with a few things around the house, and is very particular about the way these tasks are performed. This goes on for some time and the kid's faith is tested along with his endurance. After what seemed an eternity of painting fences, sanding floors and polishing cars, he figures that the old geezer has suckered him for free labor and gotten his house and cars renovated in the deal. The kid finally decides he's not getting any useful information in the ass-kicking department and starts to walk. At this point the old one reveals how the boy had been mastering the fundamentals all along. I loved that part.

Volume I of the Fretboard Logic series was an explanation of how the guitar works and it was pretty easy. Volume II was a guitar-oriented approach to the tonal elements of music, and it wasn't very easy. Now you'll be exposed to a wide range of interrelated guitar and music concepts and it'll have nothing to do with easy. But, like the kid, maybe after your faith and endurance are tested, you will have a greater impact on people.

Education is the process of moving from cocksure ignorance to thoughtful uncertainty.

Utvich

Introduction

The Fretboard Logic series originated because of a discovery that there was a specific pattern organization to the playing area of the guitar that was only partially understood by most players. The first book revealed these patterns and relationships as a result of the pitch selection of the open strings, and independent of any musical considerations such as theory, technique or style. This pattern organization is unique in the field of musical instrument design. It can be considered the instrument's interface, and the one aspect of guitar playing that all the others have in common, and so should be learned first. Because of the guitar's unusual tuning, EADGBE, and its intervallic result (4th, 4th, 4th, 3rd, 4th), three fundamental and integral form or pattern types occur: chord forms, scale forms, and lead patterns. There are five basic chord forms, five basic scale forms and two basic lead patterns. The chordal facet of this pattern organization has long been referred to as the "CAGED System." Volume I presented all three aspects as a *unified operating system* for guitar players regardless of style or level.

In Volume II the tonal aspects of music were reduced to their most basic elements in a guitar orientation. When considering pitch alone, groups of notes can only be played two ways: either simultaneously or consecutively, and are expressed as vertical or horizontal groupings when notated. When played together they are known collectively as chords, and there are two main families which have either three or four different notes. When the notes are played separately, they are known as scales and there are two primary (major and minor) and several secondary (modes and variations) types. A third tone group, arpeggios, is derived when chord tones are played separately like scales. These basic tonal elements were presented in the context of the pattern organization of the guitar as outlined in Volume I, so that each could be *constructed* by combining its music identity, or formula with a specific fretboard form. Learning them in the context of the pattern organization of Vol. I eliminated the overwhelming task of having to memorize vast numbers of seemingly unrelated patterns in order to have a useful tonal vocabulary. The different types of chords, scales, and arpeggios make up what can be considered the essential tonal materials of the musician.

With that in mind, consider that at the moment we decided to become guitarists, we entered a universe in which many systems were already in place by the time we arrived. We can choose to ignore them and continually reinvent the wheel and rediscover fire, or come to grips with them and pursue higher objectives. As varied and numerous as they are, these systems fall into two main categories: those that are man-made and those that occur in nature. An example of a man-made system is the twelve tone system whereby each octave is divided into twelve equal parts. A related system that occurs naturally is the overtone series whereby each different tone is comprised of numerous parts, or partials, which give each sound a unique and recognizable acoustical "fingerprint."

The overall strategy for maintaining cohesion in Vol. III amongst these myriad fields of information is to delineate and define them within a kind of hierarchy. That way, anytime a new area of endeavor is encountered, it will be perceived as an integral part of a whole, instead of just another in a seemingly endless line of disjointed sections and random events. This hierarchy is presented in the form of a *menu* on page 3, where the interrelated facets of the guitar and music are presented for selection from available choices to be varied and combined with others. Our tactics for implementing this approach will be the practical application of the material presented in Volumes I and II from two fundamentally different points of view: Creativity and Analysis. Basically, analysis poses the question, "What is?" Creativity poses the question, "What can be?" The tonal elements of Vol. II can be considered the *what* of music, as in what is being played, and the rhythmic, melodic, technical, sonic, etc., aspects of Vol. III can be considered the *how*, as in how it is being played. To further the analogy, Vol. I showed *where* it can be played.

As a practical matter, guitarists, like other musicians, usually find themselves in the position of either replicating the works of others or else trying to develop ideas of their own. These seemingly opposite types of circumstances often require similar capabilities expressed differently. The idea here is to enable the guitarist to approach either type of situation equipped with the right tools, skills and materials for the job, whether it is to grasp the workings of someone else's music or to construct his or her own from raw materials.

The guitar and its music will be explored here in a different way than what you may have been used to. Any guitarist who's played for a while has learned how to acquire the music he or she wants to play, usually by reading or by ear. Volume III attempts to present you with the means to understand what you are playing to the point of being able to create original musical expressions in similar styles.

In the preceding volumes, the scope of each was relatively narrow and the focus was on areas of comprehension that plagued most players because of its subtlety in the first case, and its seeming enormity in the second. From here on, our aperture of awareness must widen to encompass the many different directions that different individuals may wish to explore as a matter of personal preference. In Vols. I and II, in the interest of cohesion and as the difficulty increased, the structure of the books was *linear*, in that each section built on what preceded it. Vol. III assumes that you have absorbed and are functional with that material so that you can pursue more advanced goals and the structure is non-linear. In other words, going directly from one section to the next isn't necessarily required for comprehension. The order will be up to each individual. The use of the term "advanced" in this case means the ability to combine and vary basic elements in the creative context, and to recognize and reproduce them in the analytical context. It is not intended to convey the relative difficulty of the work as a whole or in part. However, as before, there will be both mental and physical challenges.

The overall philosophy of the series is that it is not effective to spend all your time stockpiling billions of bits of information for later usage. It makes more sense to put just a few things to immediate use in a practical application, rather than remain a warehouse for truckloads of unused ideas, techniques, and abilities. To that end, Vol. III provides material which is intended to be a vehicle for the guitarist to better understand the music with which he or she as individuals are involved.

Systems

Whenever a person makes a decision to learn the guitar, they unknowingly enter a vast network of interrelated systems that existed long before that decision was made. This section is an attempt to come to terms with a few of those systems, and put them into some kind of perspective with one another. The most fundamental division of those systems already in place is the natural vs. man made systems.

Natural - Physical and Physiological

The natural systems can be further divided into the physical, or outer world, and our human physiology, or our inner world. We use the science of physics to understand our outer world and acoustics is the branch that deals with low frequency vibrations or those within the range of human hearing. Acoustics is the science of sound which forms a basis by which we are furnished explanations for many of the properties of music. The physiological aspects we are concerned with are the ways in which we perceive and relate to sound in general; organized sound, or music, in particular. A property of sound as it pertains to the way we perceive music, is the overtone series. Overtones are a naturally occurring series of intervals, which give each sound its timbre, or individual quality by which we distinguish it from others. Every sound has overtones, or harmonics, and sounds produced by musical instruments can be distinguished by a harmonic "fingerprint" in the form of the relative strength of its overtones. The physical properties of a musical instrument determine the quality of its tone or timbre, and therefore to some extent, how we perceive the music to be played on it. The tonal qualities produced by the different types of guitars are interpreted by the listener as a kind of precondition to the music played on them. The cultural and emotive character of music produces physiological responses in us that are both separate to our social milieu and common to us as people. For example, you and your grandparents likely do not share the same tastes in popular music, but you probably would have responded similarly to the "shark approach" theme in the movie "Jaws."

Man Made - Instrumental and Musical

The first division to be made in the man made systems are those systems that pertain to the instrument and those that pertain to music. The physical properties and design of an instrument determine how sounds are produced and controlled. In each (non-electronic) musical instrument, sound is generated when an elastic body is caused to vibrate. The elastic bodies include stretched materials such as hides, metal, plastic, etc., enclosed columns of air such as are found in windblown instruments, elongated tines and tubes, and all manner of materials of varying densities and shapes. These tone generators are generally accompanied by a device or devices which both amplify and control the vibration. In the guitar, the vibrating bodies are in the form of strings usually made of metal, or plastic. The amplification has traditionally been in the form of resonating chambers of wood or other suitable materials, but modern electronics has enabled significant improvements in this area. The control of the frequency of the vibrations has been achieved by means of strips of wood, metal, etc., termed frets, placed at specified intervals along a playing surface of the instrument termed the fretboard. The spacing of these frets are a result of compromises between the optimal tuning given the overtone series, and the optimal functionality given the twelve tone system and the way we use it to produce music in note groupings termed keys.

Systems

The primary man made guitar system, meaning the one most essential to the player, is the pattern organization which results from the way the instrument is tuned string by string. It becomes an interface for the player to more adequately operate the instrument as a true polyphonic, given the limitation of four fingers and a thumb on the fretting hand.

The primary man made music system is the twelve tone system whereby the tones within a range termed an octave, or a frequency and its double, are separated into twelve relatively even divisions. The guitar's tuning system should be distinguished from the even tempered system of tuning used by all (western) instruments for about the last three centuries. Even tempering specifies the exact frequencies of those twelve tones relative to one another such that certain resultant intervals are more accurate than others. In even tempering, the octave is the benchmark interval and the others are adjusted to compensate for this.

Overlaying the even tempered tuning system is another music interface called a key. A key is a system of fewer than twelve notes, usually seven, in a specific intervallic sequence (whole and half step increments) such that one is equivalent to another. In other words, from a given starting note, termed a tonic, target note or keynote, a key is a group of notes related by their intervallic structure. The key of E is the functional equivalent of the key of Ab, which is the equivalent to F#, and so on. Their intervallic equivalence determines their functional equivalence. In yet another sense, a key is the intervallic relationship of tones with a common center which we perceive similarly as humans by virtue of a common aesthetic, or physiological interpretation.

From this reduction and centering we term a key, are derived the tonal materials we use to produce music. Those tonal materials are the interval, chord, scale, and arpeggio. Each of these tone groupings are derived from a key as independent yet related music elements.

Beyond the tonal materials are the other parts of the musical experience, including the all important rhythmic materials. The time values, beats, etc., of music are, in a sense, its life force. They give music its dynamic qualities and represent a completely separate set of systems from the tone groups.

Intervals, chords, scales, and arpeggios are among the basic tonal units which, when combined with rhythmic materials produce what we perceive as music, which when further combined with other influences, including cultural or social influences, produce music of various styles. The process of coming to an understanding of music of different types involves recognizing the various components and systems which tend to be general to the style and specific to the piece.

The menu which follows is an attempt to arrange and correlate the various systems and subsystems which are related to the guitar and music. It can be used to both understand the music of others and help you develop your own ideas.

Guitar Player Menu

Fretboard Forms

Chord Forms
Scale Forms
Lead Patterns

Tonal Materials

Target Notes
Intervals
Chords
Scales
Arpeggios

Rhythmic Materials

Durations
Beats
Measures
Tempo
Accents
Syncopation
Rubato

Tonality/Modality

Major
Minor
Dorian
Phrygian
Lydian
Mixolydian
Locrian
Chromaticism
Variations

Melodic Material

Intervallic Motion
Scale Segments
Arpeggio Segments
Compound Segments

Harmonic Material

Key Areas
Chord Progression
  Cadences
Modulation
  Secondary Dominants
  Diminished Chords
  Function Shifting
  Tonality Shifting
  Chromaticism

Arrangement

Guitar in a Group
  Rhythm Comping
  Riffing
  Lead Playing
Solo Guitar
  Trad. Voice Leading
  Alternating Bass Style
  Counterpoint
  Chord-Melody Style

Right Hand Styles

Pick Style
Finger/Nail Style
Nashville Style

Articulation Techs.

Pull-Offs
Hammer-Ons
Slides
Mutes
Harmonics
Bends
Tremolos
Vibratos

Iterations

Fours
Threes
Twos
Ones
Multiples
Direction
  Ascending
  Descending

Sonics and Effects

Amplification
Tone & Equalization
Reverb & Delay
Distortion
Flanging
Chorus
Phase Shifting
Compression
Vibrato
Tremolo
Harmonizers
Wah
Volume
Tremolo Bar

Music Styles

Classical
  Baroque
  Romantic
  Flamenco and Spanish
Popular Music
  Folk and Bluegrass
  Blues
  Rock & Roll
  Hard Rock & Metal
  Country
  Jazz
Fusions

Guitar Types

Nylon String Classical
Steel String Acoustic
Semi-Hollow Body El.
Solid Body Electric
Hybrids

Physiological Responses

Hypnotic/Head-Banging
Inspired/Religious Fervor
Exhilarated/Breathless
Excited/Dance Fever
Unmoved/Hesitant
Boredom/Disinterest
Embarrassment/Discomfort
Worry/Unease
Melancholy/Moody
Misery/Revulsion

Systems

Natural
  Physical World
  Low Frequency Vib.
  Overtone Series
Man-Made
  Twelve Tone System
    Equal Temperament
    Key

Analysis

Analysis is the separation of a whole into its constituent parts. In the field of chemistry, the term also applies to determining the proportions of those parts. The concept of (a reduction to) elements and their proportions provides us with both a qualitative and quantitative means for understanding music. In order to provide an understanding the different types of guitar music, the common elements are listed in a menu fashion. This way, the music styles that you as an individual are interested in can be seen in terms of how each piece is composed of these elements, and then consider them in terms of each element's relative significance to the overall result. The process of analysis began with the fretboard geometry of Vol. I, where the guitar's patterns were separated from everything else, and continued into Vol. II where the primary tone groupings were isolated and examined as individual sections of a larger whole. When separating music into component parts, we must always be concerned with the plurality of the systems with which we're involved. At the very least, the musical nature of things must always be balanced with the guitaristic nature. As guitar players, we are always having to think in parallel - the issues of music must always be expressed on the guitar for application's sake, and what is executed on the guitar must always be translated into musical meanings for comprehension's sake.

The method of analysis presented here varies from the conventional approach in a number of ways. First, it is guitar oriented in that there are things here that won't apply to other instruments. Second, it takes into account both traditional and more modern techniques and capabilities. In the past, music analysis has been a process of separating and categorizing primarily the pitch and time values, plus such secondary considerations as tempo, dynamics, and other expressive characteristics. Some might suppose then, that music written in standard notation is reduced to its most basic elements and therefore analyzed. Not so. Standard notation specifies much but explains little. Notating can, however, be a vehicle by which pitch, time, and other values can be interpreted. Our method for analysis will use a macro-micro perspective whereby we'll try to see the larger picture with sharpness and contrast without losing focus in the minutia.

As a matter of fact, there are a great many guitarists who are and will remain satisfied with simply being able to function well enough to perform for audiences. For them it is enough to be appreciated as performers. Nothing wrong with that. But since they usually only have a superficial understanding of the things they play, they run into comprehension problems when they try to grasp what made it worth the effort in the first place. At least part of the reason for this has to be that they don't have the necessary tools, methods, or experience to deal with it adequately. Another reason is the time and effort of the learning process itself. If they have learned by a reading method, they are usually absorbed with the ongoing effort of converting and retaining written symbols into dynamically played tone groups, with little mental energy left over for anything besides committing it to memory and polishing it up through repetition. If they've cast their lot with learning by ear, they have more than a passing familiarity with trial and error, and that can be frustrating, tedious, and exhausting as well. On the other hand, understanding the different facets and levels of what we are playing makes us more than guitarists - it makes us musicians.

Consider our eyes and ears as sensory input devices. Learning by ear and learning by reading symbols are equally valid because it is the brain that finally sorts out the information for further use. As far as validity is concerned, maybe its just the old left brain-right brain argument again. There are advantages and disadvantages to both ways. Learning to analyze music will be beneficial regardless of your preferences with regard to input. The object, perhaps, is to be able to think on the level of the composer who thought enough of his ideas to commit them to some form of media in the first place.

Functioning within the fretboard pattern organization and constructing the tonal elements seemed to be the La Brea tar pits of comprehension for a lot of guitarists. To keep from getting similarly bogged down in the next levels, we're going to separate the other aspects and then recombine them for learning purposes. The metaphor of the Chinese menu is how we'll relate to the different areas of involvement. In essence, we've provided sets and subsets of the guitar player's tools, materials, and methods, and you can select from these possibilities to understand the music you like. In this fashion, you'll be able to analyze other people's music and later reverse the process and try to develop some ideas of your own as a matter of creative selection and variation from available choices.

It will soon become obvious that Vol. III does not aspire to be merely a collection of pieces to be learned for performance. If you want to learn a particular piece of music, to paraphrase the slogan, just learn it. Our efforts are in the direction of enabling you to make sense out of things, ie., no more "guitarist see - guitarist do." The idea is to offer various things of significance for guitarists ready to cross over to a higher level of understanding in different areas. If what is being demonstrated is obvious to one guitarist, it may be just on the edge of comprehension for another, and completely out of reach of yet another. Although each of us is limited by our own experience (and lack of it) we constantly rely upon our frames of reference to further our abilities and understanding. The ability to reduce a piece of music to its component parts can enable us to understand and appreciate the thinking of other composers.

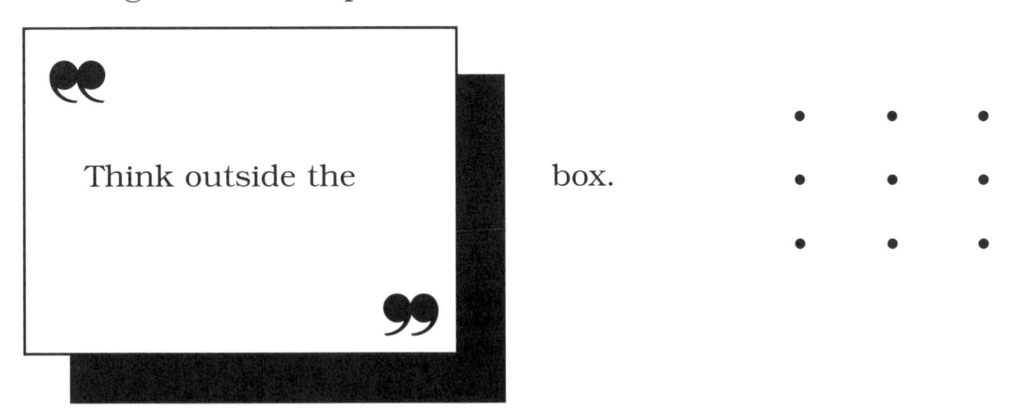

I think this oft-repeated quote originated years ago when the popular brain teaser above was making the rounds. I'm going to include it in hopes you haven't yet seen it. The object of the puzzle is to connect all the dots with only four straight lines and without lifting your writing implement. The solution is printed elsewhere in the book. You can use your brain and work it out or flip pages hunting for the answer - your choice - and perhaps destiny.

Creativity

When it comes to creativity, people usually fall on either side of a line that divides what you might call intellectual optimists and pessimists. The intellectual pessimist is perhaps somewhat over-educated and easily sees the copying done by their less insightful and shorter-memoried counterparts. The intellectual optimist views the world as an oyster, and doesn't need a lot of rules and regulations to weigh him down while he scours oceans of opportunities for inspirational pearls. Somewhere in between the soft-heads who think that every little thing they do is new and special, and those hard-heads who say with complete certainty that there's nothing new under the sun, is a world of learning and imagination that propels us into the future insight by insight.

The question becomes how to determine what constitutes truly creative effort and what falls short. From my own nebulous experiences with the invention business and the PTO (Patent and Trademark Office), I learned a few lessons that may be of use in addressing that question or at least better understanding what's at stake. As you can probably imagine, along with a few truly original ideas, the PTO gets a lot of useless and preposterous stuff sent their way. They also get scams that are simply attempts to corner a particular market for profit since patents can be very profitable things. On the other hand, it costs money to get patents, so you don't see too many people trying to simply reinvent the wheel. However, a lot of folks wouldn't hesitate to retread it and submit it for a 17 year monopoly to manufacture.

So how does the PTO separate the wheat from the chaff? First of all they categorize the different areas of endeavor so that their examiners don't have to be experts in every possible field. Such categories include mechanical designs, chemical compounds, electronics, plant hybrids, etc. The important part of the examination process deals with an invention meeting three simple tests: utility, novelty and non-obviousness; simple criteria, but not easily understood or met.

The utility part means that first of all, it has to function as described, and do something useful. This is a means of preventing people from getting into what could be termed the "patent application business" where they take out a patent on every idea under the sun and wait till something gets produced and try to license it as their intellectual property. The bottom line is that you don't get patents (or copyrights) on ideas per se, but on *the expression of an idea*, and if you don't remember anything else, remember that. The difference between an idea and the form that idea takes is a fundamental creative issue for the PTO.

The novelty part means an invention must exhibit a newness and uniqueness that separates it from what already exists. The novelty aspect of the patent process is somewhat subjective on the part of the examiners, but they work hard to keep from looking like idiots to their bosses and review boards, and yet still issue patents where merited. The novelty aspect of an invention is more than just common sense, but in fact is not too difficult to judge since they can look up whether it or anything similar has been done before. Not only must the examiners use their experience and training to judge whether an invention meets the newness criteria, but the patent applicant must actually disclose all he knows pertaining to the subject, where he learned it, and how his invention improves on everything else in the field.

The non-obviousness criteria is by far the most subtle part of a patent application. It can also be the most hotly contested when an examiner disallows claims based upon it. Non-obviousness means that an average person termed "skilled in the art" wouldn't have thought of the invention. This is a kind of creative leap that separates true imagination from ordinary smarts.

The criteria of novelty, utility, and non-obviousness are certainly not necessary to demonstrate originality in music, but it is a pretty good overall strategy. In the music business, our creative output usually conforms to a particular genre such as the song, sonata, concerto, opera, etc. Most guitarists will find themselves writing songs as a vehicle for their self expression. As musicians we'll either be working solo, or with others. In the case of collaborative efforts, the creative process can take on new dimensions. In a larger sense, the job is to come up with new sounds and new ways of saying old things.

The idea of creativity can perhaps be viewed as an awareness of available resources rather than some unattainable genius ability conferred upon a precious few individuals. There is ample evidence that creativity is not limited to the super intelligent or gifted. In other words if you have a place to work, plus the raw materials, tools, and techniques, creativity can be a matter of choices from available options. After all, what is it that constitutes the difference between what is considered advanced and basic? It's possible that advanced guitaring should be considered nothing more than creative combinations and variations of the basics. To that end you are invited to explore the guitar player menu. These options will include resources, tools, and methods. From the menu we can make conscious selections of what is available until the process becomes familiar and more essential considerations can be explored.

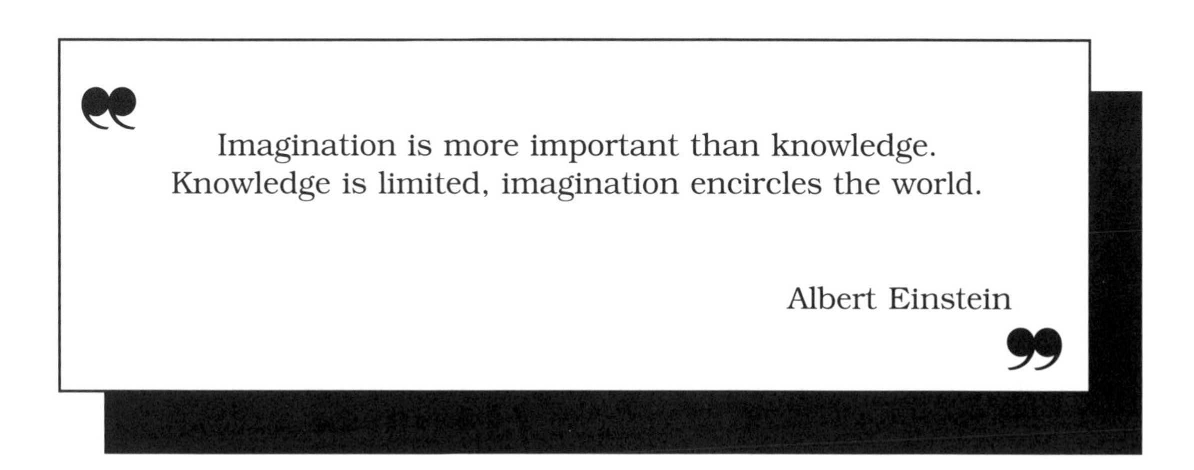

Learning and Memory

At some point in the development of this book, it became apparent that in order for progress to be made, it would be necessary to get involved with things that could not be anticipated at the outset. The whole time this series was being developed, it seemed that there was something missing - perhaps a common thread to hold everything together. Eventually the universal characteristic became evident, and that was, at its essence, playing guitar is a learning experience. Seems less than earth shattering, maybe, until you try to define what learning really is. We all recognize when we know something, but we seldom contemplate the things we don't know, because we aren't sufficiently aware to consider them in the first place. It is easy to take for granted the learning process. For example, why does it work when it works, and why doesn't it *always* work? As teachers and students, we have to accept that in order for better progress to be made, both parties have to become progressively better at what we do. Assuming one teaches guitar, how can he or she do this job better without at some point focusing on the teaching itself? On the other hand, how can one learn guitar, without also knowing more about the learning part? Monkey-see, monkey-do only goes so far.

There are some things that should be taught and some things that are better left up to each student to determine for him or herself. Knowing which is which is not easy. What is easy for both parties, is falling into that trap that insists "The right way is this way" - meaning *my* way or more commonly, the way *I* learned. An example of a fundamental approach is whether a student should use a pick or his fingers to vibrate the strings with his right hand. Many instructors have no hesitation instructing students to do it one way or another not realizing that to a great extent it is the teacher's own personal preference and is not really a matter of what the student needs or finds easiest. Even sensitive teachers would suggest this is simply a matter of what style of music is being played but that ignores the innumerable exceptions that make the rules.

Deciding what and what not to teach is no mean feat, and it pervades every level of endeavor. For example, say I recommend that a student use a pick, do I also say what kind of pick to use and which fingers to hold it with; how to hold it, and whether to aim the leading edge upward or downward and so on ad infinitum? I believe these are among the things that should be decided and implemented for oneself, and then constantly audited and improved upon. The catch is, that to accomplish certain things, it is necessary to follow certain guidelines. For example, in order to be able to, say, play a "false harmonic," it is necessary to hold the pick in such a way that the side of the thumb contacts the string on the way past. You could read an entire book about it, look at a thousand pictures, watch the teacher do it over and over and still, you'd have to employ a certain amount of trial and error until you can make it happen for yourself. Every student should consciously and aggressively critique what teachers teach for its intrinsic value, relevance and rightness, and remember that reduction to practice, as the patent office terms it, is his or her own responsibility. If you don't necessarily agree with the way things are done here or anywhere else, try another way. To some extent, it boils down to who makes the decisions, and ultimately we each make our own.

With that said, I want to try to give you a value for the learning experience and a perspective you may not have considered. I haven't met too many people who don't have a lot of day to day problems, and with few exceptions, think that most of those problems could be solved with money and lots of it. In growing up in our era (and most others I suspect) we've grown accustomed to believe that money is THE THING. Granted, with perhaps the exception of the computer, it is our most evolved tool. But if you think about it, intelligence is worth way more than money. If you have (the right) intelligence then you can get money, but not the other way around or else you wouldn't always hear about fools and their money being soon parted. But what exactly is intelligence? Most psychologists agree that more than anything else, it is the ability to learn. If you can learn, then you can have intelligence to get money and almost anything else you need. So when it comes down to it, learning is THE THING.

So what is this thing, learning? If, like most people, you've never actually tried to put it into words, learning can be considered the process by which changes in behavior result from experience or practice. This behavior includes any response by means of feelings, thoughts, or actions. This also includes muscular and also glandular activities, which we won't go into. I believe the essence here is change and its process. Changing the way we do things is fundamental to learning. The process varies.

It is also interesting to note that learning is not considered temporary. When we say, "Its like riding a bike - once you learn, you never really forget," we are referring to a change in our abilities that is more or less permanent. Learning and memory are integral to one another. When you learn to make a G chord, as in when you learn to ride a bike, definitive learning has occurred since you have changed what you can do through experience and practice, and you'll never completely forget how it is done. On the other hand, I freely admit that I've recognized questions in Trivial Pursuit or on Jeopardy that I'd even heard the answers to before, and yet I miss them time and again. (Eg. from Trivial Pursuit: How many "bouncing Johnsons" were on the court for the 1986 NBA championship playoffs?) The problem, I believe, is that I don't have a place for many kinds of information in my frame of reference. I suppose I could try to memorize the answer for the next time but usually the questions weren't all that relevant to me. We shouldn't forget that we are products of an education system that features an emphasis on performance in the form of test taking, in which students are motivated to retain a broad range of surface information just long enough to make the grade. Later on we tend to forget what we studied for lack of application. True learning involves a permanent change in the way we do things.

It is generally accepted that there are at least four discernible types of learning. They are known as classical conditioning, instrumental conditioning, multiple response learning, and insight learning. In each of these methods there is something of value, so we'll examine what each type is first and then how it relates to us as guitar players.

Classical conditioning is the Pavlovian thing. In case you haven't yet heard of Ivan Pavlov, he was a Russian scientist who experimented with dogs by ringing bells etc., at their feedings over a period of time so that the dogs would eventually "learn" to salivate any time the bell itself was rung. Ok, so we got into a gland thing. The key elements of classical conditioning are the stimulus, the response, and the reinforcer. Whenever the dogs learned to salivate to a bell, the reinforcer was the food, the stimulus was the bell and the the response was dog drool all over Ivan's floor. This type of learning is noteworthy because the stimulus and the response can be of widely divergent natures and conditioned learning may still occur.

Learning and Memory

Instrumental conditioning is the type of learning usually associated with B. F. Skinner. It is also known as shaping and trial and error behavior. I heard an amusing story about instrumental conditioning a long time ago, about a class of college kids who conspired to shape a novice professor. Before the first class they all agreed that no one would respond to his lecture unless he happened to raise his voice, and then they'd all perk up for a short while. Throughout the period, the professor tried valiantly to engage his bored class until finally by the end of the period, he was pretty much yelling at the top of his lungs without realizing it. Mr. Skinner's research focused on an element termed an operant whereby a learned response operates within an environment to produce an effect of some sort. Here's a sobering example to remember the next time you're squared off against a one-armed bandit in a Las Vegas casino. When a person plays a slot machine, the occasional chump change payoff (the operant) elicits the desired response of having the environment (the chump) put more money into it. Skinner used rats to demonstrate his theories on learning. He'd put a hungry rat with a willingness to learn into a cage with a lever connected to a food supply and pretty soon it could pass the bar exam. (Couldn't resist.) The term *shaping* refers to the proximate aspects of this type of learning. The rats wouldn't just walk up and stomp on the lever and when they did hit it accidentally, they didn't automatically put two and two together. The process was gradual and the rat's behavior was shaped to hit the lever over a period of time. At first it was rewarded for being in close enough proximity to hit the lever without intending to. The intent resulted later as a learned response to the lever-food relationship.

Multiple response learning involves combining simple movement sequences together to create more complex chains of movement patterns. Learning to use a typewriter or keyboard is an example of multiple response learning. An untrained typist will poke at individual keys and letters using only one or two fingers at first. This inefficient method must sooner or later be replaced by a system that specifies certain keys be struck with certain fingers from basic hand positions. Through repetition of this method, the typist is eventually able to type out words as wholes. The whole word level continues until sentences come together as wholes. Each level uses a combination of sequences derived from the previous levels until, if you're Isaac Asimov, you sit down at the typewriter and get up later with an entire book. Since rats don't type, they put 'em in mazes. When a rat is in a maze, he'll always come to a point at which he has to make a choice to, say, turn left or right and only one choice is correct. His learning is a sequence of correct turn choices combined and remembered. It is also notable that the beginning and the end of the maze is significantly easier to learn than the middle. This is true of many endeavors such as chess, jigsaw puzzles, and guess what else.

Insight learning is closely associated with problem solving. It occurs by understanding the separate components of a problem and their relationships to one another. Insight is often the result of pondering something for a period of time until all at once a not-so-obvious solution becomes apparent. We've all heard success stories where people say "The idea hit me like a bolt from the blue!" and the like. These types of statements serve to underscore the sudden impact this kind of learning can have on us. A psychologist named Wolfgang Kohler experimented with chimps and documented cases of insight learning. The primates, who share 97% of DNA with humans, were presented with out-of-reach food, a stick and a box. First they tried to jump to the food but it was too high. The stick was usually next but it was too short by itself. They would try the box by itself, but it was also too short. The chimps eventually tried combinations of stick-jumping and box-jumping until after a while they tried the stick and the box together and reached the food. They were able to reason through the relationship between the stick and the box to solve the banana problem.

I have personally experienced insight learning on a few occasions and I'm not convinced that it is always a totally conscious process. In one instance I'd been trying to design yet another gizmo for the guitar market. I wanted to convert one of those Skil cordless screw guns for use as a powered guitar string winder for music stores, roadies, and lazy rich kids. The problem, of course, was that they were geared for driving screws which meant high torque and low speed, which was the opposite of what was needed for winding the strings onto the machine head posts. A friend of mine happens to be a brilliant mechanical engineer so I put the problem to him saying I wanted to double the speed and halve the torque (which was too specific, I later found out). He looked the gearbox over and quickly calculated that it couldn't be done without changing the shaft placement which was totally impractical, so I just dropped it altogether - or so I thought. A few weeks later as I was waking up, I “saw” the gears in an orientation that would do the job. It wasn't precisely double the ratio but in fact, higher with even lower torque which wouldn't break strings. I had the problem in the back of my mind as they say, and my subconscious produced an insight solution for me. The interesting thing in retrospect is that my conscious mind was convinced that it couldn't be done. Ooh, it makes me wonder.

What is the key to retaining what we have learned? First of all, it is fairly well established that in learning, we build upon what we already know: our frame of reference. The concept of a frame of reference pertains to the background of firm knowledge necessary to be able to understand and apply new ideas and information. For example, you aren't going to have much luck solving calculus problems without having requisite skills in algebra, etc. Before you can do algebra, you need to know the basic math functions of addition, subtraction, multiplication, etc. Basic math is a frame of reference for algebra, and algebra provides one for calculus. On the other hand, we've all experienced teaching systems that could accurately be termed garbage because a load of information gets dumped into students's brains as if they were merely filling up a container. Then they slam down the lid with a test, and expect the student to grasp and integrate it all out of fear of failure. A presumption is made that the student already has the necessary frame of reference to proceed and that isn’t always the case. Beyond the necessity of a foundation upon which to build, there are three types of memory which we employ to retain what we learn. These are sensory memory, short term memory, and long term memory.

Sensory memory is the ability to retain information which we receive through sight, hearing, touch, smell, and taste. If you think about it, it's easy to remember the taste of ketchup, the smell of popcorn or the feel of sandpaper. The trails sparklers leave at night are a visual form of sensory memory. Short term memory is the “desktop” we use to hold a bit of unsupported information such as a telephone number we just looked up, just long enough to complete the call. Long term memory is that “file cabinet” of seemingly limitless amounts of information we store indefinitely. Long term memory takes three main forms: procedural, episodic and semantic. Riding a bike is an example of procedural memory. Remembering where you bought your first guitar is an episodic recollection. Semantic, or meanings memory is the ability to recall facts and figures such as names, dates, meanings of words, etc.

Learning and Memory

The most difficult things to remember, not surprisingly, are the ones which haven't occurred yet. The term for things to remember to remember, is prospective memory. Prospective memory can be both short and long term, and has given rise to an entire industry of devices such as calendars, datebooks, PDAs and day planners, in many forms from low to very high tech, all designed to help us recall the future.

There is another, more delicate aspect of learning that I feel needs to be discussed, since it is at the very heart of both the process and what we are about. It's not something we usually think about when we think of the learning experience, but that may be because it isn't about *thought* processes per se. It concerns both how we feel about what we're learning, and how we feel when we're learning it. Our emotions play a pivotal role in the learning process and that can work for or against us. When we feel good about what we are learning, it doesn't matter how difficult the work is, because we will rise to the occasion. If we don't feel good about it it doesn't matter how easy it is either because it will impede our progress to the point where we may question the very purpose of our endeavors and the validity of continuing any further. When learning, we are also subject to our present moment feelings. It's hard to be tired, stressed out, nervous or in any way emotionally off balance, and have an effective learning experience. The solution is to monitor ourselves and try to determine if anything is getting in the way of our ability to learn effectively and deal with it as directly as we can. In case you hadn't noticed, we seldom learn under ideal conditions.

Have you ever noticed that we tend to think in specific terms when discussing thinking and more generally when speaking of our emotional state? We always say "*What* do you think?" and "*How* do you feel?" to describe our states of mind and heart. Saying "How do you think?" and "What do you feel?" seems to go against logical convention, but perhaps there is something to be gained by changing the emphasis so that we directly address the way we feel and are less certain about our thought processes.

Many learning disabilities can be traced back to earlier emotional trauma of some sort or another, some related to the learning process itself. Few, if any of us, run the gauntlet of our education systems unscathed. In fact many of us get damaged by ignorant, insensitive or impatient teachers (and dare I say parents?) who fail to grasp that we each have special needs, speeds, and abilities. In fact, if we have had enough unsuccessful learning experiences, we may be pre-programmed to fail because we've lost confidence in ourselves, the teachers, or the system itself. Naturally, most of us manage to muddle on anyway, or if we're lucky, we get repaired by those wonderful people who take the job of teaching seriously, intelligently and sensitively. My personal observation is that the learning process is at once, stimulating and exhausting. What's more, when learning, we all put our self esteem on the line, and set ourselves up to occasionally look stupid. If the teacher understands the amount of inherent risk and stress this involves, they may make the extra effort to try to relieve it and make the process more relaxed and enjoyable. Humor works wonders. Funny teachers, like most funny people, are exceptional human beings. And even if they aren't always funny, at least their attempts to redistribute the vulnerability will be appreciated by all but the most cynical - as long as it doesn't get in the way of the learning. The effects of learning are cumulative and restorative, and just one profoundly positive experience can more than make up for several so-called failures.

Learning and Memory

I've always felt that excelling in the public and private joys of music is a good way for the rest of us to compensate for not having the physical advantages or the jocks or the mental advantages of the honor students.

So, having discussed learning and memory in general, we'll now attempt to relate the different types to our more specific efforts with the guitar. Classical conditioning obviously works best for the classical guitar. (Heh. Just wanted to see if you were still awake.) Classical and instrumental conditioning are types of training where a significant amount of repetition is necessary for the learning to occur. They are reward-dependent but in different ways. Pavlov's experiments were a direct association between the sounds and the food repeated over a period of time. Skinner's boxes were an indirect association between the levers and the food that became a direct association after a sufficient number of repetitions. These types of learning have much in common with the technical or physical requirements of the guitar. There is no substitute for repetition in order to acquire physical coordination (conditioning) on a musical instrument and the guitar is certainly no exception. With very few exceptions, beginning students grossly underestimate the physical requirements of the guitar. As we each approximate rightness in our playing, we convert an indirect learning experience to a direct one. As stated earlier, many of the physical aspects of playing defy analysis and simply have to be attempted, failed and re-attempted to be understood. This process of constantly shaping our own behavior is even more essential than the task itself as it forms the method by which we measure ourselves against each successive task. As the various objectives approximate rightness, not only are we able to perform with increasing precision, but we can carry over those new found abilities to more demanding future goals. The frequency of repetition is the essence of the procedural mastery necessary for guitar virtuosity. In other words, how many times and over what period of time will you have to repeat something before you can do it to your own satisfaction with little if any possibility of error? Secondly, how long can you maintain that level of accuracy without having to practice (or worse, reacquire) it again? Answer number one: many. Answer number two: not very long. What you have is a conditioning continuum where each piece of music not only has to be acquired but also maintained or else it degrades. With time and consistency of effort, we can hope to eventually bask in the comfort of the overall technical accomplishment that is so often associated with guitar mastery. But don't count on it.

The learning method most easily associated with guitar is multiple response learning. Naturally. The idea of joining small fragments, such as movement sequences, into progressively larger chunks to make a whole, can be appreciated by guitarists at any level. In music, much harmonic and melodic development consists of sequences of smaller sections grouped to create larger ones. In lead playing, smaller phrases or licks are grouped together to form larger phrases. (In more formal music circles, the terms motive and theme are used similarly.) The idea of learning by combining musical and physical subassemblies together is at the heart of what we do when we learn a piece of music by reading or by ear. When reading, at first we are bound to a note-by-note plodding until through experience, we are able to recognize groupings of tones and rhythms that we've seen before. When we learn by ear, we aurally latch onto the largest perceivable phrases or groupings until we can find the appropriate location on the fretboard and the correct rhythmic feel. The difference in the two approaches can be thought of less as philosophical ones, as those of specificity. If it is easier for us to appreciate the exactness of the written specification, then we will gravitate toward a reading habit. If we prefer to listen to a section over and over until each aspect becomes clearer and more specific, then we will tend to want to learn by ear. Because of the nature of multiple response learning, the earlier and later stages of both approaches tend to be easier and more accessible than the middle ones.

Insight learning can be related to virtually any endeavor including the musical and guitaristic ones. Insight and creativity are first cousins. Creativity is necessary in, among other things, problem solving and producing new works. When we recompile the raw material necessary to produce new expressions of old ideas, new uses for old tools, or new applications for old methods, we are acting in ways that can be considered insightful. When songwriting for example, small but significant changes to common phrases can quickly become popular sayings used to make hits. Having a background of a great deal of diverse information can become a wellspring of new ideas if you use your imagination to combine things of a divergent nature. As we struggle to increase our abilities, new possibilities open up, not the least of which are those created from our mistakes. Insight learning is on the menu in every restaurant of our existence and once we've tasted it, we hunger for more. It can be as common as getting a joke or as profound as a miracle. In fact, some would say no experience can compare. It sprouts from insatiable curiosity and is cultivated with intensity of awareness. It is also the type of learning at which successful musicians seem to excel.

In every type of learning there is an underlying factor that produces the fuel to power our intellectual engines. Something enables us to overcome the inertia of the status quo. Something compels us toward an ever distant finish line in our race to catch up, overtake and excel. That something can be characterized as heart, persistence, courage, drive or perhaps best, willpower. You can't buy it on late night TV and can't cultivate it by just wanting to be the guy on stage bad enough. I don't even know if it can be learned. I'm pretty sure each one of us has it but doesn't always know what to do with it. I do know that when we see it in action, willpower can be awe inspiring.

Ultimately the job is to use whatever we have to play and produce more and better music. But it is not enough just to play for ourselves. A significant conversion occurs when we play for others. Over the years I've developed a half-serious list of graduations for most (popular) guitarists based pretty much on where their equipment resides. It goes like this: The first graduation is when you move it out of your bedroom and into a garage with your friends equipment. That, of course, makes you part of a long standing American institution known as the garage band. The second graduation is getting it out of the garage and into a local club, however seedy and disreputable. That turns you into a pro and a heavy equipment mover. The next graduation is when it sleeps in trucks and travels from city to city. By then you develop a relationship with that twisted maniac known as the roadie, who will occasionally help you move your gear. The last graduation is a simple matter of touring your albums and clawing your way up from opening act to headliner, hit by hit. Then you have to start paying your roadie what he's worth because he owns you, but you don't have to bang gear anymore. Or so I'm told.

Whenever an audience hears us play, they don't judge us by how many books we've read, or how many hours a day we practice or how much we've sacrificed for the guitar or on any of the formative aspects of learning that precede the performance. They judge us based on how they hear us and to some extent, how they see us. How they perceive us in general is mainly an issue of how they feel about us as we play. They perceive us in terms of how they relate to us, and more importantly, in how well they feel we are relating to them. When as guitarists, we can learn to relate to our audience on their terms, then we have succeeded as musicians.

Ok. That's it for this section. At least one of us feels better. Some people may view this part of the book as less than guitar-specific, but it's a matter of coming to grips with things. Can a guitar teacher help someone learn *guitar* better without helping them become a better *learner* also? There was a thought that kept occurring to me over and over. What would the ideal learning situation be like? What characteristics would the perfect student and the perfect teacher possess? Perhaps the perfect teacher would always teach exactly what was needed, exactly when the student needed to know it. By the same token, the perfect student would always completely and permanently understand, integrate and retain everything the teacher taught the first time every time. On a personal note, I also believe that both teacher and student would be both passionate and witty about the subject to a point that it was effortless and enjoyable, yet profound and life affirming. Right. When monkeys fly out of my Macintosh. The reality is, we all muddle on as best we can.

To save a buck, I learned drafting so I could render designs for guitar stuff. An interesting thing about it that I've never forgotten, is that you only dimension a line in one place, one time, and that place should be the optimal location to convey your intentions to the person who has to make the part. That kind of singular specificity is perfect for keeping misunderstandings and losses in translation from occurring between designers and builders. Then, if a part gets made and doesn't work, everyone sprints for the print to see who screwed up and has to pay. What we're attempting to do here is similar in intent, anyway. Anytime a new idea is presented, an attempt is being made to put it in the right place at the right time on a section by section basis. That is the teacher's part. The student's part is to first, determine which section is next in line given his or her frame of reference, and second, to accept that for real learning to occur, a certain amount of repetition is necessary for new ideas to take hold. So this is the deal. I'll do my part to insure that the specifications are in order, if you agree to simply repeat everything until it sinks in permanently. This includes going back and rereading and replaying the first two books until you know them cold.

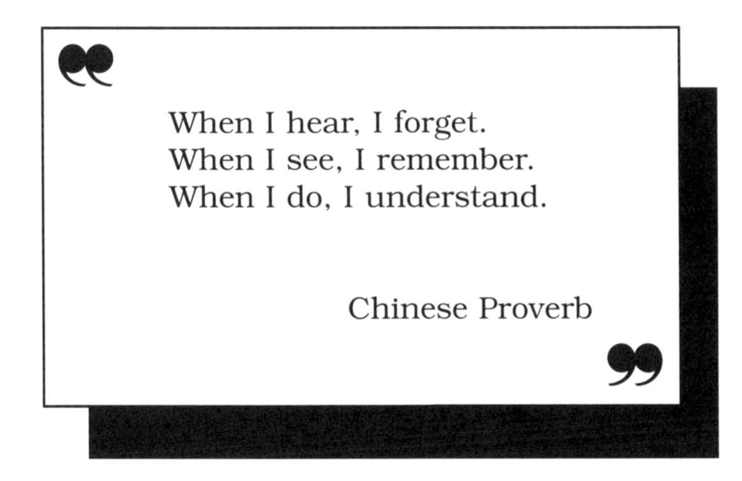

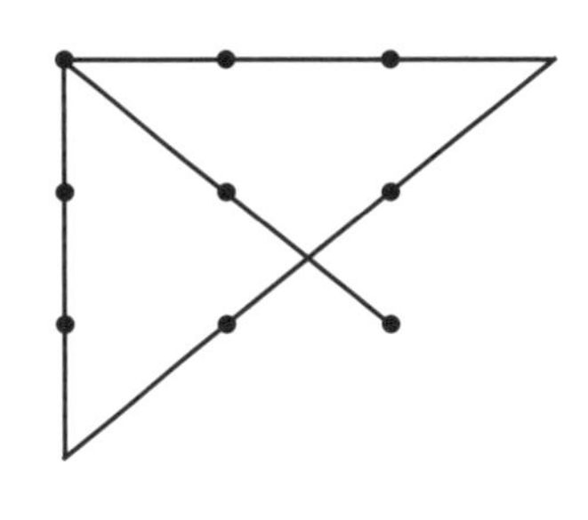

Theory

The theory chapter of Volume III is broken up into four main sections: Notation Formats, Rhythm, Keys, and Intervals. Notation Formats presents the various means of writing and illustrating music that is used throughout the method. The Rhythm section discusses the terms, symbols, and meanings used to denote durations, beats, and other rhythmic materials in music. The section on Keys deals with how to derive the notes available in a given key area for the purpose of enabling each key to be used as an equal in different situations. Intervals explores two note combinations in a guitar oriented format with some common usages.

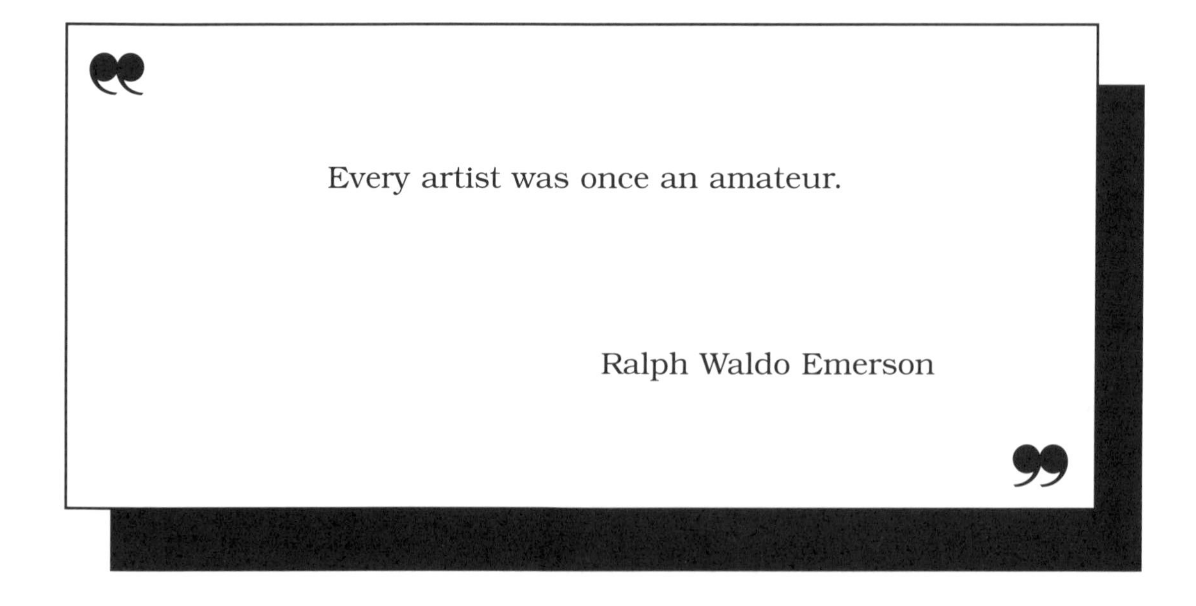

Notation Formats

In order to pursue the creative and analytical applications of the material in Vols. I and II, we have to agree on a format or formats to specify and illustrate the way notes, intervals, chords, scales and arpeggios are described. Pitches are notated one way and rhythms another and they have to be rendered within a time frame. The problem is that there are several ways to do this and not any one way is best for everybody.

What is termed **standard notation**, or the standard method of notating music, involves the use of simple graphic symbols based primarily on dots and lines called heads and stems. Each note is specified by a combination of these which defines both pitch and how long notes are sustained relative to one another. They are grouped into units of beats called measures (of time).

In standard notation, pitches are specified by placing them either higher or lower (representing frequency) on the page within a group of 5 lines called a staff. This system evolved as an all-purpose method for use with practically any instrument. In fact it works fine for most instruments, but the guitar's tuning system produces problems that increase the difficulty of interpretation. The appropriate string on which to play the note is not always obvious, and so requires a separate means of specification. Also the 2nd to 3rd string interval prevents string to string symmetry. The form this additional specification takes in modern guitar notation is a number within a circle near the note stem and/or a roman numeral indicating the position. These specifications are not always employed, however and the player must constantly reason through the available choices in order to arrive at the optimum or intended string when two or more are within reach. In some ways this is like *arranging* each piece you are learning. It is mentally taxing and the only relief seems to be to memorize everything as soon as possible and store it as a frame of reference for later. I don't believe this mental effort actually stunts the creative process, but it is seldom that you find guitarists that are outstanding at both.

This process can be daunting especially for beginning and intermediate guitar players, and has led to the resurgence in popularity of an equally ancient, string-specific method of notation known as **tablature**. In tab the horizontal lines represent the guitar strings themselves and, of course, there are six instead of five. The pitches in tab are notated less for musical purposes, than to specify an exact location. This is done by means of a number indicating the fret to be *stopped* overtop a line representing a string. (This is another guitar-oriented approach as contrasted with the music-oriented standard notation.) Tab relies on the same rhythmic symbology as standard notation to specify durations. Tab by itself suffers from the inablilty to clearly distinguish between certain durations such as quarter notes and half notes. This method of writing music is graphically somewhere between the dynamic standard notation and the static fretboard "snapshot" method used in Vols. I and II.

So what we have now, is two standards for illustrating both pitch and time on a fretboard: standard notation and tablature. In today's fast paced music industry, a kind of organizational "skeleton" is widely used, called **charts** or **lead sheets**. Charts vary in the amount of information they contain and there is not really one set format. It consists of whatever the session player needs to jot down at the time or whatever has been prepared for him. Generally a lead sheet has words, chords, and melody, and collections of these are known as fake books since experienced musicians can fake their way through songs they've never actually played, for audience requests, etc.

Notation Formats

Sometimes it is nothing more than a number sequence that refers to a chord progression so the key can change to accommodate the range of the singer. This method of sketching the minimum amount of information is useful for several reasons. For one thing, it is quick to write out and saves time in the studio when music is being worked out on the fly, often to the tune of hundreds of dollars per hour. More importantly it allows the experienced session players a chance to improvise and try different ideas when its his turn to contribute, instead of just sticking to a script. To this end a contractor or artist may select a guitarist because of a unique type of sound that he thinks will work well in the song. For example, guitarist Edward Van Halen was called in to do a solo on Michael Jackson's "Thriller" album. (I considered this unusual combination evidence of some shrewd musical instincts on the part of whomever was responsible.) For a chart they just told him where to start playing and when to stop. For the purpose of illustrating or teaching basic strumming patterns, what is commonly termed a **slash sheet** is also used. Slash sheets use chord symbols plus diagonal lines showing the number of beats each chord gets.

There are other **symbols** to describe the traditional ornaments, etc., as well as more modern technical articulations, many of which have become popular due to evolution in styles of playing and innovations in instrument design. More traditional symbols such as turns, mordants, and fermatas, have been joined by bends, vibratos, hammer-ons, tremolo dive-bombs, etc., and each has their own unique designation which indicate effects rather than pitch or time values. Another minimalistic symbology for notation via the fretboard, is a simple two number **fraction** specifying intersections of string and fret numbers. Finally, don't forget the **graphs** of Vol. I and II that are partial fretboard representations lacking specifications for all but where to put your fingers. With all the different standards and options for writing and reading music, its no wonder that so many guitarists get frustrated and just wear out tape trying to figure it out by ear. In some ways it is a more direct approach since fewer man made contrivances stand between the music and the musician. The difference in psychology of the two approaches is that learning by ear deals with possibilities, whereas learning by reading symbols deals with specifications. Paradoxically, an indirect vs. direct approach.

For the purpose of enabling as many as possible to learn on their own terms, the musical examples will be rendered in context sensitive formats. At various times these may include graphs, fractions, symbols, charts (including number sequences), tablature, and standard notation. There is no one way that works best for everyone at all times. There are different types of thought processes for different types of learning circumstances, musicwise and otherwise. If you're on stage performing something you've played a thousand times before, you aren't using the same thinking that you'd use when you're alone in your practice room hammering out the first few lines of a complicated piece you just started. Contrary to what you may have heard, the relationship between the guitar content and the musical content is not cart and horse. The only appropriate metaphor seems to be chicken and egg. In other words, what takes precedence is whatever is relevant at the time. We won't be limited to one type of format here. The format(s) that appeals to one person may not necessarily work for the next. A benefit to the student, is that the formats with which he or she is least familiar may be de-mystified by seeing it in peaceful coexistence with others more familiar. Maybe for the by-ear guys, standard notation and tab will stop looking like a page full of squashed mosquitoes, and a lead sheet won't look like a blank page to the readers.

Notation Formats

Below is the five-lined staff of standard notation, and the six-lined strings of tab.

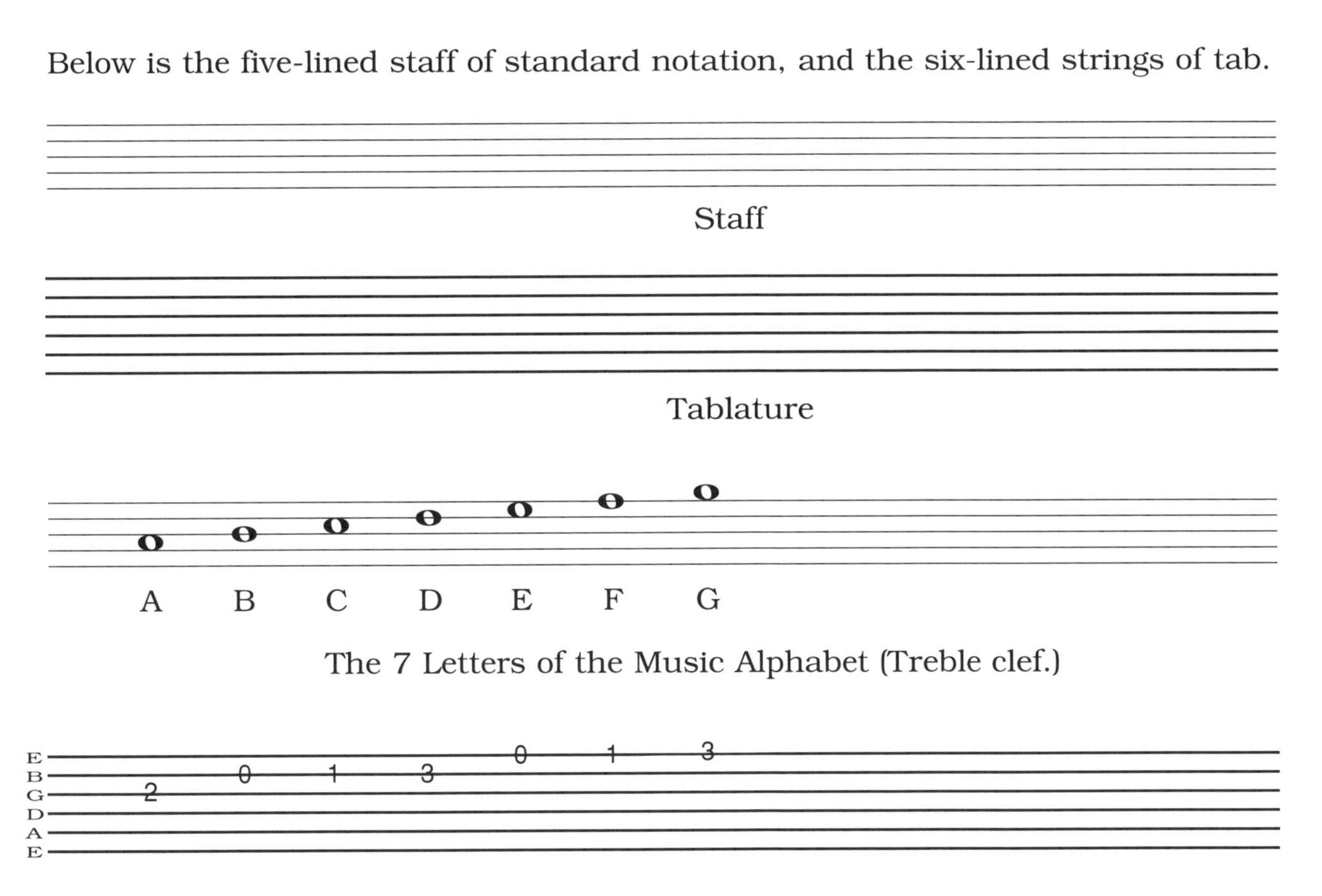

Tablature Orientation (Open position.)

In standard notation the pitches are specified by their placement on the staff. In tablature each note is specified as an intersection of a string and fret or stop. The advantage of standard notation is conveyance of pitch and time relationships. The advantage of tab is that unequivocal fretboard positions are related. At the very beginning of a piece of music written in standard notation is a symbol called a clef which determines the pitch range of the staff for the different instruments. The most common clefs are treble and bass clef. The symbols are hard to recognize as such, but they are nothing more than old style calligraphic letters. Treble clef is a fancy "G" and bass clef is an "F".

The G in the treble clef circles the second line from the bottom and the F in the bass clef refers to the second line from the top. The notes increment alphabetically relative to the clef using both lines and spaces. (Although this is a simple system, it is not necessarily intuitive. I'll bet I wasn't the only kid one who thought the treble clef "sat" on the E line and the bass clef "hung" from the A line.)

Notation Formats

For beginners, the hard part is going backwards or down the staff since as a rule, we aren't used to saying or using the alphabet in reverse. Although music only uses the seven letters A through G, it can make you wonder just how well you learned your ABCs. Since the range of the guitar is limited, only the treble clef is used. The notes, by convention, are written an octave higher than they are actually played. This spreads them more evenly on the staff and so requires fewer **ledger lines** or the added lines that extend above and below the staff for notes out of its range. The symbol 8va (octave) can be substituted for ledger lines indicating to play the note an octave higher.

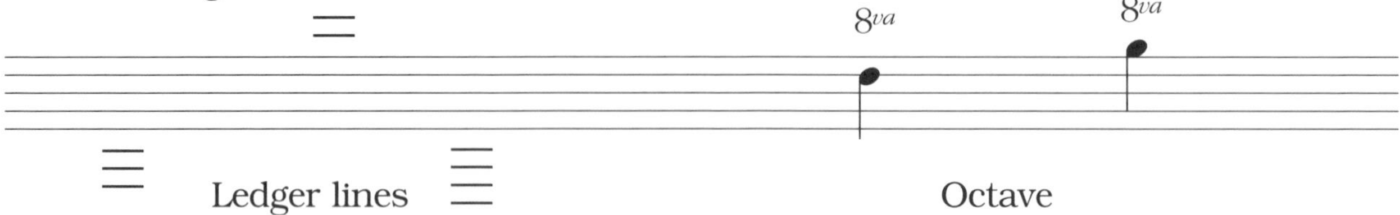

Below is the dual format now in common usage for notating modern guitar music. The vertical lines are called **measure lines** or **bar lines** and denote an equal time period regardless of the amount of physical space represented or the number of notes included. Double lines symbolize the end of a section. Symbols and graphs provide further specifications.

Slash lines or rhythm marks are an efficient shorthand for chord progressions with minimal rhythmic information. The slashes indicate the beats but not the way to strum them. In other words just playing down stroke strums for each slash mark is not what is intended. They indicate only the beats and where the chord changes are in relation to them.

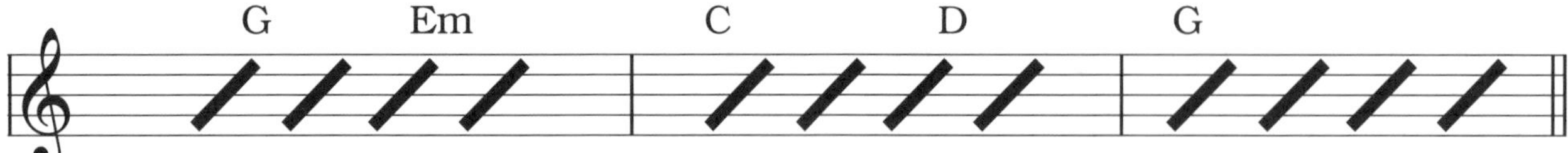

Next is a brief introduction to the time values most commonly used in music. These time values are called divisions of the beat, since they are relative only in the context of a steady beat or pulse. These are continued in the Rhythm section.

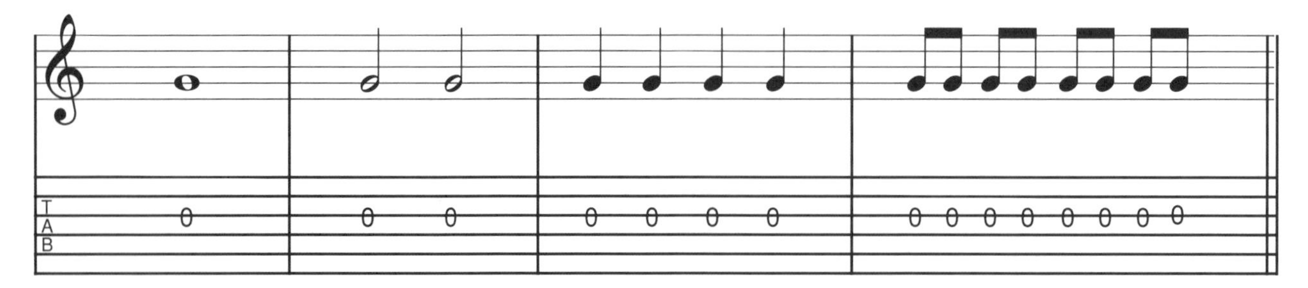

Notation Formats

Thus far we've only discussed the notation of natural, or unaltered notes. The other notes are termed accidentals because apparently, someone a long time ago seemed to feel that sharps and flats were notes that occurred "by accident".

Western musical instruments are designed and tuned in a manner called equal temperament, meaning that they are grouped and oriented in octaves. The term octave pertains to an eighth letter and scale tone repeated (ABCDEFG-A). In between all but two pairs of notes (B-C and E-F) are the accidentals. Seven natural notes and five accidentals add up to twelve tones. Octaves, or a pitch and its double (or half) are divided into twelve tones, each division termed a half-step. The half-step is the smallest unit of pitch in western music. Indian, Chinese, African, etc. music have various tonal systems with more or less divisions of the octave. More on this in the section on guitar tunings. The accidentals alter notes by half-steps. A sharp raises (toward the body) a note one half-step higher in pitch, and a flat lowers (toward the headstock) it one half-step. A half-step is the equivalent of one fret, and two frets is called a whole-step.

The note one half-step lower than B, is called B♭(B flat). The note a half-step above F is called F♯(F sharp). The natural notes with accidentals in order are: A A♯ B C C♯ D D♯ E F F♯ G G♯ and back to A. Using flats, the notes in reverse order are: G G♭ F E E♭ D D♭ C B B♭ A A♭ and back to G. It is the same starting from any note.

When notating accidentals, the ♯ or ♭ symbol is placed in front of the note to be altered. Within a measure, once a note has been altered with an accidental, that note continues to be sharp or flat until the next measure or until it is cancelled with another accidental. The natural sign (♮) cancels a sharp or a flat and reverts the note to natural. *If a natural sign is not used to cancel a sharp or flat, it is automatically cancelled by the next barline.*

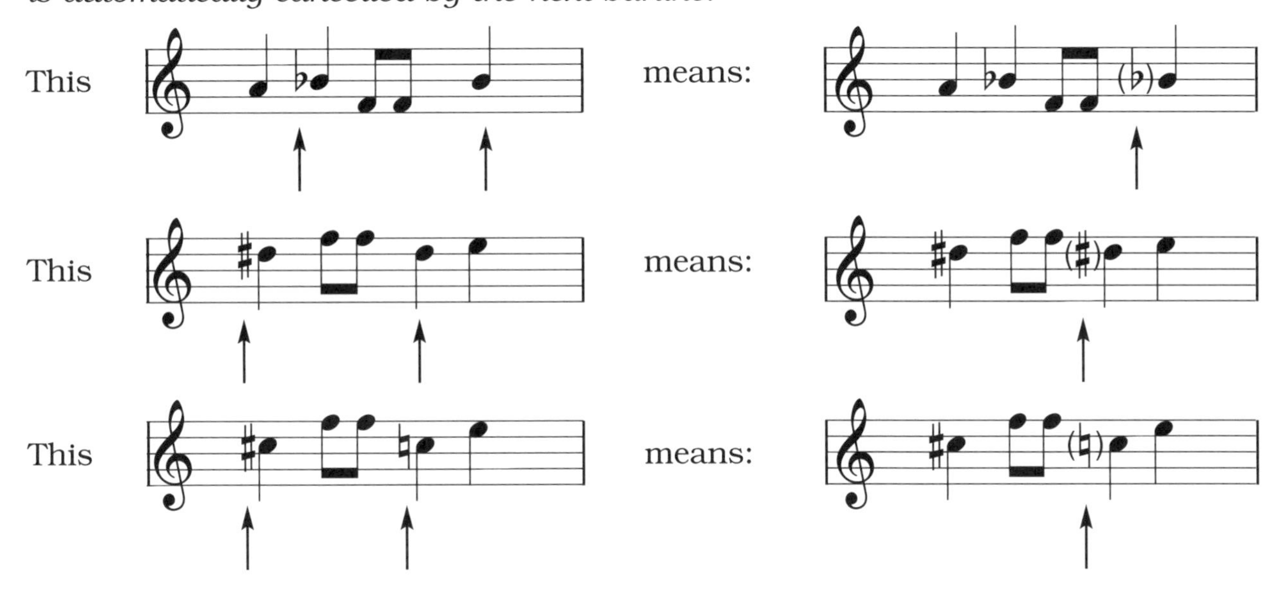

Notation Formats - Traditional Symbols

ppp pp mp p **Pianissimo, pianissimo, mezzo piano, piano** - Very soft to soft.

fff ff mf f **Fortissimo, fortissimo, mezzo forte, forte** - Very loud to loud.

𝄋 **Segno** - Sign. Indicates the beginning or end of a section to be repeated. **Dal Segno** or **D.S.**- From the sign.

𝄌 **Coda** - Marks separate part of music used for final ending

♯ ♭ ♮ × 𝄫 **Sharp, Flat, Natural, Dbl. Sharp, Dbl. Flat** - Raises and lowers pitches in half step increments.

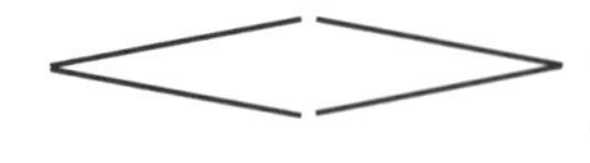

Crescendo, Decrescendo (diminuendo) - Gradual increase or decrease of volume.

Rhythm marks - ad lib rhythm usually with strummed chords

Mordent - A short trill with varying interpretations.

Grace note - A note of inconsequential (uncounted) time value printed in smaller type usually with a slash, and located adjacent to the primary note.

Turn - A musical ornament placed above a note indicating to play four notes: the tone above, the principle tone, a tone below and end on the principle tone.

8va **Octave** - Indicates to play the passage one octave above (8va) or below (8vb) what is notated.

Fermata - Hold note indefinitely, or until conductor signals release

Repeat measure - Repeat the previous measure

Double bars - Light bars are used to denote the end of a section; heavy bar denotes the end of a piece.

Repeat - Repeat notes and measures in between the double bars.

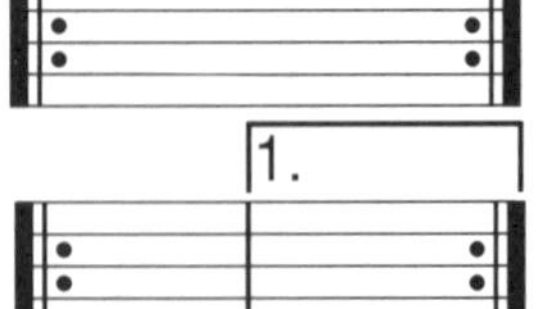

First Ending - Play notes under bracket then return to double bar

2.

Second Ending - Follows 1st ending. After first ending return to double bars, skip over first ending and play second ending.

Rhythm

Rhythm is a term used to described durations of pitches in general, and the countless ways of combining patterns of durations. A composition's rhythm is specified in terms of divisions of what are called beats. **Beats** are analogous to our own pulse in that they are a consistently repeated temporal units that have a speed which is relatively fast or slow. In standard notation, a piece's rhythm is specified by a pair of numbers at the beginning of a piece or new section termed the **time signature**. The number on the top designates the number of beats per measure, and the number on the bottom says what type of note gets a beat. In the example below, four-four time, there would be four beats per measure and the quarter note would get a beat. Next, the different types of note durations are illustrated. All but the whole note have stems, and the shorter the time value, the more flags or beams the note will have. Flags and beams are the same, but beams are faster to notate, and so get used more often except in the case of vocal melody lines. The direction of the stem depends on whether the note is above or below the middle staff line such that the note doesn't extend too much beyond the staff. Middle line note stems go either way.

The next order of business is to establish the basis for the number system of the rhythmic half of music. It is fundamentally a base seven system in that seven different types of durations are commonly used (only six shown below). They are the whole note, half note, quarter note, eighth note, sixteenth note, the thirty-second note and the sixty-fourth note. Starting with the whole note, each type is successively both a doubling of the number of notes per measure, and a halving of the amount of time with which to play them. Below are the number of each type in one measure of four-four time.

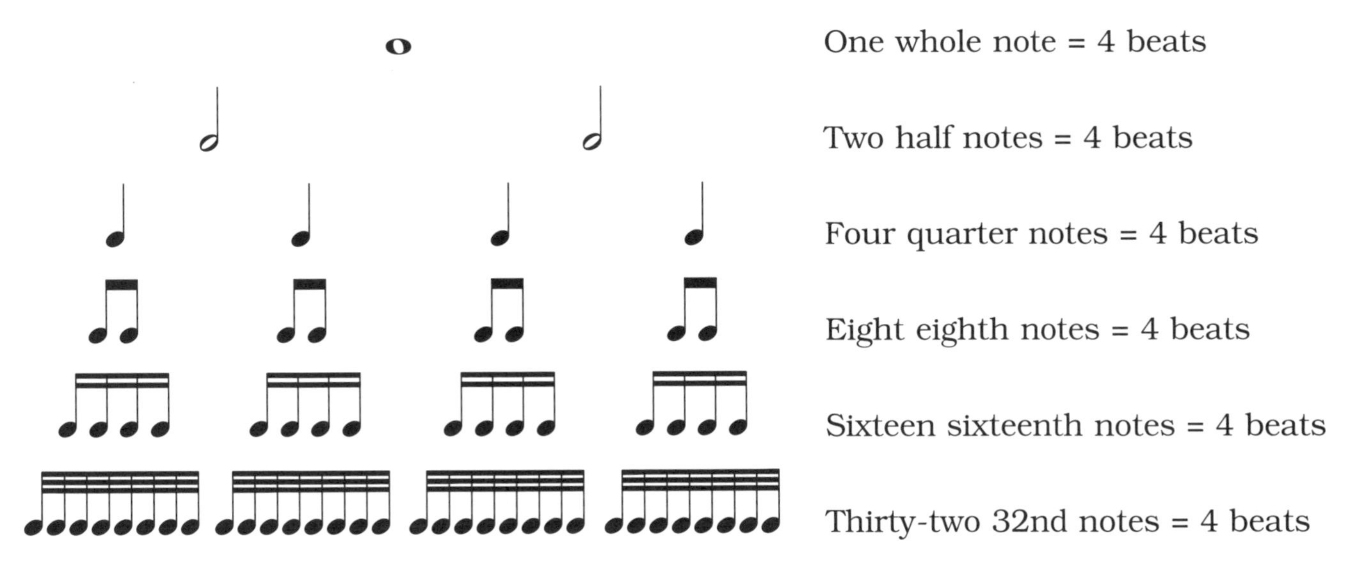

Rhythm - Rests Dots and Ties

Within a measure, the sum of the time values must always total the value specified by the time signature. When that value has not been realized by notes, a kind of place holder termed a rest is used to account for the remaining time. A **rest** is a symbol that indicates a cessation of tonal activity, or silence, for a specified period of time. There are equivalent rests for all of the seven basic durations. The commonly used symbols for rests are illustrated below along with their tonal counterparts. The nonuniform nature of the rest's symbology is cause for some consternation, but here again, its best to just accept the situation and learn them any way you can. Hopefully, when newer technologies replace these systems, the designers will learn from past iconic inconsistencies. Ok, maybe that bears restating. The symbols don't really indicate anything by their individual or collective designs. The eighths through sixty fourths make sense, but none of the others have any apparent semantic consistency.

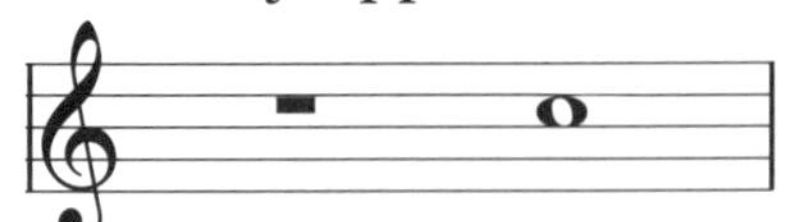

The Whole Rest and the Whole Note
Both equal four counts or beats.

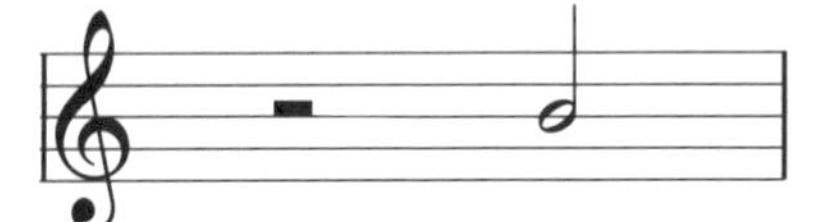

The Half Rest and the Half Note
Both equal two counts or beats.

The Quarter Rest and the Quarter Note
Both equal one count or beat.

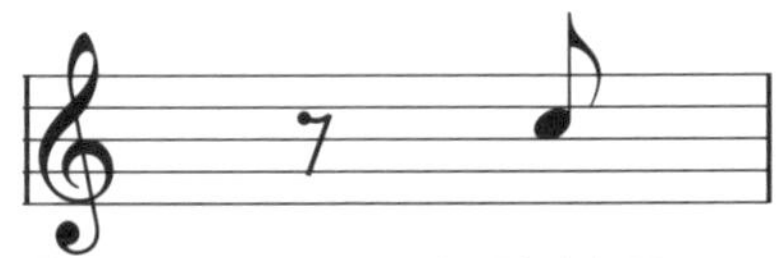

The Eighth Rest and the Eighth Note
Both equal 1/2 count or beat.

The Sixteenth Rest and the Sixteenth Note
Both equal 1/4 count or beat.

The Thirty second Rest and the Thirty second Note. Both equal 1/8th count or beat.

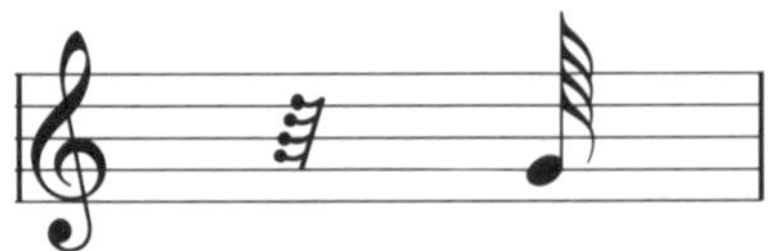

The Sixty fourth Rest and the Sixty fourth Note. Both equal 1/16 count or beat.

Notes that need to be held for intermediate periods of time are designated by the dot and the tie. A **dot** increases the durational value of a note by one half of its normal value. The **tie** is a curved line that links two notes and adds their time values together even across bar lines. Ties and dots have somewhat overlapping abilities and composers use whichever makes the most sense to them. Dots don't cross over barlines, and ties are intended to join notes of different beats. It is interesting that you seldom see dotted or tied rests. Below are examples of dotted notes and tied notes.

The Dotted Whole and the Dotted Half Notes
A dotted whole note gets six beats (4 + 2).
A dotted half note gets three beats (2 + 1).

The Dotted Quarter and the Dotted Eight.
A dotted quarter note gets 1 1/2 beats
A dotted eighth note gets 3/4 beat.

Dotted sixteenth, thirty second, and sixty fourth notes. Dotted 1/16s gets 3/8 beat.
A dotted 1/32s get 3/16 beat.
A dotted 1/64s get 3/32 beat.

Below is the same measure of repeated time values with various sections tied.

Rhythm - Time Signatures and Tempo

The terms *meter* and time are more or less synonymous in music. The time signature specifies a piece's meter. Next we'll present some different types of time signatures and what their numbers signify. Four-four time is used so often it is termed “common time” and is usually abbreviated with the letter "C." Two-two is also known as “cut time” and is abbreviated also with a "C," but with a line *cut* through it. Three-four time is called *waltz* time. Examples are illustrated below.

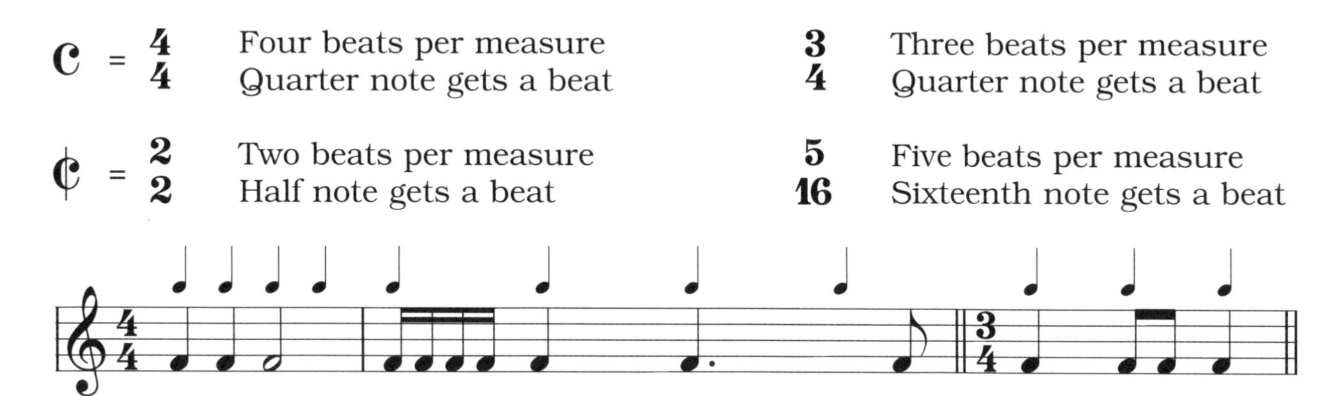

When written properly, rhythms are notated such that within the physical space of the measure, they are distributed evenly in a manner that best conveys the time signature's intent. Since musicians read in groupings rather than single note units, this makes it easier to readily interpret a section's rhythmic meaning. When learning to write music, get in the habit of spacing your notes evenly from the beginning. When learning to read music, get in the habit of interpreting entire beats at a glance.

A piece's **tempo** is the relative rate at which the beats occur in time. Again, the beats of a measure are designated by the lower number in a time signature. These beats are what we tap our feet to when a piece of music gets us going. They are also the back and forth motion we create when we dance. Traditional terms for the relative speed of the beats are Italian words such as *allegro* for fast, or *largo* for slow. There are many such terms which have no quantifiable definition, and so we've adopted a more specific system for determining a composition's tempo. It is based on an invention by a man named Malzel, called the metronome. His device was a clicking, spring -loaded mechanical pendulum, which could change speeds. It was designed to click from about 40 beats per minute to about 208. Now tempos are specified by the letters "M.M." (Malzel's Metronome, or metronome marking), with a note type, and a number. This indicates how many and what kind of note per minute. The M.M. is not always included when specifying tempo.

M.M. ♩ = 120 means 120 quarter notes per minute

M.M. 𝅗𝅥 = 60 means 60 half notes per minute

M.M. ♪ = 200 means 200 eighth notes per minute

Rhythm - Common Groupings

Now that we've established the basic values, the important thing to do is to enable the player to think rhythmically and respond to common rhythms that are likely to be encountered. Since the beat of a piece of music is the basic unit of rhythm, we'll take some common beat groupings and practice them until they become easy to recognize and play. The thing that seems to prevent us from keeping accurate time is an unfamiliarity with certain common rhythmic expressions. To learn this we will practice counting rhythms beat by beat.

Counting is a two part affair. It involves simultaneously keeping a steady beat while tapping, saying, or playing the rhythms notated. Keeping the beat means tapping (or setting a metronome, drum machine, etc.) to just the main pulse. In 4/4 time that means four beats per measure (on the quarter note). In 3/8 time it means three beats per measure (on the eighth note), and so on.

Counting conventions attribute a specific terminology or rather verbalization to each beat. For example, when counting out loud, the strong quarter notes in 4/4 time are simply "1 2 3 4". Eighth notes are termed "and". This would make a series of eighth notes in 4/4 time "1 and 2 and 3 and 4 and". A 4/4 measure of sixteenth notes are counted "1 e and a, (pronounced one-ee-an-uh) 2 e and a, 3 e and a, 4 e and a". The plus symbol (+) is the equivalent to the word "and". Both are pronounced using the more monosyllabic "an". The tapping, or beat keeping is generally one tap per beat.

These exercises will be based on the single note open G string to allow us to concentrate on the rhythms. Use alternate picking on the eighth and sixteenth notes.

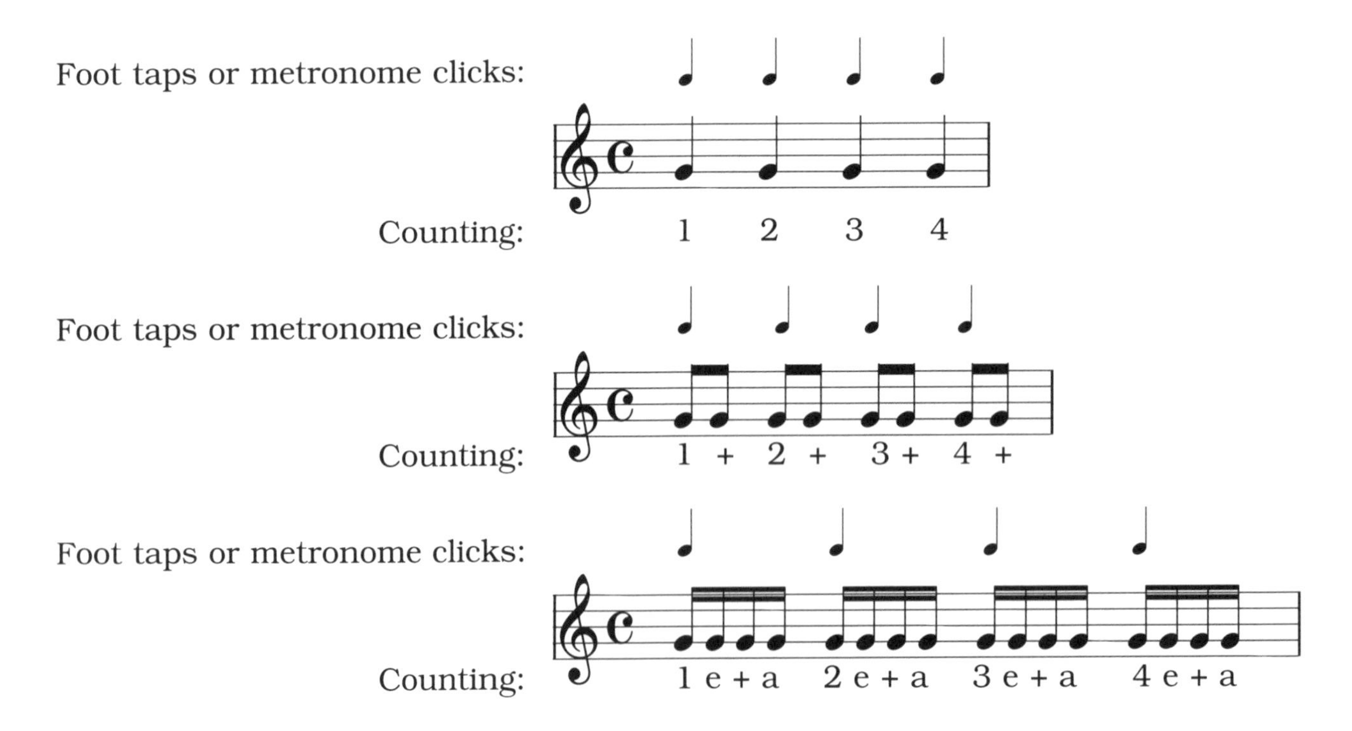

Rhythm - Common Beat Groupings

By combining dotted eighths and sixteenths, you get a familiar rhythmic combination also known as a *shuffle*, probably because it brings to mind a drag-footed gait.

Below are the three most common sixteenth and eighth note groupings. A measure of each is illustrated. In each case a sixteenth other than the first is missing. Among durations, the quarter, eighth and sixteenth durations tend to get used most often.

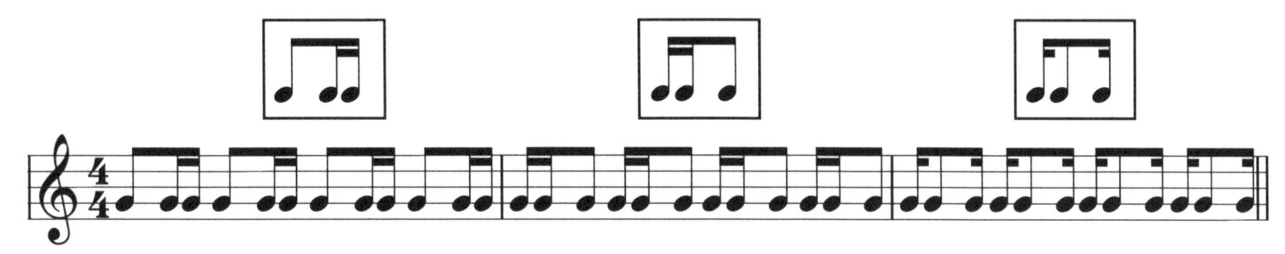

The next most common rhythmic grouping is the triplet. Triplets are three notes that are played in place of two of the same value. They are indicated by a number "3" and often a slur or brackets. A **slur** is a curved line over a group of notes indicating they are to be played **legato**, or in a connected fashion. These methods of notating rhythms can be used also for fives, sixes, sevens and various uneven groupings. Composer Frederic Chopin would often place a cascade of notes over a beat or beats and simply group them with a number over top. He is to have said that he wanted his music to be played "like water" and felt he couldn't really "hear" how his compositions sounded until his pal Franz Liszt, perhaps an even greater virtuoso, played them. With groupings of five and seven it is often easiest to relate to them as threes and twos, and fours and threes or vice versa.

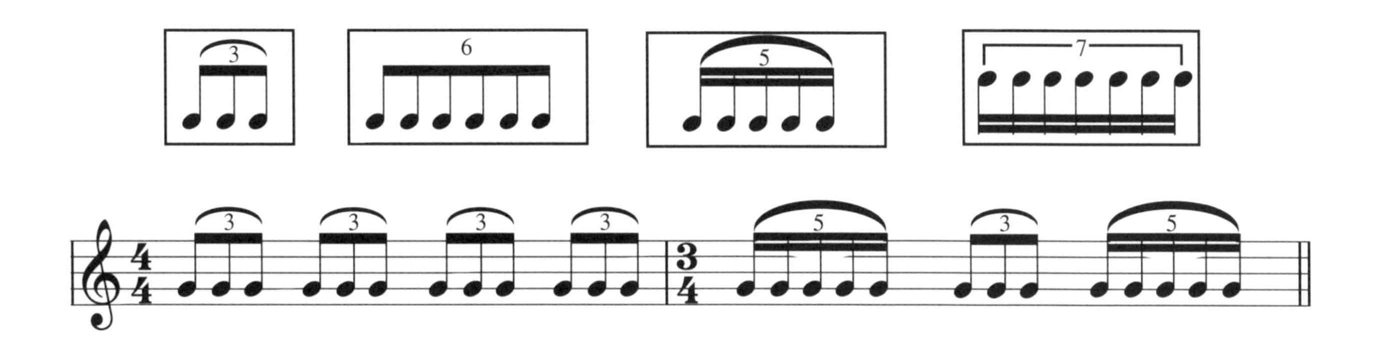

Rhythm - Exercises

What follows are some exercises using various note values. Before beginning to count and play, let a measure or two of metronome clicks or foot taps go by to get a steady feel for the tempo. If the tempo isn't right, change it to something you are comfortable with, but I never had to tell a student to speed up to learn something new, if you catch the drift. The exercises start with easy combinations of the values we've discussed and move toward more coherent rhythmic passages.

So again, if you're just starting out, the key to acquiring rhythms from notation is to look for recognizable groupings instead of just one note value at a time.

Keys

Among the natural systems already in place when a person starts to learn guitar are physics, physiology, acoustics, and the overtone series. The man made ones are the twelve tone system, the guitar's polyphonic design, the geometry of the fretboard, and notation symbologies. The concept of key is a product of both the twelve tone system and our human physiology. As a practical matter, keys are what chords, scales and arpeggios are derived from.

A **key** is a group of notes derived from the twelve tone system, that are arranged in half step and whole step increments such that each group is equivalent to another. In another sense, it is a group of centered tones that are agreed upon by an common aesthetic. In yet another sense, a it can be considered an interface for the twelve tone system. Keys are specified by the notes contained within them and their distance from one another in half steps. (You should distinguish key and scale in the same manner as note and tone; the **note** is an abstraction we use in theory and symbology, and the **tone** is what we hear when something moves in such a manner as to vibrate our eardrum, activate our nervous system, etc. Similarly, a key is a concept and a scale is one expression of that concept.) Keys are named by a combination of the first seven letters of the alphabet and a system of "accidentals" termed sharps and flats. There are 15 keys - seven using flats and seven using sharps plus one that has neither.

In general use, the terms key, tonality and mode are as inbred as those guys in Deliverance, and their meanings are difficult to distinguish. For one reason, the terms are context sensitive, but here goes, anyway. A key is a group of centered tones such as Major, minor or dorian, but then so is a mode or a tonality. Modes generally refer to the seven most common tonal orientations (Ionian, Dorian, Phrygian, Lydian, Mixolydian, Aeolian, and Locrian). Tonality refers to these plus all the major and minor variations as well as the numerous chromatic variants. In another sense, tonality is distinguished from modality, and in yet another it denotes tone centering as opposed to atonality or no discernible tone center. Now that I've cleared all that up for you...

In practical usage, a key has a name and type similar to intervals, chords, scales, and arpeggios. A key's name would be its letter name and accidental (when applicable). Its type would be Major, minor or Mixolydian, for example. A key would be referred to as "Ab Major", "C minor" or "D# dorian". The combination of name and type gives not only a tonal center and a whole step - half step specification, but also a humanistic quality such as happy or sad.

The concept of key as an interface for the twelve-toned system is a means of taking the individual tonal elements, and reducing them to a manageable number. If each key works the same as another, then **modulation**, or a change of key within a piece, can produce added tonal interest with ease and simplicity.

Ok here goes. What follows is important. If you are to proceed beyond the beginning levels of music theory, it will be because you have a firm grasp of the fundamentals, and are able to combine and vary them in creative ways, and recognize and understand them in the music of others in analytical ways. Being able to function in any key is a necessary ability for a musician. As a practical matter, keys are the most basic unit of tonal orientation with which the musician works. Now more than any other time, you should overcome any reservations you may have and just learn this material. Its significance can't be overstated although perhaps it may have been attempted.

Keys

The goal is to be able to recognize a key by its signature, identify the notes in a key, and develop intervals, chords, etc., from those notes.

The sharp keys in order are: (C), G, D, A, E, B, F#, and C#. The flat keys in order are: (C), F, Bb, Eb, Ab, Db, Gb and Cb. The order represents the incrementing number of accidentals. The key of C can be considered a "zero" key since it belongs to neither the sharps or the flats, but it will be the starting place in the counting system to follow. The zero key in both cases has no accidentals. The first sharp key, G, has 1 sharp. The second sharp key, D, has 2 sharps. The third sharp key, A, has three sharps, and so on. The first flat key, F, has 1 flat. The second flat key, Bb, has 2 flats. The third flat key, Eb, has 3 flats, and so on.

The next issue is the order of sharps and flats as they are added on to successive keys. The sharps in order are F#, C#, G#, D#, A#, E#, and B# or FCGDAEB (all sharp) The order of flats is the same as the sharps but in reverse: Bb, Eb, Ab, Db, Gb, Cb, and Fb or BEADGCF (all flat).

To derive each key's **signature** or the specification of accidentals, combine the number of sharps (or flats) with the order of accidentals. To get to the next sharp key, count up in fifths; to get to the next flat key, count up in fourths. For example, the key of G is the first sharp key (five up from C), and so has a signature of one sharp-F#. That means the notes in the key of G are: G A B C D E and F#. The key of D is the second sharp key (five up from G), and so has a signature of two sharps-F# and C#. Therefore the notes in the key of D are: D E F# G A B and C#. The key of A is the third sharp key (five up from D), and so has three sharps-F#, C# and G#. That makes the notes in the key of A: A B C# D E F# and G#. Remember that you add on another sharp in the order: FCGDAEB (all sharp).

The signatures (and notes) for the rest of the sharp keys are as follows:

The key of E has four sharps- F# C# G# & D#. The notes are: E F# G# A B C# & D#
The key of B has five sharps- F# C# G# D# & A#. Notes: B C# D# E F# G# & A#
The key of F# has six sharps- F# C# G# D# A# & E#. Notes: F# G# A# B C# D# & E#
The key of C# has 7 sharps-F# C# G# D# A# E# & B#. Notes: C# D# E# F# G# A# & B#

Whereas the sharp keys increment in fives, the flat keys increment in fours (or fives in reverse). For example, the key of F is the first flat key (four up from C), and so has a signature of one flat-Bb. That means the notes in the key of F are: F G A Bb C D and E. The key of Bb is the second flat key (four up from F), and so has a signature of two flats- Bb and Eb. That means the notes in the key of Bb are: Bb C D Eb F G and A. The key of Eb is the third flat key (four up from Bb), and so has three flats-Bb, Eb, and Ab. Therefore the notes in the key of Eb are: Eb F G Ab Bb C and D. Remember that you add on another flat in the order: BEADGCF (all flat).

The signatures (and notes) for the rest of the flat keys are as follows:

The key of Ab has 4 flats- Bb Eb Ab & Db. The notes are: Ab Bb C Db Eb F & G
The key of Db has five flats- Bb Eb Ab Db & Gb. Notes: Db Eb F Gb Ab Bb & C.
The key of Gb has six flats- Bb Eb Ab Db Gb & Cb. Notes: Gb Ab Bb Cb Db Eb & F.
The key of Cb has 7 flats- Bb Eb Ab Db Gb Cb & Fb. Notes: Cb Db Eb Fb Gb Ab & Bb

Keys

As with intervals, chords, scales, and arpeggios, unless otherwise specified, a key is assumed to be Major.

Next the job is to see if we can determine the notes in any key so we can function with it. To find the notes in the key of A, first determine what the accidentals are as specified by the key signature. Here it is in dialog format:

1) Is A a sharp or flat key? Answer: Sharp. (The sharp keys are G D A E B F# & C#.)
2) The key of A has how many sharps? Answer: three. (It is the third sharp key.)
3) Which ones are they? Answer: F# C# & G#. (The sharps in order are F#, C#, G#, D#, A#, E#, and B#.)
4) If those are the accidentals, then what are all the notes in A? Answer: A B C# D E F# & G#.

If you don't know that "A" is the third sharp key, and so has three sharps, then you'll have to count in fives from C (zero sharps) until you arrive at A. C counted up five = G (add a sharp - F#); G counted up five = D (add another sharp - C#); D counted up five = A (add a third sharp - G#). Key Signature of A: 3 sharps - F# C# and G#. (Counting on your fingers helps if you use two hands. Point with a finger of the opposite hand instead of a thumb, or you're liable to miscount.)

We'll do it once more with a flat key: Bb. To find the notes in the key of Bb, first determine what the accidentals are as specified by the key signature.

1) Is Bb a sharp or flat key? Answer: Flat. (The flat keys are F Bb Eb Ab Db Gb Cb & Fb.)
2) The key of Bb has how many flats? Answer: two. (It is the second flat key.)
3) Which ones are they? Answer: Bb & Eb. (The flats in order are Bb Eb Ab Db Gb Cb & Fb.)
4) If those are the accidentals, then what are all the notes in Bb? Answer: Bb C D Eb F G & A.

The job now is to go through all 15 keys and name the signature and the notes of each. If it is your first time with keys, it will no doubt be arduous, but don't put it off. If you are having trouble, as always, go back to the beginning of the section and reread from the start. You may see something you missed the first time.

Being able to determine the notes in a key means we can build on them in a melodic and harmonic context. The first melodic extrapolation we will take up is the directional motion of one note to another. This is discussed in the chapters on intervals and melodic phrasing. The first harmonic extrapolation we'll discuss are the chords in a key and how they progress in a musical context, and to attach a chordal function to the notes in a key to produce the chords in a key. These are found in the chapter on chord progression. Throughout this series, the term key area has been frequently used. The use of this term is to draw attention to the difference between a temporary or brief change of key within a progression, and a complete modulation into another key altogether. For example one E chord played in the key of Eb constitutes a change of key area, but not a change of key.

Keys

If you find the systems outlined for determining the notes in a key too convoluted, you can make up your own method or simply learn them by rote. Below are the keys, signatures and their notes in table format.

Sharp Keys

Key	Key Signature	Notes in Key
C	No accidentals	C D E F G A B
G	F#	G A B C D E F#
D	F# C#	D E F# G A B C#
A	F# C# G#	A B C# D E F# G#
E	F# C# G# D#	E F# G# A B C# D#
B	F# C# G# D# A#	B C# D# E F# G# A#
F#	F# C# G# D# A# E#	F# G# A# B C# D# E#
C#	F# C# G# D# A# E# B#	C# D# E# F# G# A# B#

Flat Keys

C	No accidentals	C D E F G A B
F	Bb	F G A Bb C D E
Bb	Bb Eb	Bb C D Eb F G A
Eb	Bb Eb Ab	Eb F G Ab Bb C D
Ab	Bb Eb Ab Db	Ab Bb C Db Eb F B
Db	Bb Eb Ab Db Gb	Db Eb F Gb Ab Bb C
Gb	Bb Eb Ab Db Gb Cb	Gb Ab Bb Cb Db Eb F
Cb	Bb Eb Ab Db Gb Cb Fb	Cb Db Eb Fb Gb Ab Bb

Now for a glimpse of a practical guitar-oriented application of all that theory. Several years back, Steely Dan launched their careers with the song "Reelin' In the Years", that featured some nice guitar work by studio legend Eliott Randall. The solo was played over the repeated progression G to A. So what key did he play his solo in?

You might suppose that he'd have to switch keys every time the chord changed, but that wasn't what happened. The solo was played in the key of D. If you can figure out why, you're able to make all this information work for you. There are two types of logic behind why it worked so well. First, the G and A chords are the 4 and 5 chords in the key of D. On the other hand, the key signature of G has one sharp (F#), and the key signature of A has three sharps (F# C# & G#). The reason D worked is because it had the key signature closest to both of those: two sharps (F# & C#). It was a good compromise that resulted in a great solo on a hit song.

Intervals

Intervals are any two notes sounded either simultaneously or in succession. When played simultaneously, they are termed **harmonic intervals** and when played in succession, **melodic**. Intervals derive their name from both: 1) the distance between the two pitches (inclusive) in terms of scale steps (unison, second, third, fourth, fifth, sixth, seventh, octave, ninth, etc.), and 2) from the half step variations in (musical) character similar to triadic chords (diminished, minor, major, augmented, and perfect.) The intervals within an octave are termed "simple", and beyond an octave are termed "compound".

Combining their numeric pitch distance and musical character from lowest to highest, the intervals in half step increments are: unison, minor 2nd, Major 2nd, minor 3rd, Major 3rd, Perfect 4th, tritone (aka augmented 4th, or diminished 5th), Perfect 5th, minor 6th, Major 6th, minor 7th, Major 7th, and octave (Perfect 8th). Starting from the unison, each successive interval is one half step "wider" than the preceding one and so can be specified by the number of half steps (inclusive). There are 12, (13 if you include the unison) simple intervals. You can save yourself a lot of time and confusion if you skip the countless why's and wherefore's of the terminology and just learn them. In practical usage, 4ths and 5ths are deemed to be Perfect unless otherwise specified; 3rds, 6ths, and 7ths are similarly deemed to be Major unless otherwise mentioned. This is not unlike when someone says "Play a G chord", we understand it to be Major until we hear otherwise.

Compound intervals are generally limited to two octaves. You can, of course, play wider intervals, but there aren't any new names for them. An easy way to identify compound intervals is to add seven to the simple intervals. This makes the compound Major 2nd a Major 9th, the compound Major 3rd a Major 10th, and so on. The compound intervals, again in order, are: octave, minor 9th, Major 9th, minor 10th, Major 10, Perfect 11th, (double) tritone (aka aug. 11th or dim. 12th), Perfect 12th, minor 13th, Major 13th, minor 14th, Major 14 and (double) Octave. In practical usage, musicians often forgo these terms referring to the more familiar simple intervals, octave understood.

On the fretboard, melodic and harmonic intervals can be derived by a variety of methods, two of which we will use. Melodic intervals are easily accessed within the appropriate scale forms, and smaller harmonic intervals can be produced from adjacent string pairs. For adjacent strings only two cases exist: the 2nd-3rd pair; and all the other pairs (1st-2nd, 3rd-4th, 4th-5th, 5th-6th). Remember that each adjacent string pair is a naturally occurring (Perfect) 4th except the 2nd and 3rd which is a (Major) 3rd.

From smallest to largest, each will be illustrated in its harmonic and melodic guitar orientation. Intervals are subject to **inversion**, or the exchanging (of relative positions) of the higher and lower tones. When a 2nd is inverted it becomes a 7th; when a 3rd is inverted it becomes a 6th; when a 5th is inverted it becomes a 4th, and so on. An interesting difference about intervals on the guitar as opposed to a keyboard, is the smaller the (harmonic) interval, the longer the reach which brings us to the **unison**. A unison is the same tone played in two separate places. It is indistinguishable from a single note for guitar purposes, and because of the inordinate reach it won't be illustrated.

Simple Intervals - Sixth String

The strategy for the melodic intervals is to derive them from the appropriate scale form. From the sixth string, the Major and perfect melodic intervals (2nd, 3rd, 4th, 5th, 6th,7th and Oct.) are derived from the E diatonic scale form.; the minors (min. 3rd, min. 6th and min. 7th) from the G diatonic scale form; and the min. 2nd and the tritone from the chromatic scale.

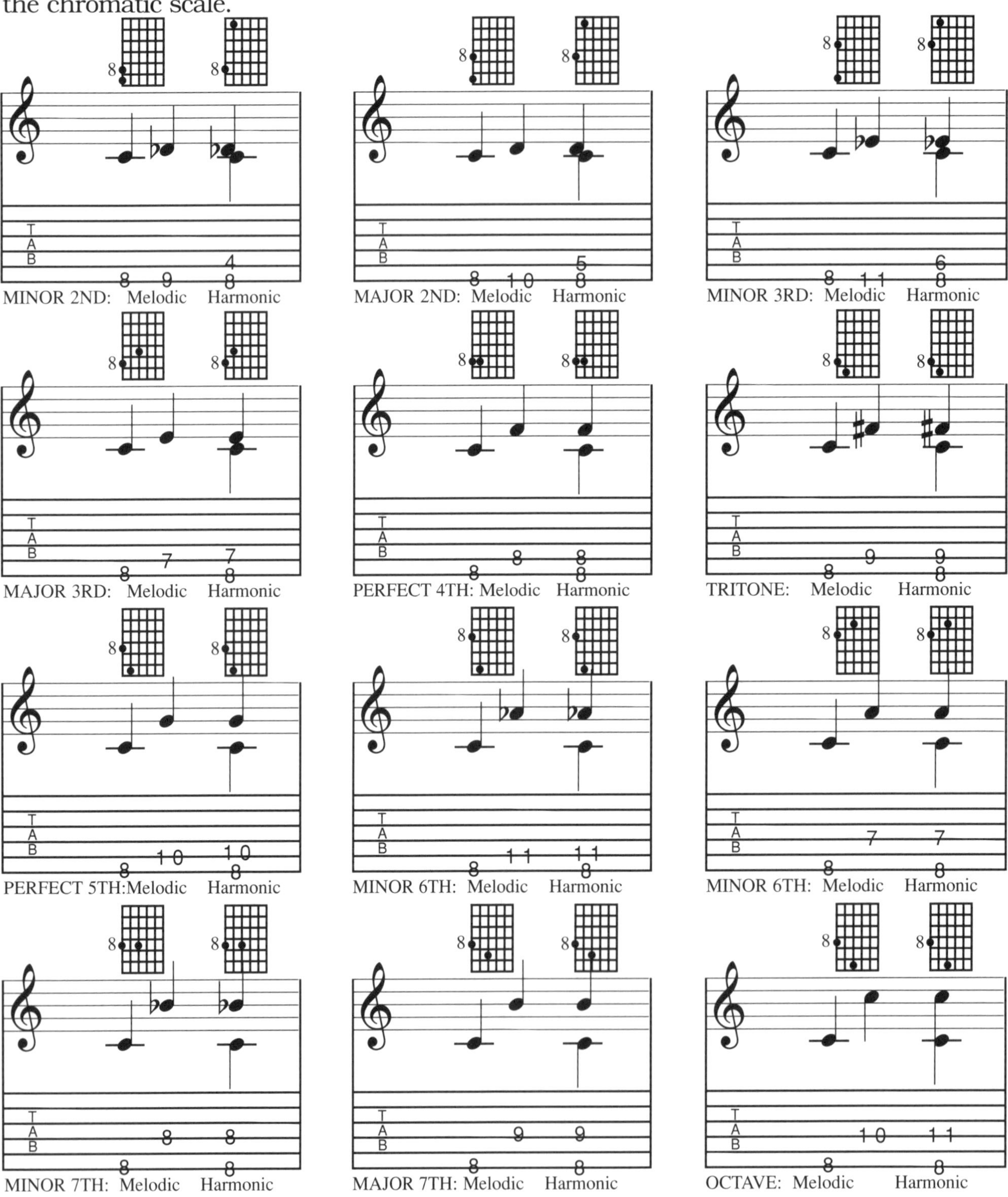

Simple Intervals - 5th String

From the fifth string, the Major and perfect melodic intervals (2nd, 3rd, 4th, 5th, 6th,7th and Oct.) are derived from the A diatonic scale form. The minors (3rd, 6th and 7th) are derived from the C diatonic scale form; and the min. 2nd and the tritone from the chromatic.

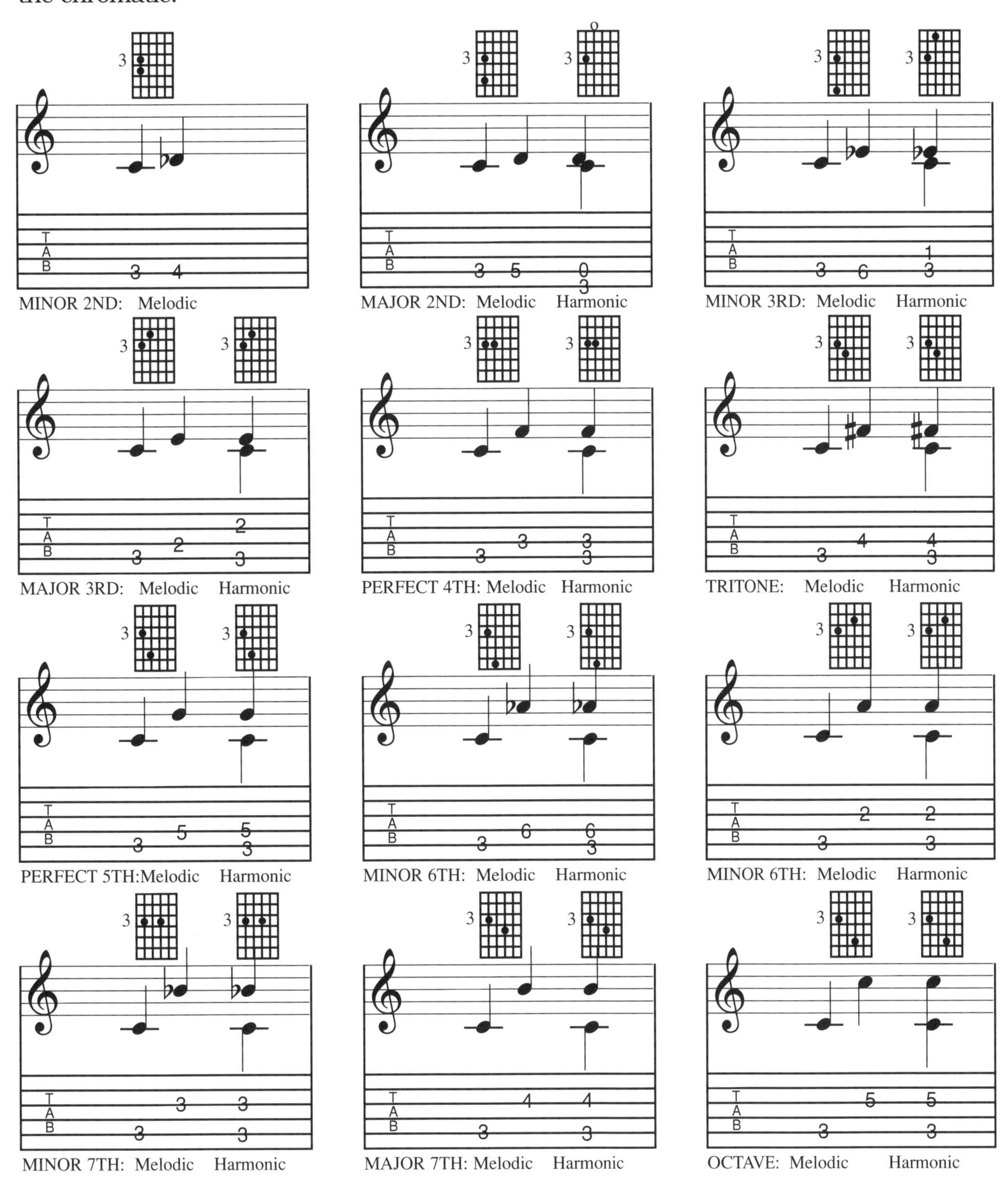

Simple Intervals - 4th String

From the fourth string, the Major and perfect melodic intervals (2nd, 3rd, 4th, 5th, 6th,7th and Oct.) are derived from the D diatonic scale form. The minors (3rd, 6th and 7th) are derived from the E diatonic scale form; and the min. 2nd and the tritone from the chromatic scale.

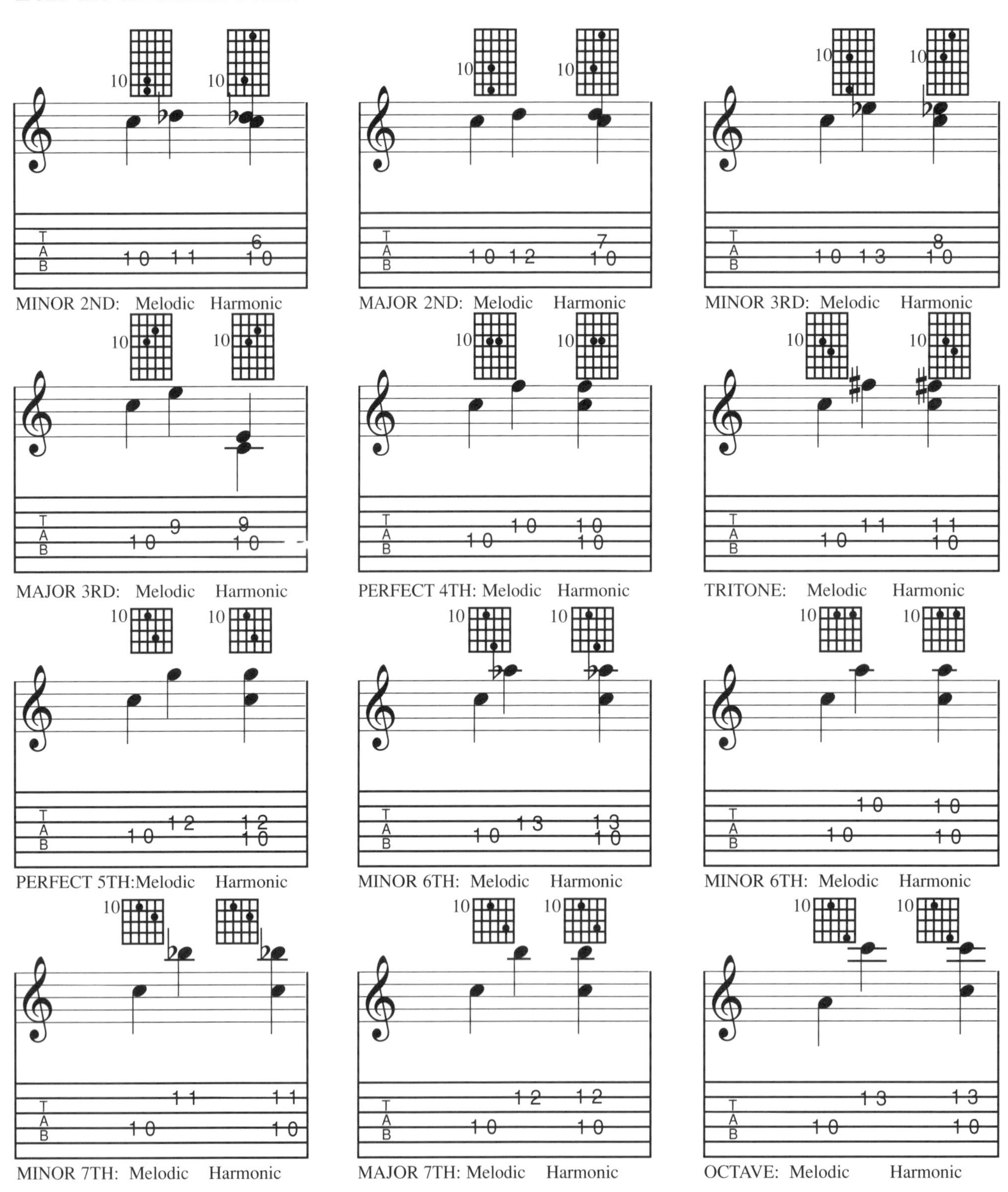

Simple Intervals - 3rd String

From the third string, the Major and perfect melodic intervals (2nd, 3rd, 4th, 5th, 6th,7th and Oct.) are derived from the G diatonic scale form. The minors (3rd, 6th and 7th) are derived from the A diatonic scale form; and the min. 2nd and the tritone from the chromatic.

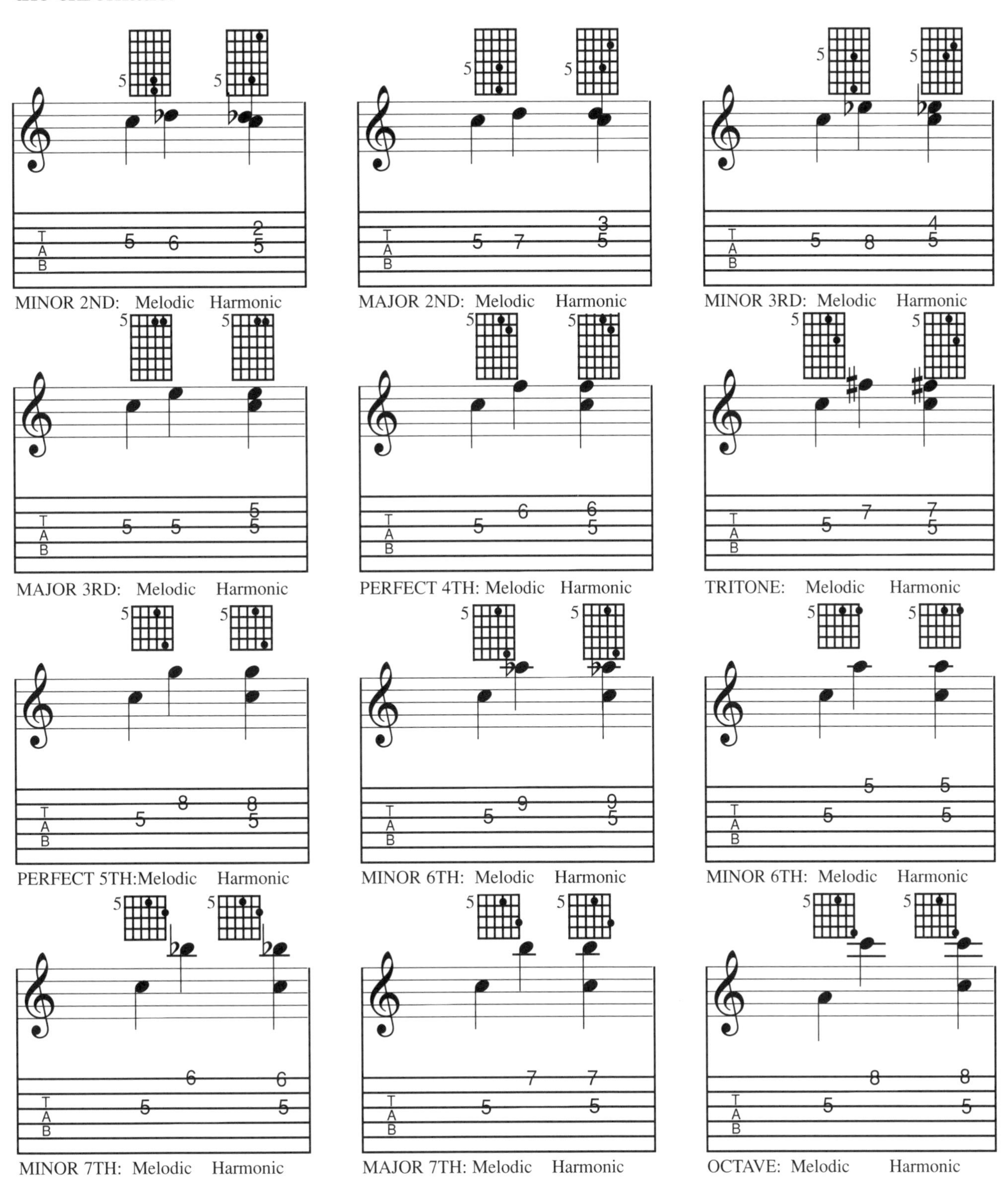

Compound Intervals - Sixth String

As with the simple intervals, the major and perfect compound intervals from the sixth string are derived from the E diatonic scale form; the minor 10rd, 13th and 14th from the G diatonic scale form; and the minor 9th and double tritone from the chromatic scale.

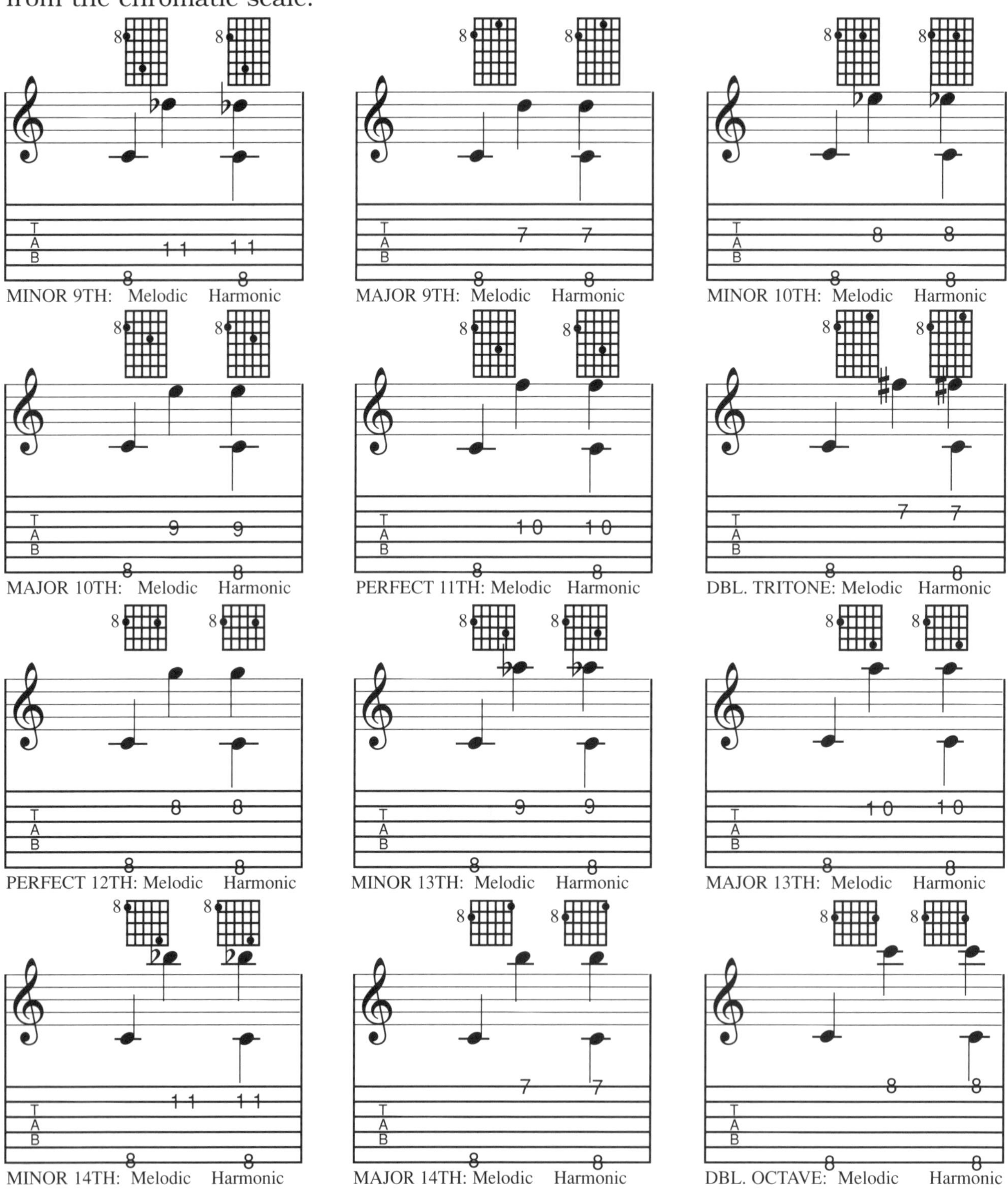

Compound Intervals - 5th String

From the fifth string, the Major and perfect compound intervals are derived from the A diatonic scale form. The minors (3rd, 6th and 7th) are derived from the C diatonic scale form; and the min. 2nd and the tritone from the chromatic.

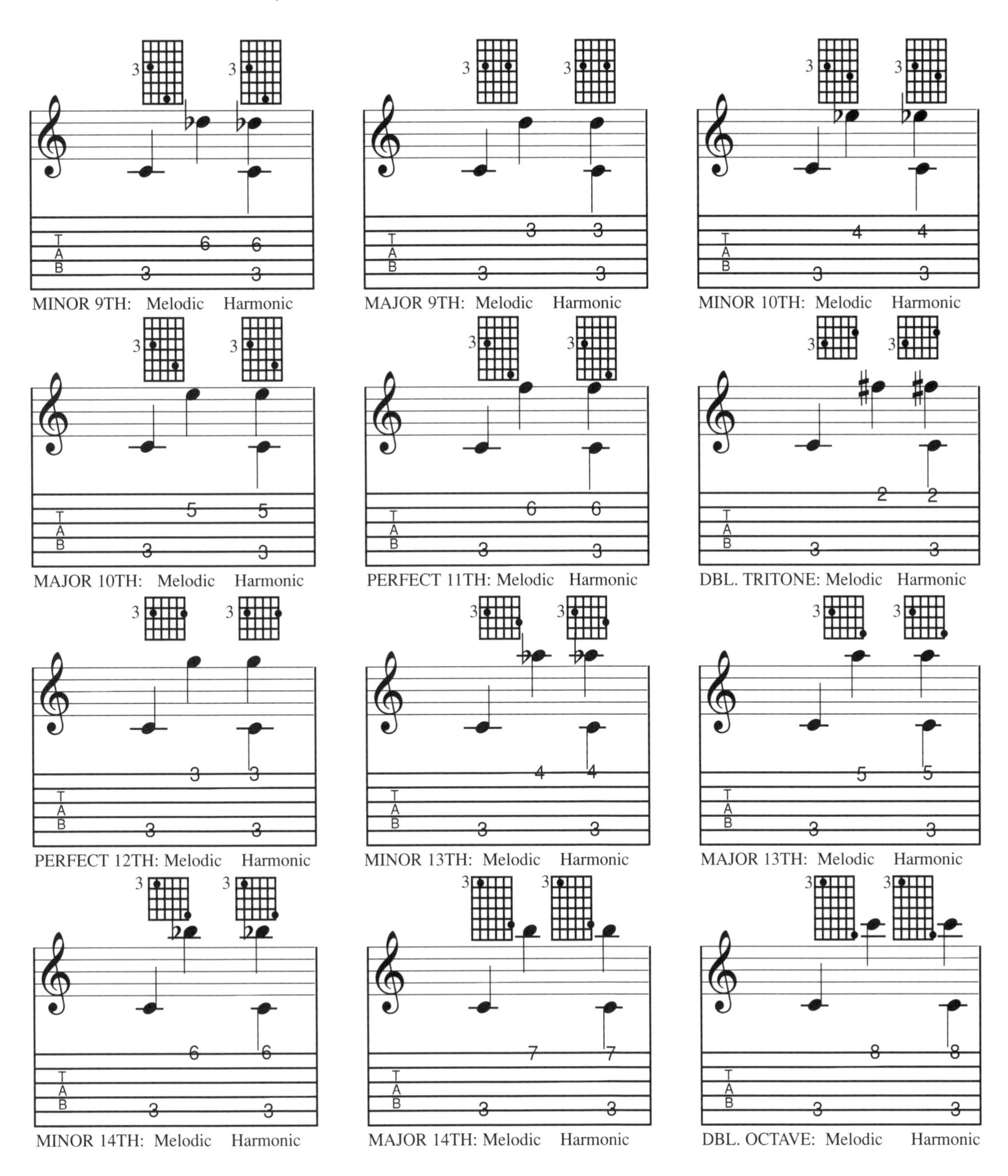

Intervals - Diatonic Progression

Diatonic stepwise motion in thirds are termed couplets, and are presented below on both types of naturally occurring adjacent string pairs. The guitar pattern series in the first measure will work for the string pairs 6-5, 5-4, 4-3, and 2-1. The pattern series in the second measure works only on the 3-2 pair. Both are in the key of A. These intervallic progressions are a combination of scalar stepwise motion and chordal diatonic progression. Keep in mind both W-W-H, W-W-W-H, and Maj. min. min., Maj. Maj. min. dim. as applied to intervals. The Whole-Half motion is from the lower string. Try to recognize the guitar form of which each interval is a portion.

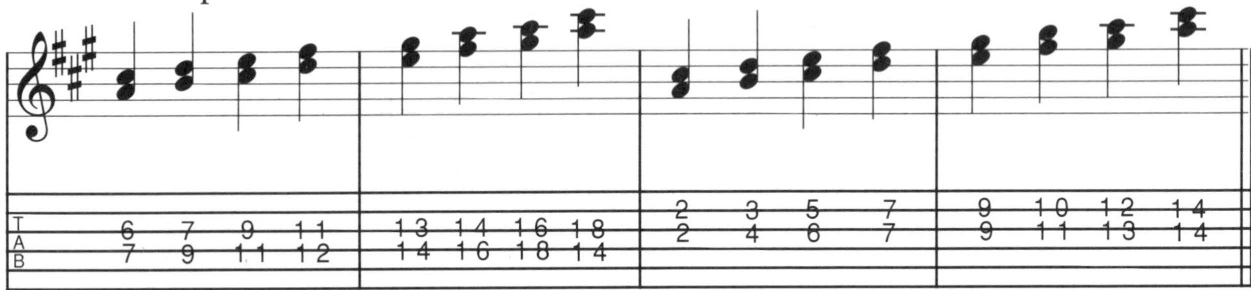

In the next series, the couplet progression is inverted to sixths instead of thirds. Major thirds invert to minor sixths; minor thirds invert to major sixths. This time the Whole-Half motion is in the higher string. The guitar pattern results one way for the string pairs 3-1 and 4-2, (directly below) and another for the pairs 5-3 and 6-4.

Below are the sixths on the 5-3 and 6-4 string pairs. The sixths are played on non adjacent strings to avoid the unnecessary reaching that would occur on adjacent pairs. Although the entire length of the neck isn't illustrated for each string pair, you should be able to use the sequences printed to access both the neck's entire length and changes from one string pair to another. Once the patterns become familiar in this key, apply the progressions to a couple of others.

Intervals

Intervals fall into two categories in terms of how we relate to them individually. If an interval per se, is pleasing to the ear, it is termed consonant. If not, it is considered dissonant. Traditionally the consonances were thirds, sixths, and octaves. The dissonances were the seconds and sevenths, leaving the others considered neither fish nor fowl. As this was somewhat less than objective, another more specific definition has been adopted. If an interval or its inversion exists within a triadic chord, then it is deemed consonant. These are the major and minor thirds and sixths, plus perfect fifths and fourths. Otherwise it is a dissonance, which includes major and minor seconds, sevenths and the tritone. Even within these parameters, some consonances are more appealing and stable than others. Dissonances tend to produce physiological tension, motivating a resolution toward consonance. It is this specificity of tension vs. resolution which gives intervals unique qualities separate from chords. In practical application, an interval is richer than a single note in a melodic sense and only slightly less definite than a chord in a harmonic sense.

Using seventh chords as our basic unit, we will take another look at the relative value of each chord tone for the purposes of discussing certain types of intervallic progression. If you are familiar with altered and extended chords, then you know that some degrees are more important than others to the essential nature and character of a chord. When producing altered and extended chords, it is often necessary to leave off less important tones to permit the addition of others. The first to go is the fifth degree. It has the least significance to the chord in terms of distinguishing value. The next to go is perhaps surprisingly, the tonic. The tonic is important because it references the tones, but not as important as the ones which remain. The remaining third and seventh degrees become the main determinant of character when reductions are necessary or when intervals become the unit of currency.

The third degree establishes the single greatest distinction of a chord, and that is whether it is major or minor oriented. If the third is unaltered, then it is, of course, major oriented. The major oriented quatrads are Major 7th, augmented 7th, and dominant 7th. If the third is flatted, it produces a minor orientation. The minor oriented quatrads produced are the minor 7th, minor 7b5, and diminished 7th.

The seventh degree is the second most essential chord tone. It has been termed the leading tone since it pulls strongly toward the tonic. Without a tonic note, the seventh degree at least suggests one, by way of leading our ear toward it, if in a tensioned manner. The seventh and its alterations also identify the character of the chord with the dominant chord and its extensions in particular. Recall in Vol. II we related the major-ness or minor-ness of the various modes by the character of the last interval. If the last interval was a half step, then the mode sounded more major. If it was a whole step, then it came across as more minor.

By combining the essential intervals with the most basic cadence, the five-one resolution, we produce two types of intervallic progression that are distinctive, useful, and easy to remember. In the spirit of gonzo guitar we are going to term these exploding and imploding chromatic 5-1 intervals. Ok, call it literary license. Exploding and imploding just means that the physical motion of both degrees on the fretboard is outward and inward, but some words are easier to remember than others. Musically the motion is simply contrary for both. They are illustrated on the next page.

Intervals - Contrary Motion

The key we will illustrate this intervallic motion in is C, and the diagrams follow CAGED sequence starting with the C form. The 5-1 in the key of C is G to C, or G dom.7 to C Maj. 7 using quatrads. The third and seventh degrees of the G chord are the notes B and F , which is the interval of a tritone. By moving outward in contrary motion, or exploding the interval by a half step in both directions, we can conveniently resolve to the 1st and 3rd degrees of the C chord as shown in the first illustration.

C7 Form Tritone G/E Form Min. 6th

A7 Form Tritone E/D Form Min.6th

G7 Form Tritone C Form Min. 6th

E7 Form Tritone C/A Form Min. 6th

D7 Form Tritone G Form Min.6th

Next are the imploding intervals. The musical motion is outward just as above, but with these, the physical motion of the forms is inward.

C7 Form Tritone E Form Min. 6th

G7 Form Tritone C Form Min.6th

E/D Form Tritone G Form Min. 6th

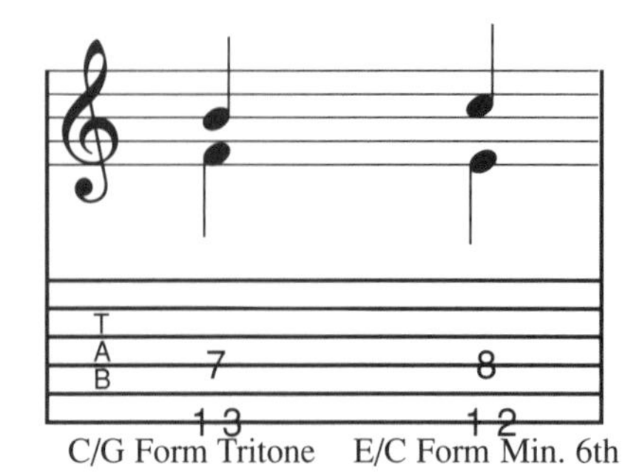

C/G Form Tritone E/C Form Min. 6th

Intervals - Contrary Motion

These 5-1 progressions can be continued indefinitely by simply moving the resolved "1" a half step in either direction, making the tritone and continuing as before. you will here this type of harmonic activity in a great deal of classical and baroque music.

Technique

What is meant here by the term technique is the overall physical aspects of playing. When people refer to the plural "techniques," it usually pertains to more specific articulations such as slides and trills. A technical issue is generally a physical issue. If you know the three Ls of real estate, you can probably guess the three Ps of technique. The goal here is to 1) establish technically oriented practice habits, 2) put iterative note sequences into practice, and 3) practice guitar-specific articulation techniques. In Vol. II, a lot of tonal material was provided but without a method for applying it in a practical context. This area is intended to provide answers to the oft asked question, "How should I practice the stuff in your books?" It is obvious that in order to make use of those materials, we've got to do more than just be able to play them as simple forms. In a general sense, the goal of technical studies is to enable us to do things we couldn't do before. I don't subscribe to the teaching philosophy that says "My way or the highway." Too many opposing methods work in too many different circumstances. I've got to get my hands to work for me, and you have to get yours to work for you. Maybe this is what all those so-called "self-taught" players really mean. But don't forget that we can learn wrong just as easily and permanently as right. What is meant by the term "wrong," is anything which prevents us from attaining our goals.

As a child I took piano lessons from the proverbial "little old lady down the street" who always stressed proper technique. (Another thing she always stressed was the furniture, since she weighed in at about 280, but let's just say she left a lasting impression on us both, and leave it at that.) At the time, holding your hands as if you had oranges in them was taught as the way to achieve proper technique. In retrospect, I don't think I could dream up a more ridiculous approach. No wait, how about like you're holding mashed potatoes... no, unpinned grenades... uh, shark bait? Wait a minute. How about holding your hands as if you were maybe... playing a piano? Nah. As you can imagine, not only do strategies for technique go in and out of style, techniques for approaching different styles of music vary greatly from artist to artist and teacher to teacher. So proper (roll the first "r" please) technique is not something that one should expect people to agree upon. On the other hand, it is important not to down play the significance of technical ability. To a certain way of thinking, technique is what puts the virtue in virtuosity. How to get there is anybody's game. I remember reading about a performer who once said in an interview that the night before every concert, he'd squeeze a tennis ball 5000 times or so in each hand. The first thing that popped into my head was, "Well that's a way to get good at squeezing tennis balls, but I don't think it would prepare him as well as playing his guitar." Later I realized that if he thinks this is what he needs, and feels it helps him, well ok. Whatever works, works. Our physiology, emotions, and psychology are all a part of what goes into our guitar playing. After all, guitarists are at least as superstitious about their careers as your average minor league ball player. If you believe something besides practice is improving your overall technical ability, then by all means go for it. On the other hand, the people who play really well also seem to practice an awful lot.

The physical requirements of playing the guitar are such that anyone who takes it seriously is going to commit themselves to an ongoing daily struggle with strength, coordination, extensibility, concentration, endurance, and velocity, to name a few. To address these requirements, this section will attempt to provide specific technical studies, aka etudes, general developmental concepts and an overall system of goals for both individual practice sessions and longer range objectives.

Since the job of the left hand is fundamentally different from that of the right, it makes sense to examine them as two separate issues. Synchronizing them is a third and more significant issue altogether. All things being equal, scales are more demanding than chords, and arpeggios are more demanding than scales. That goes for each hand individually and in sync.

Left hand scale and arpeggio requirements will usually be in groups of fours, threes, twos, and ones in terms of the number of notes played per string (position crossovers, single and double string play notwithstanding). As the number of notes per string decreases, the string to string activity on the part of the right hand increases.

As a general statement of technique with respect to the material in Vol. II, right hand techniques can be divided into chordal and scalar approaches, where chordal pertains to picking in one direction with (normally) one pickstroke per string. Scalar pertains to the alternating direction convention usually termed alternate picking. The analog for strings picked with the fingers (and/or nails) is similar. Notes played with a scalar technique are plucked with alternating fingers (usually index-middle, or index-thumb) on the same string. Right hand chordal technique is where a finger (or thumb) plucks just one string per ascent or descent.

Since arpeggios are a hybrid of chords and scales, they can be articulated with either right hand approach. When encountering two or more notes per string using the chordal approach, play the tones that follow with techniques such as hammer-ons, slides, and pull-offs. When playing arpeggios using the scalar technique, reverse the pick direction for each note regardless of the number of notes per string.

If there was one overall, golden rule for technique (in both hands), it would probably pertain to economy of motion. This can mean anything from putting your left hand fingers closer to the strings about to be played, to preventing the pick from travelling any further past the string than necessary.

We all recognize a polished player when we hear one. I have my favorites and you have yours. The technical abilities these players possess is among the things that set them apart from ordinary guitarists and get our attention. I've heard many students say something to the effect, "I'd kill to play like [fill in the blank]" but would they do something even more outrageous? Would they practice, experiment and push themselves just as much as [fill in the blank] does?

> A laborer works with his hands. A craftsman works with his hands and head. An artist works with his hands, his head and his heart.
>
> Anon.

Technical Development Exercises

The technical development exercises that follow are designed to produce and sustain synchronization between the left and right hands. They will also prepare them for almost any single note, string to string activity likely to be encountered. The right hand part can be played using fingers or any type of pick(s) you are interested in or already comfortable with. The right hand motion of particular interest involves the change from playing on just one string to playing on adjacent ones, because of the differences of the two activities. For those who use a flat pick, moving to another string is a longer, necessarily more elliptical motion, which has to blend in with the shorter, more linear ones of the same string. This is the so-called circular picking, of which many players speak. For players who use their fingers, this motion will be somewhat more easily absorbed by having as many as four or five fingers range the plane of the strings. The main difference then will be between the direction of travel of the fingers and the thumb. In other words, going from string to string using thumb and finger is a kind of balancing action, whereas using successive fingers tends to draw the right hand out of position.

Although there might seem to be quite a number of string to string possibilities, in a directional sense there are actually only four: down-down, up-up, down-up, and up-down. Most people will do these exercises with a pick. As a matter of course, flatpick users learn to associate downstrokes with strong beats (accents) and upstrokes with weak beats. As a result, most will usually begin each series with a downstroke. Make it a policy to also play starting with an upstroke 50% of the time. It will pay off when there are regular accented upstrokes such as with three notes per string, and when there's an irregular number of notes from one string to another such as with harmonic minor lead patterns.

Continuing along the lines alluded to early on, the studies that follow are designed to increase your physical awareness, coordination, and velocity. They can be used, for example, as a preparation for practice sessions and performances, or for velocity studies. There are relatively few guitarists who can pick up the instrument and be playing at the top of his or her ability right from the start. The rest of us must warm up for a period of time to get to that point, and thirty to sixty minutes is about average. These are not intended solely as velocity studies, but they're fairly well suited for it. Regardless of your intentions, the approach should be to begin dead slow at first, meaning no errors. A simple way to determine what speed to begin at is to ask yourself this question. "At what speed do I play it so that I cannot possibly make an error." Determine that, and then start a notch or two slower. Establish a baseline velocity and if you make an error, start over and decrease it. Learn to distinguish between speeding up your brain and speeding up your fingers. As with all practice, strive for comprehension first, control and accuracy second, expression next, and speed last. Only increase the rate of the exercise when there is little if any possibility for error in doing so, and only in metronome or nominal increments. Most of us tend to do something slow once, ignore our errors, then immediately start to accelerate to warp speed. Control means accuracy; and repetition produces a certainty which enables velocity. One more note about right hand alternation: These exercises are scalar in a technical sense, and as such utilize alternate picking in the right hand. If you use a pick, alternate down and up pick strokes at all times. First start with downstrokes then repeat the entire exercise starting with upstrokes. If you use your fingers, alternate index and middle or thumb and index, then repeat the exercises reversing the order.

Technical Development Exercises - Fours and Threes

1. Fours - Start on the sixth string, first position (four fingers - four frets positioning) and play every fret on every string in order 6th to 1st string and then go back 1st to 6th again starting with the 4th finger. Only the first of about twenty positions, are illustrated in these exercises. Next move up a fret and repeat the exercise. Continue advancing a fret at a time until you run out of playing area for your particular guitar. Then repeat the exercises in the other direction (back down the neck, fret by fret) starting with a picked upstroke or a different right hand finger than before.

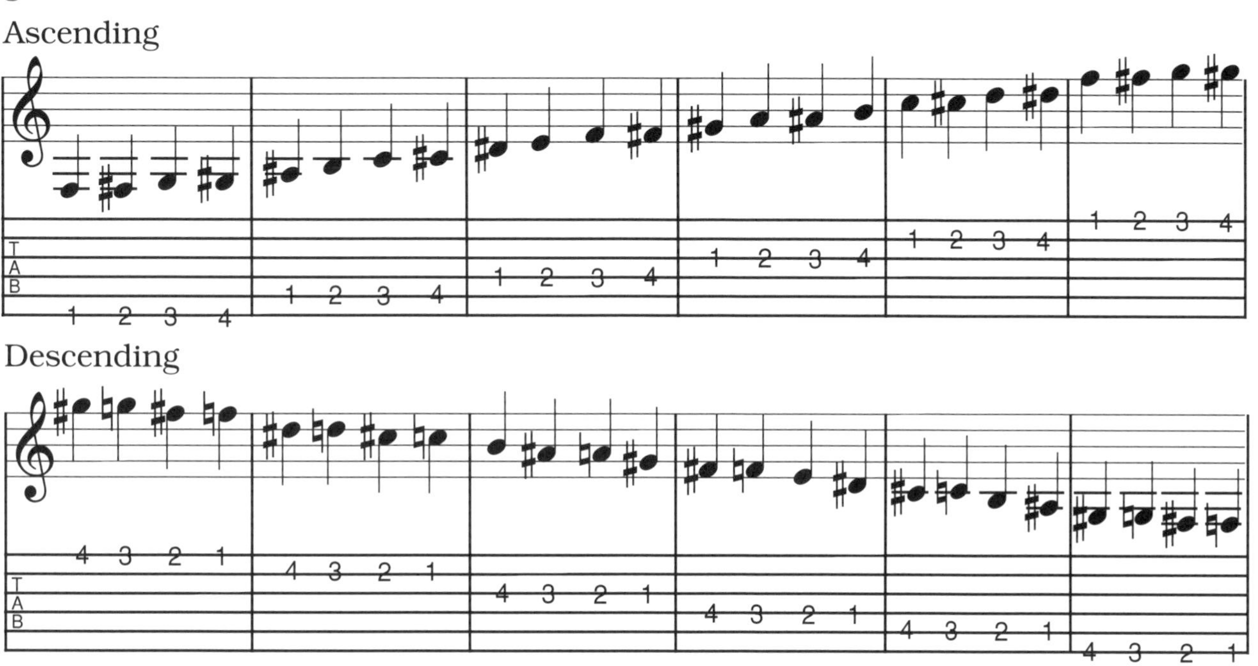

2. Threes - Start in the first position on the sixth string and play three notes per string in the same manner as above. The exercise illustrated below uses the 1st 3rd & 4th fingers. (The various options for these exercises are discussed later.) The descending part is illustrated on the next page. Don't forget that only the first position is being illustrated in these exercises. These studies involve practicing the string to string motion illustrated in as many positions as you can access on your instrument. Exercise number 2 is continued on the following page.

Ascending

Technical Development Exercises - Twos and Ones

Descending

3. Twos - Again start in the first position on the sixth string but this time play only two notes per string. The twos can be played using any combination of two fretting fingers, with the 1st and 4th illustrated ascending and descending, below.

4. Ones - The object here is to treat each string with scalar, or alternate picking. These can be played using any chord form or none at all. The E form is illustrated below. These could be considered a kind of "faux arpeggio" or chord forms played like scales.

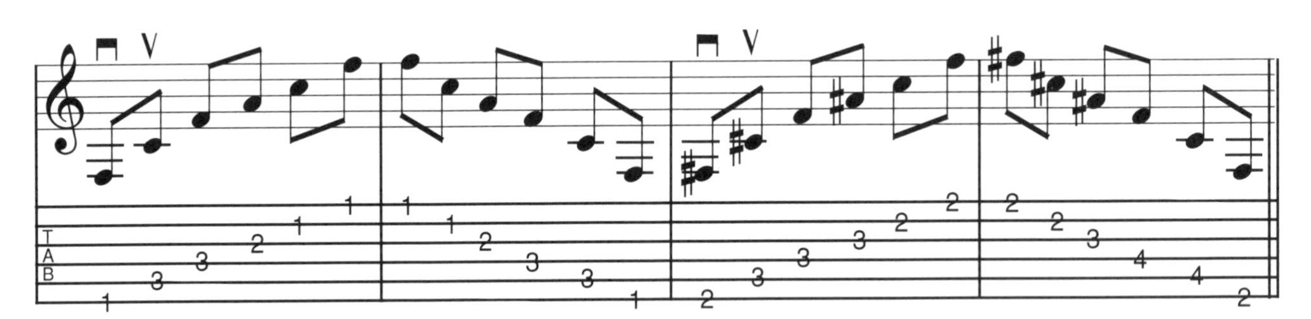

Since the pinky is our shortest and weakest finger, we tend to favor it, so the variations you select should bring it into play as often as possible. You may have noticed that the exercises seem to entail a lot of notes when played all the way up the neck and then back down again fret by fret. On a twenty four fret neck with two variations of all four, it comes to just under 10,000 notes and takes about 30-60 minutes to complete. But then your hands are nicely synchronized and you're ready for just about anything. Including a nap.

Technical Development Exercises - Variations

There are numerous ways to create variations of the technical material presented as numbers of notes/fingers per string. By keeping that one characteristic constant and changing others, we begin to have an understanding of the concept of creative choice, and more importantly, the physical manifestations of those choices. Don't forget that our hands are constantly sending signals to our brains about, among other things, their mistreatment and the unreasonable demands we place upon them. For many of us these messages can get in the way of production, and lead to slow downs, sick outs, and work stoppages. But don't ignore possible medical problems, either.

Among the left hand variations that can be made while keeping the number of notes per string constant are: 1) changing the tonal direction, 2) changing the note/fret order, 3) changing the string order, 4) including pattern/finger extensions, 5) using string articulation techniques, and 6) combinations of these. As the number of notes per string gets lower, the number of possible variations is reduced also. As always, it is up to each of us to find new ways of looking at the same old things. Remember the idea here is to allow the player to concentrate on the physical aspects of the guitar to the exclusion of pretty much everything else. Later we'll combine these acquired technical abilities with some tonal and rhythmic materials to make something that sounds like music. What follows are examples of the above variations.

Fours: Note/Fret Order Variation - Ascending

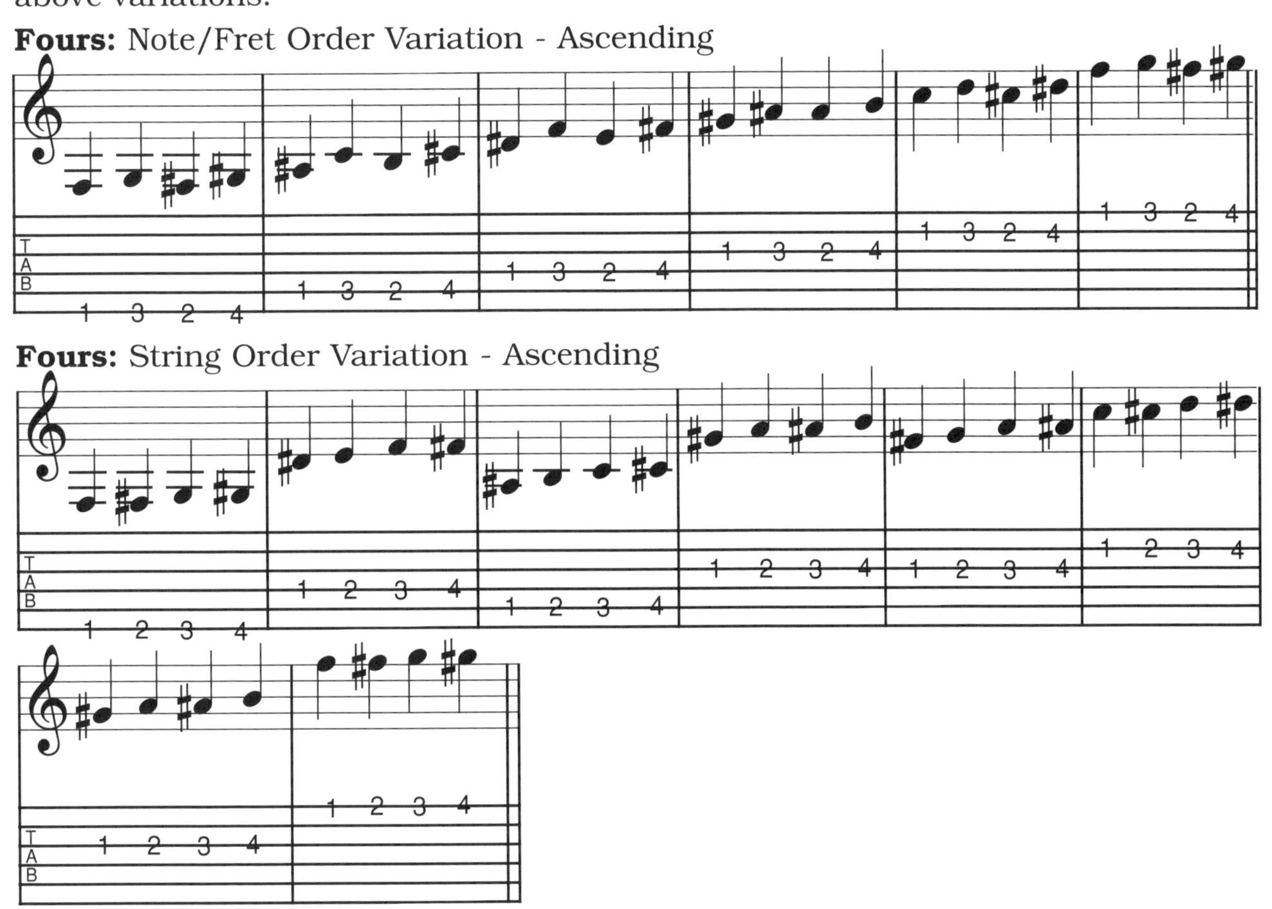

Technical Development Exercises - Variations

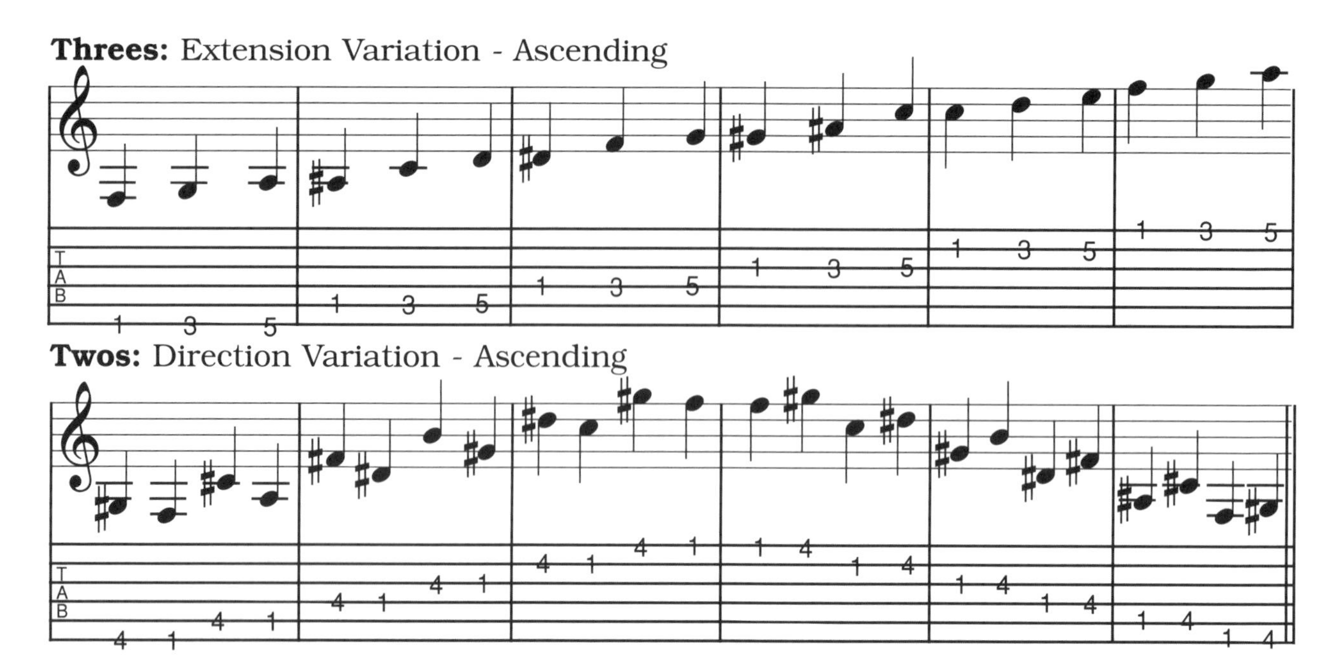

To pursue the variations further, we'll list some of the permutations of each that you can incorporate into your own technical studies. Progress from adding just a single variation, to combining two, then three, and so on. This part of the TDEs is the most important. Think of it as both a creative and self-reliant endeavor. Combinations help bridge the technical gap between simple dexterity exercises and tone groups such as scales and arpeggios.

1) Changing directions. Here you are limited to either ascending or descending. This means going from where you are tonally, to higher or lower in both a specific sense such as note to note, or a more general sense such as phrase to phrase.

2) Changing the note/fret order. Remember that on the left hand, index = 1, middle = 2, ring = 3, and pinky = 4. Playing four notes per string, the following permutations of order are possible: 1234, 1243, 1324, 1342, 1432, 1423; 2341, 2314, 2413, 2431, 2134, 2143; 3412, 3421, 3214, 3241, 3142,3124; 4123, 4132, 4231, 4213, 4312, 4321. Three notes per string: 123, 132; 231, 213; 312, 321. Two notes per string: 1-2; 2-1; etc.

3) Changing the string order. The order of strings can be altered in a manner similar to the changing of the note/fret order. Since there are six strings, many permutations of this are possible. Use the permutations of the fours above as a guide for these.

4) Pattern/Finger Extensions. A space of one fret can be placed between the four fretting fingers: index and middle, middle and ring, and ring and pinky.

5) Articulation Techniques. The ones that will be most useful for these exercises are the hammer-ons, pull-offs, slides, and bends. Hammer-ons can occur when the note to note direction (per string) is higher; pull-offs can be used when the direction is lower; slides and bends can be used in either direction.

6) Alternate No. of Notes Per String. Play four notes on the sixth string, then three on the fifth, then four, then three, and so on. The next variation is to alternate three types of "notes per string" finger groups.

Articulation Techniques

This section covers guitar-specific techniques that are known by various names including slurs, technical devices, guitar tricks, etc. To beginning players whose fingers are not yet guitar-strong, they may be considered crude physical demands, but they will soon come to represent some of the most expressive aspects of playing the instrument.

The symbols are mostly graphic representations that are intended to be iconic, in the sense that they convey meaning without words. They are in fairly common usage having become somewhat standardized over the years. There are surprisingly few basics, but by varying and combining them you can start to appreciate the broad range of non-musical expression that is possible when you have complete access to an instrument's tone generators - in this case, strings. It makes the restrictions imposed by the mechanics of a keyboard key seem woefully limited by comparison.

The basic articulation techniques are: Pull-Offs, Hammer-Ons, Slides, Mutes, Harmonics, Bends, Tremolos, Vibratos, and Rasgados. For the left hand techniques, this is roughly in order of difficulty, also. These techniques will be absorbed by constant repetition and experimentation until they are understood on not so much an intellectual level, as a tactile one. This area falls under the heading of multiple response type learning, and there is no way to "psych" the techniques out or just "grok" them. They must be played many more times than you would like to think. As with the other areas in which repetition is a necessity, think in basic units of hundreds, and serious units of thousands. What follows is a symbol legend of articulation techniques to be practiced individually until easily recognized, applied, combined, and improvised.

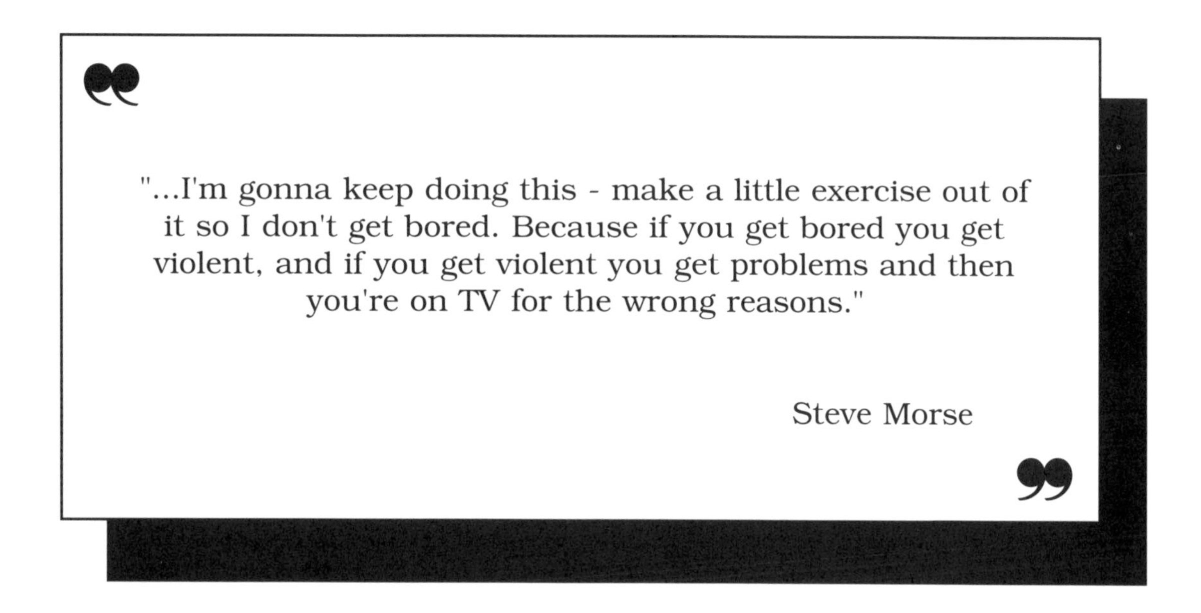

Articulation Techniques Legend - Basics

PULL OFF- With both fingers fretting the string, pick only the higher note and sound the lower note with the higher fretting finger. Push or pull away so the string is plucked and not just released. Pull offs can also be played without first being picked.

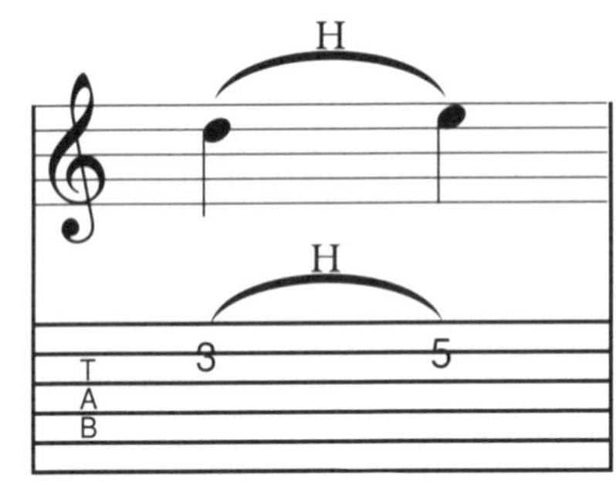

HAMMER ON- Pick the lower note then percussively fret the higher note as to sound it without picking again. Hammer ons can also be played as a first note without picking.

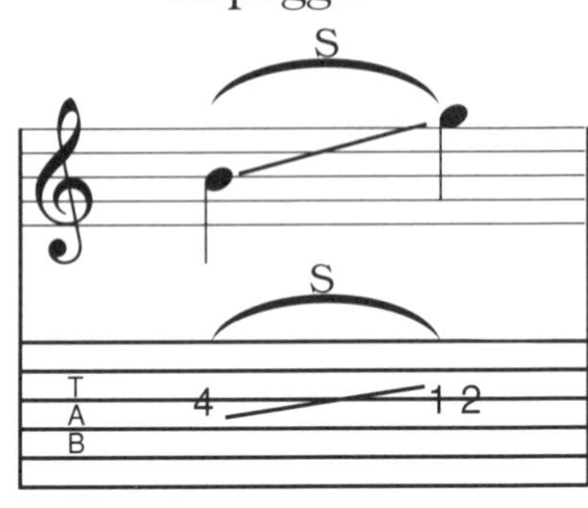

SLIDE (Legato)- Pick the lower note then drag the fretting finger against frets to the higher note. Tie (curve under S) indicates pick note only once for smoothness. AKA Glissando.

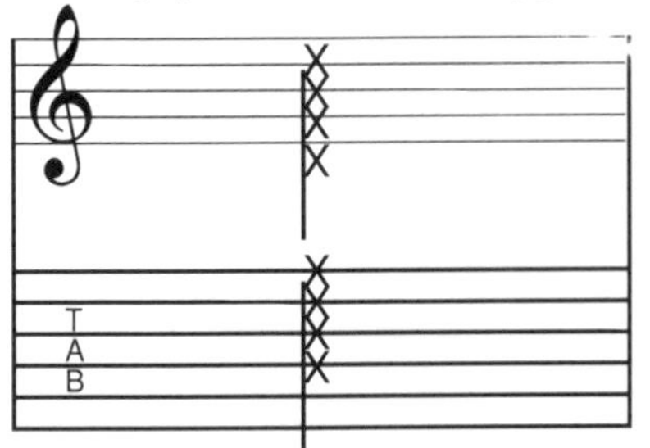

MUTE (Left hand)- Lay the fingers of your left hand across the strings unfretted to produce a percussive non-tonal sound when picked.

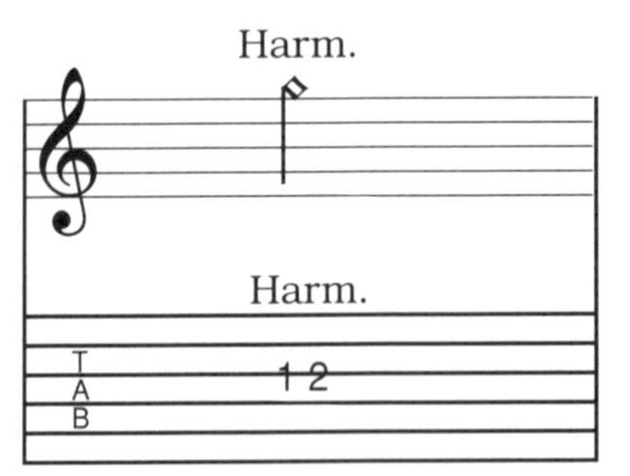

HARMONIC (Natural)- Lightly touch the string exactly over the fret then pick the string and remove finger quickly.

BEND- Pick the note and push or pull the string the specified number of half steps moving adjacent strings out of the way with fingers. Bends can also be microtonal or less than 1/2 step. AKA portamento.

TREMOLO- Using alternate picking, pick the note(s) continuously as rapidly as possible.

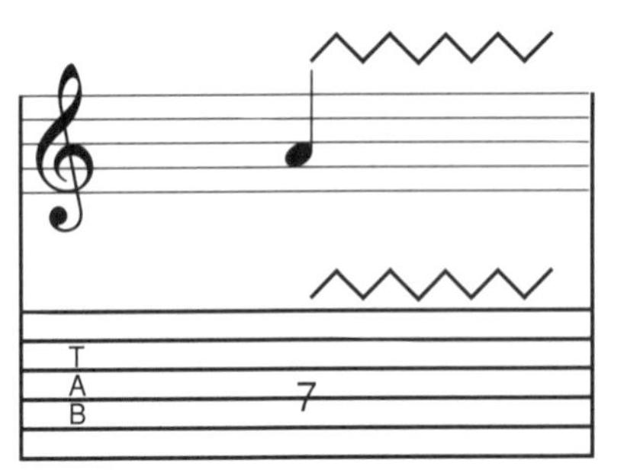

VIBRATO (Moderate)- Repeatedly bend and release the string with the fretting finger(s) or use the tremolo bar likewise. Effect can be subtle, moderate, or exaggerated as line indicates.

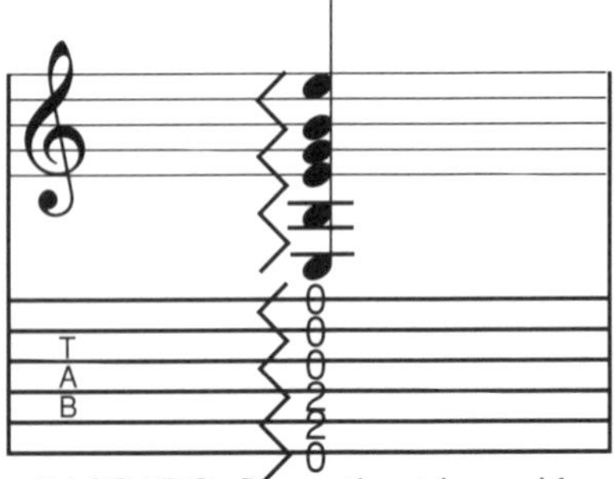

RASGADO- Sweep the strings with successive fingernails (or thumb) to produce rapidly arpeggiated or scraped chord.

Articulation Techniques - Variations and Combinations

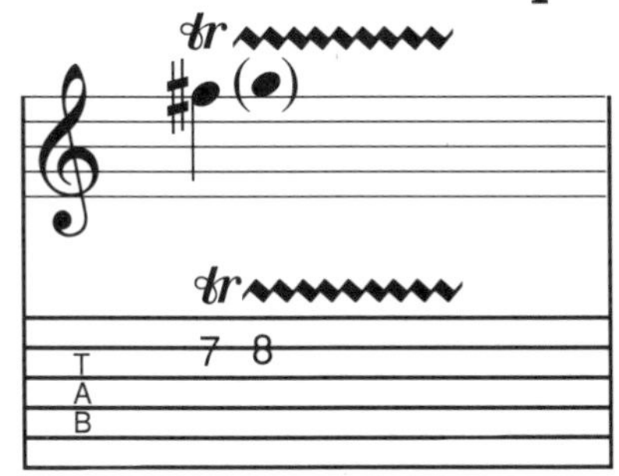

TRILL- Play a rapid succession of hammer-ons and pull-offs using the first note and the parenthetical note.

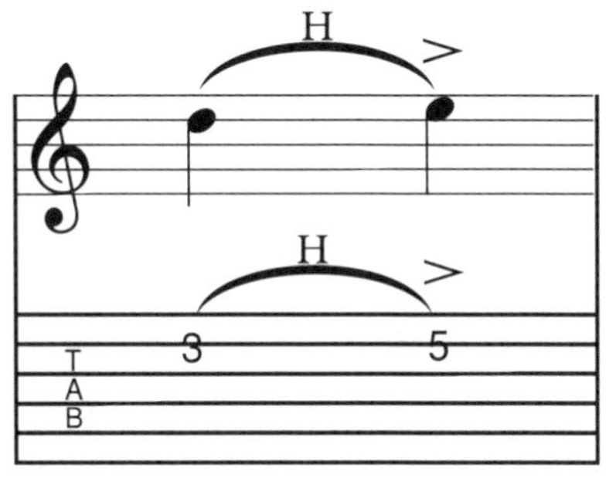

ACCENT- Play the indicated note or notes with added emphasis.

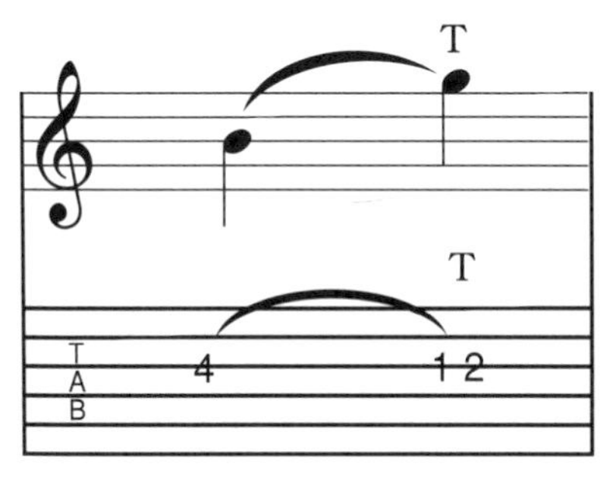

TAP- Hammer on with the index or middle finger of the right hand. A right hand tap is usually followed by a pull off or slide.

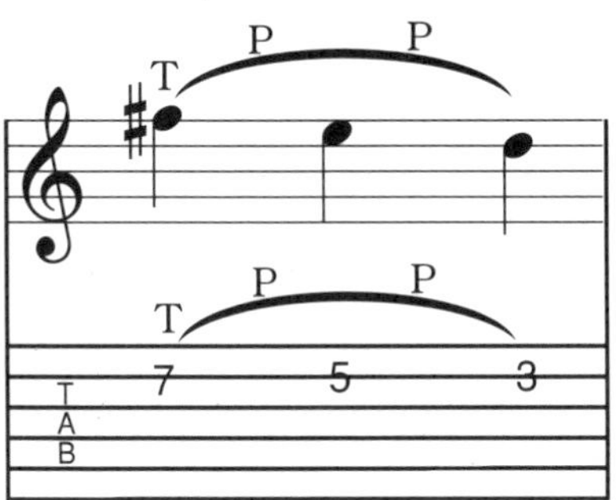

TAP-PULL OFF- Tap the first note with a finger of the right hand and pull off the following note or notes with the left.

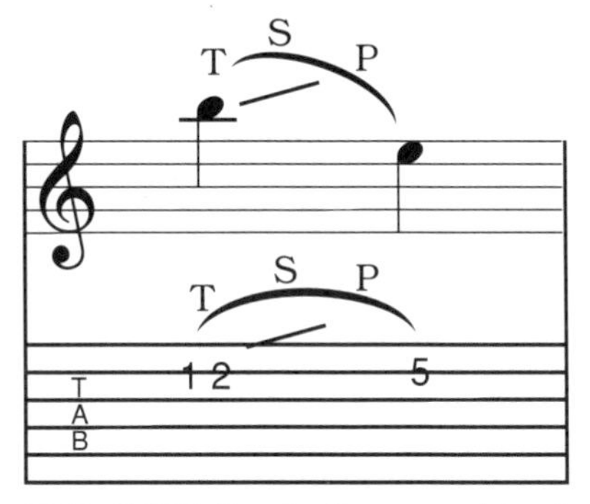

TAP-SLIDE- Tap the first note with a finger of the right hand and slide in the direction indicated. The tap-slide is usually followed by a pull off.

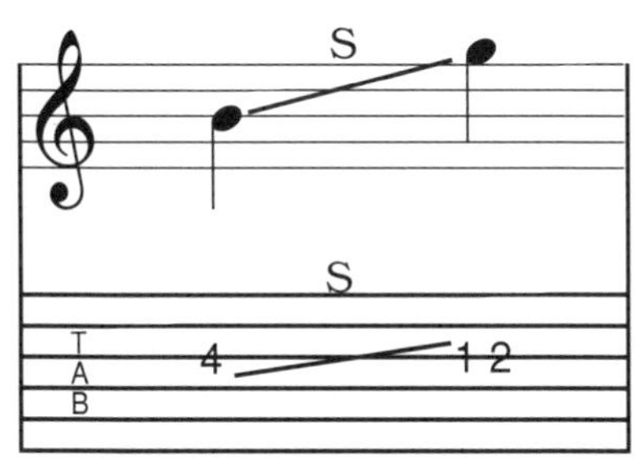

SLIDE (Portato)- Pick the lower note then drag the fretting finger against frets to the higher note, also picked.

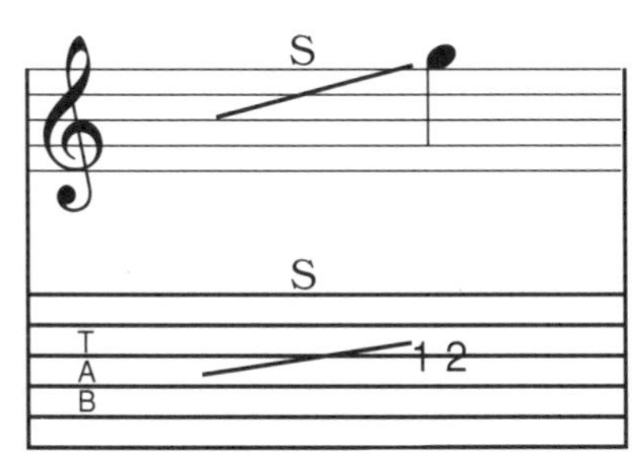

PRE SLIDE (Indefinite)- Slide from a non-specific point to the indicated note.

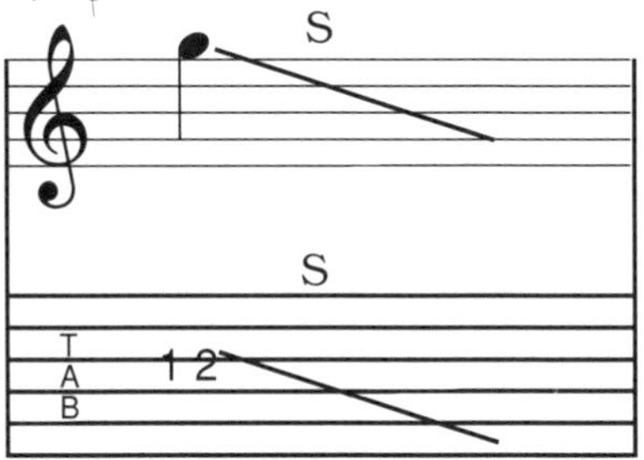

POST SLIDE (Indefinite)- Slide from the note specified to an indeterminate point in the indicated direction.

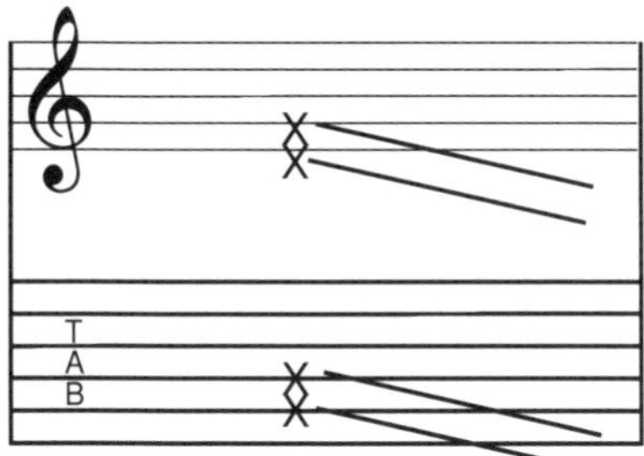

PICK SLIDE- Drag the edge of the pick along the string(s) (against the windings) in the indicated direction for a scratchy sound.

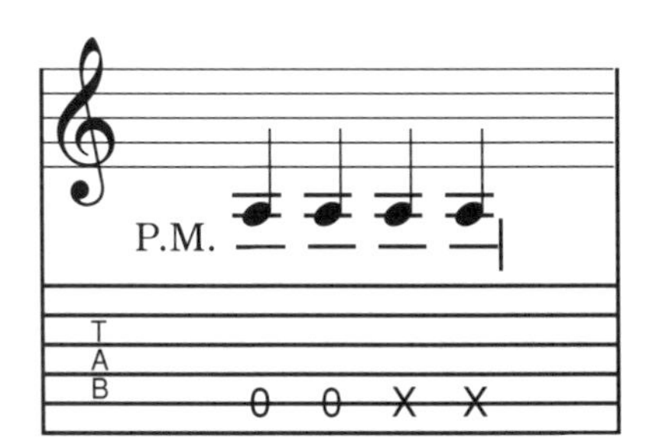

PALM MUTE- Lay the palm of your picking hand over the strings while playing. Lighter touch permits more tone to come through (0). Heavier touch is more percussive as notated (X).

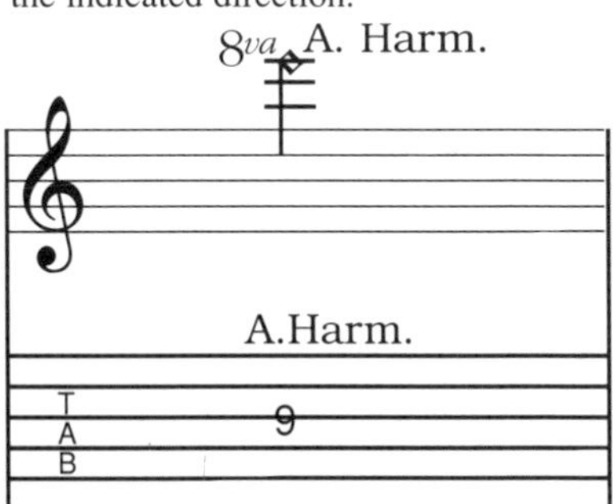

HARMONIC (Artificial)- Fret the note normally and as you are picking, lightly contact the string with the side of the picking thumb on the way past. Can also be produced with right hand by both touching and plucking the string with the right hand.

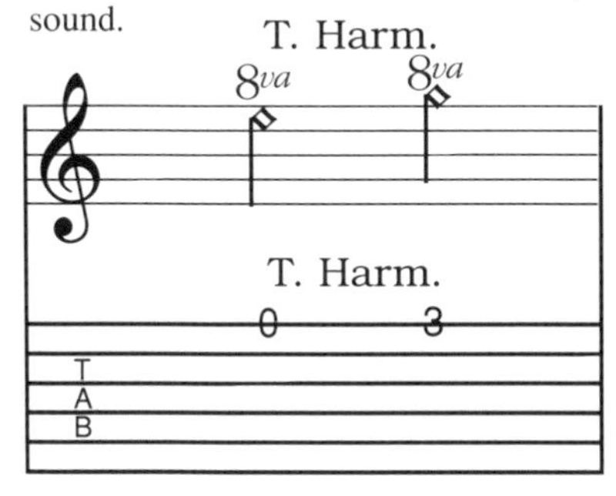

TAPPED HARMONIC- Fret the note normally then tap the note with a finger of the right hand percussively on the fret an octave higher than fretted.

Articulation Techniques - More Variations and Combinations

REVERSE BEND- Prebend the string to the specified number of half steps then pick the string and release down to original tone.

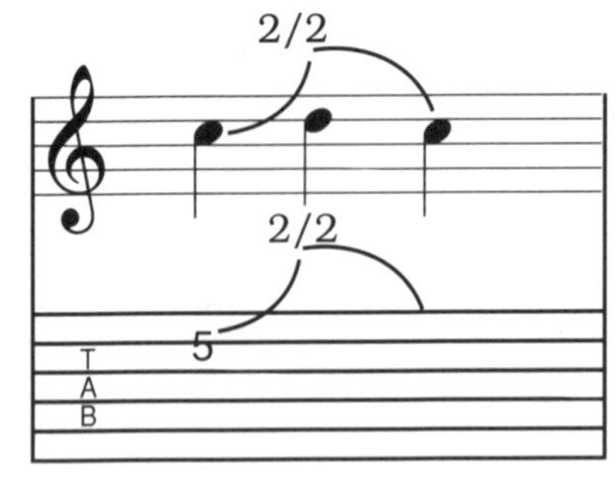

BEND RELEASE- Play the first note, bend to the second then release to the original note again.

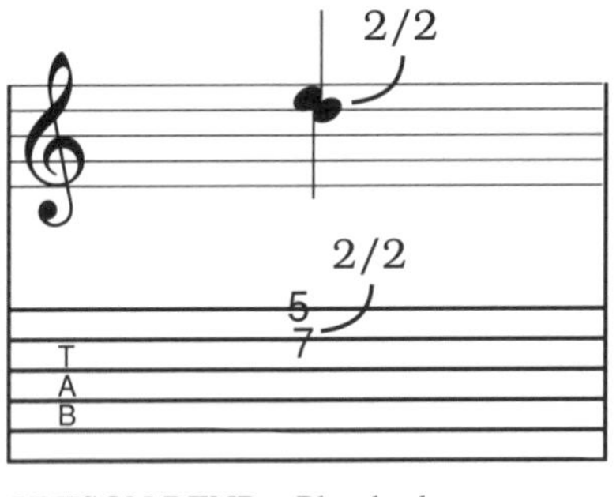

UNISON BEND- Play both notes at once and bend the lower one up to the pitch of the higher.

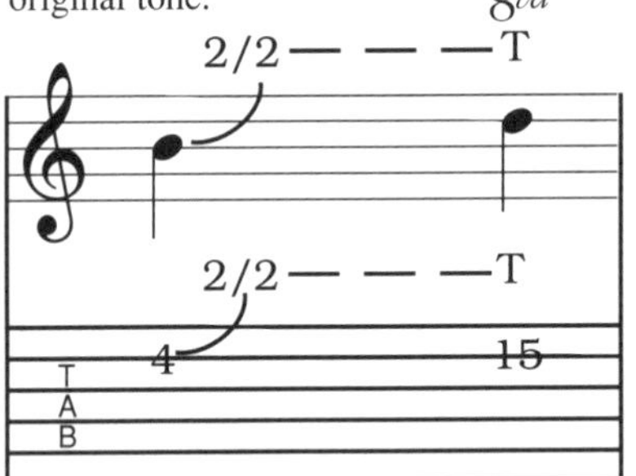

BEND TAP- Bend the first note the specified number of half steps, sustain the bend and tap the higher note with the right hand.

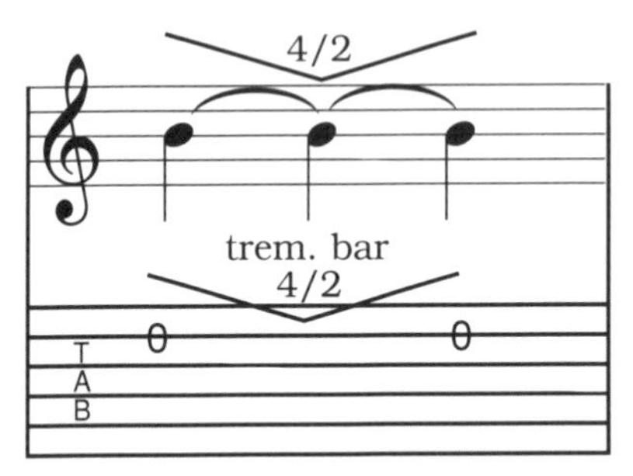

TREMOLO BAR- Push or pull up on bar to lower or raise the pitch of the note(s) by the specified number of half steps in the direction indicated. Can also be an unspecified amount.

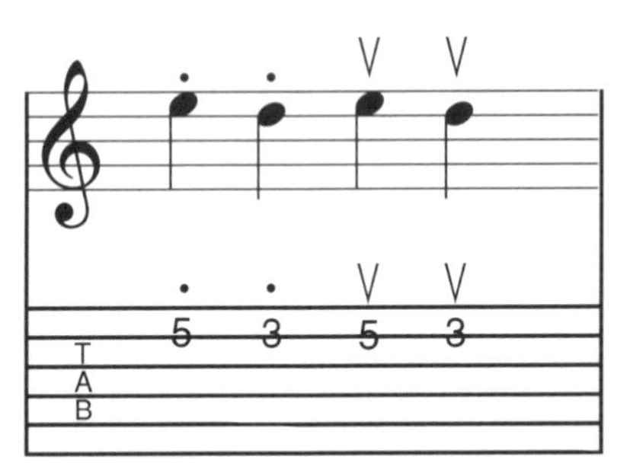

STACCATO- Dot indicates to play the note with a shortened time value. Wedge indicates shortened time value plus accent.

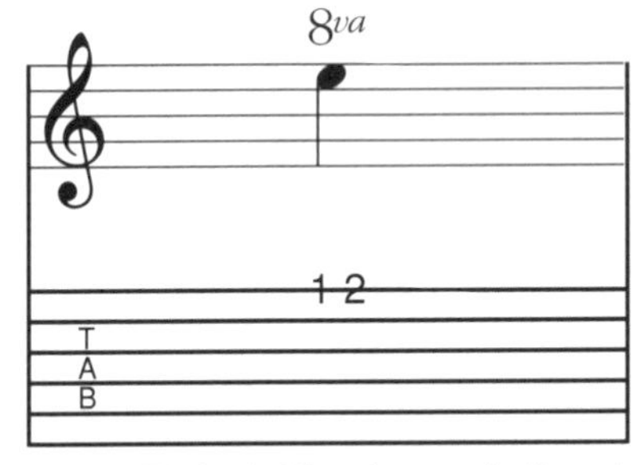

OCTAVE (8va)- Play the note indicated one octave higher than notated.

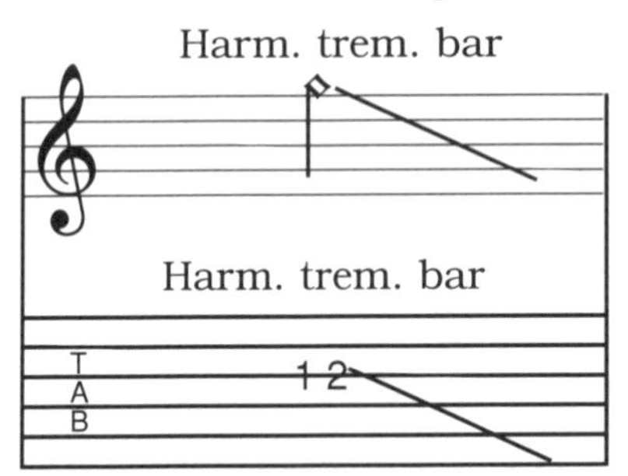

TREMOLO BAR HARMONIC- Play harmonic as indicated then pull or push bar in direction(s) indicated for the number of half steps specified. May also be unspecified.

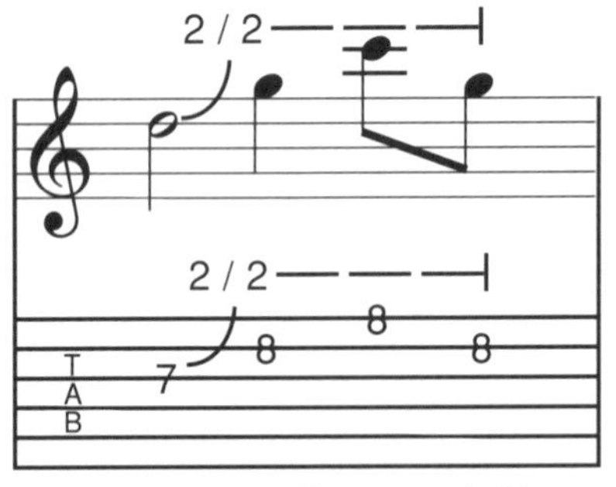

SUSTAIN- Dotted lines mean hold present value until another value is met. In example, hold the bend until the following notes are played.

The variations and combinations of the seven or eight basic techniques are practically limitless and the legend is designed to provide a practice guide and a feel for the symbology you can expect to encounter, as opposed to an exhaustive representation of what one can do in this area. Consider it an inducement to encourage you to come up with some new and interesting variations and combinations of your own. As you may have noticed, a little imagination goes a long way in this business. These devices are another link in the guitar-music chain, and form a separate area of endeavor from the ones presented thus far.

Make it a point to practice these both as separate items from the other areas, and in conjunction with one or more others, as you become better acquainted with them on an individual basis.

Rhythm Playing

Rhythm playing at its most basic, is a combination of chord progressions played with a defining rhythmic arrangement. For guitarists, the rhythmic arrangement includes both the right hand approach and the overall style. The chapters on rhythm and chord progression are combined in this section so it might be a good idea to have studied them first. This section also relates closely to the Styles chapter, and the student is encouraged to refer to it for further information concerning the influence of rhythm on the different styles of music. Since this section deals mainly in right hand strumming patterns, the tablature will be replaced with arrows indicating downstrokes and upstrokes.

As a practical matter the rhythms presented here should be used for a variety of purposes limited only to one's imagination. If you have a tape recorder, especially a multitrack, you can put together an extended or loop track, and practice playing lead. If you are a songwriter, you can vary, combine, and incorporate these ideas into your own material to come up with something original. If you are learning arranging and transposition for the guitar, you can play the progressions in different keys using different form/position schemes and different right hand arrangements. Start by substituting an appropriate seventh chord for the triad. To initiate the creative process, it is sometimes necessary to take the rudiments of an idea and combine it with others. Variation also is essential.

For the time being, it is a basic policy to play chords with the root as the lowest tone except when otherwise specified. It is also fundamental to play downstrokes on the beat and upstrokes off the beat unless otherwise specified.

We've all heard the stories of record company executives who listen to demo tapes for five or ten seconds and decide whether they need to hear any more or not. The rhythmic character of the piece combined with the chord progression gives us the ability to tell the style, tempo and character of a piece instantly. In song form, the chord progression makes up the bulk of the harmonic activity, but at the very heart of rhythm playing is the rhythm itself, which gives the music its feel. As a result, a rhythm is responsible for much of what makes the music work when it works. Without a strong rhythmic and harmonic background, there cannot be an effective melodic foreground and there is little if anything upon which to base an overall arrangement.

In performance situations, its been demonstrated that you can miss notes or chords and still carry on, but if you drop the beat the whole thing can fall to pieces right away. If you're a working guitarist, you're familiar with the structuring of sets so that your dancing audience has a variety of rhythms and tempos. You'll come to realize that this listener response is the result of a combination of factors driven on the most fundamental level by the beat and tempo.

This chapter has three sections, Forms and Progression, Chord Progression, and Rhythm Playing.

Forms and Progression

In this section, the diatonic progression of both triads and sevenths is illustrated using each of the CAGED forms. In each case a single form is used throughout the progression starting from the open position until it repeats at the 12th. To play in sequence, first go down the left column and then down the right, as was the case in Vols. I and II. The triads are shown on the left half of each page and the sevenths are on the right.

Each diatonic progression that follows is a combination of the chords in a key and a single basic chord form. Each key is the same as the letter name of the chord form. This exercise combines the concepts of building the chords in a key on the notes of the key, with the basic chord forms in various positions. It is also useful for demonstrating the whole-step and half-step scale relationship in a chordal context. As usual, some of the stretches will be difficult if not impossible for some. This exercise is a practical application of theoretical principles, and is a good intermediary between the chords as constructed, and chords as used in progressions.

A logical next step is to combine the diatonic progression of chords with various chord forms. The object is to enable the guitarist to think in terms of both the forms and the function within a key at the same time. After that it becomes a matter of progression as an entity with musical character or style- the guitar considerations becoming secondary in importance.

Diatonic Progression - Triads & Sevenths
C Forms

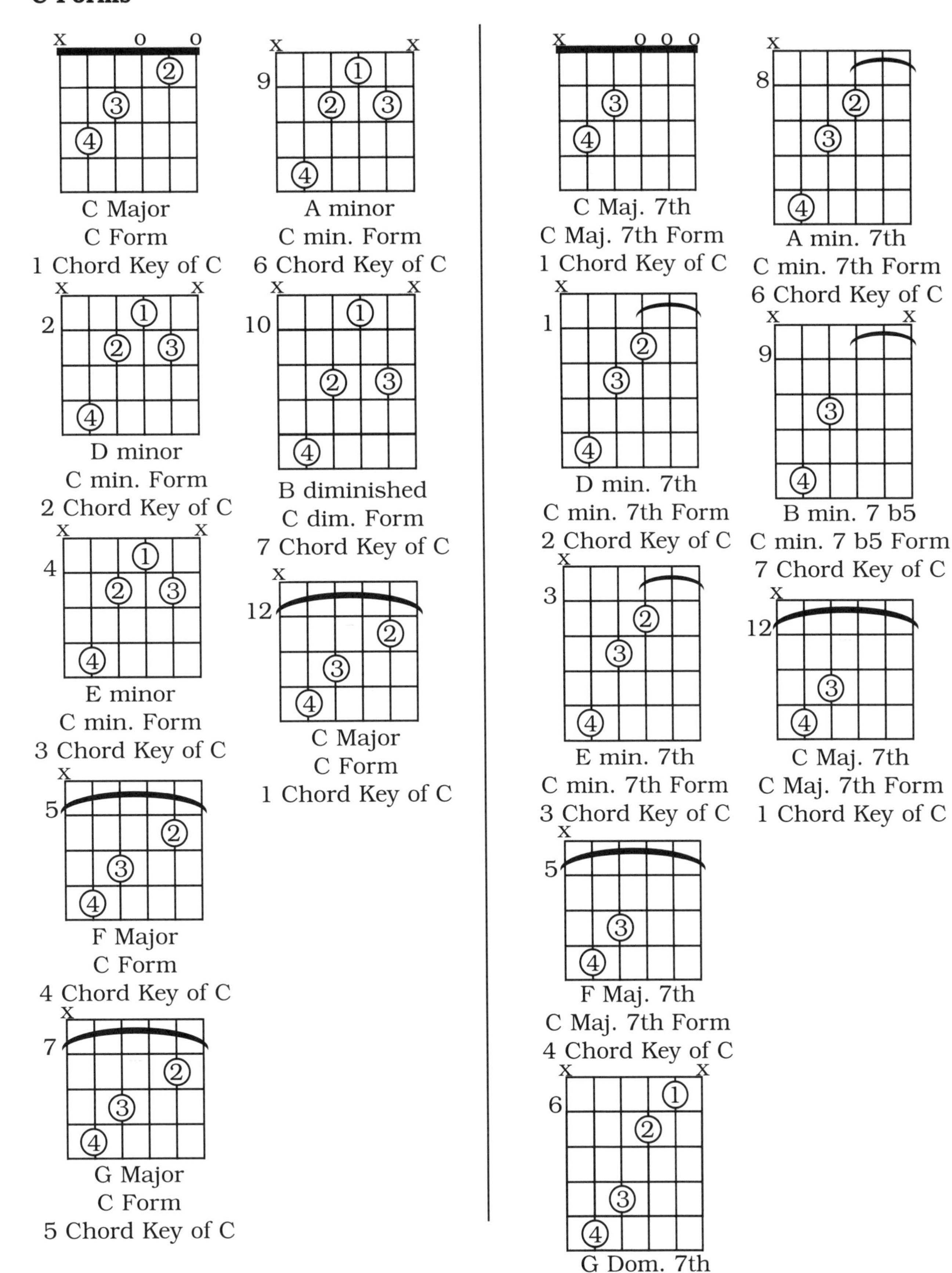

Diatonic Progression - Triads & Sevenths
A Forms

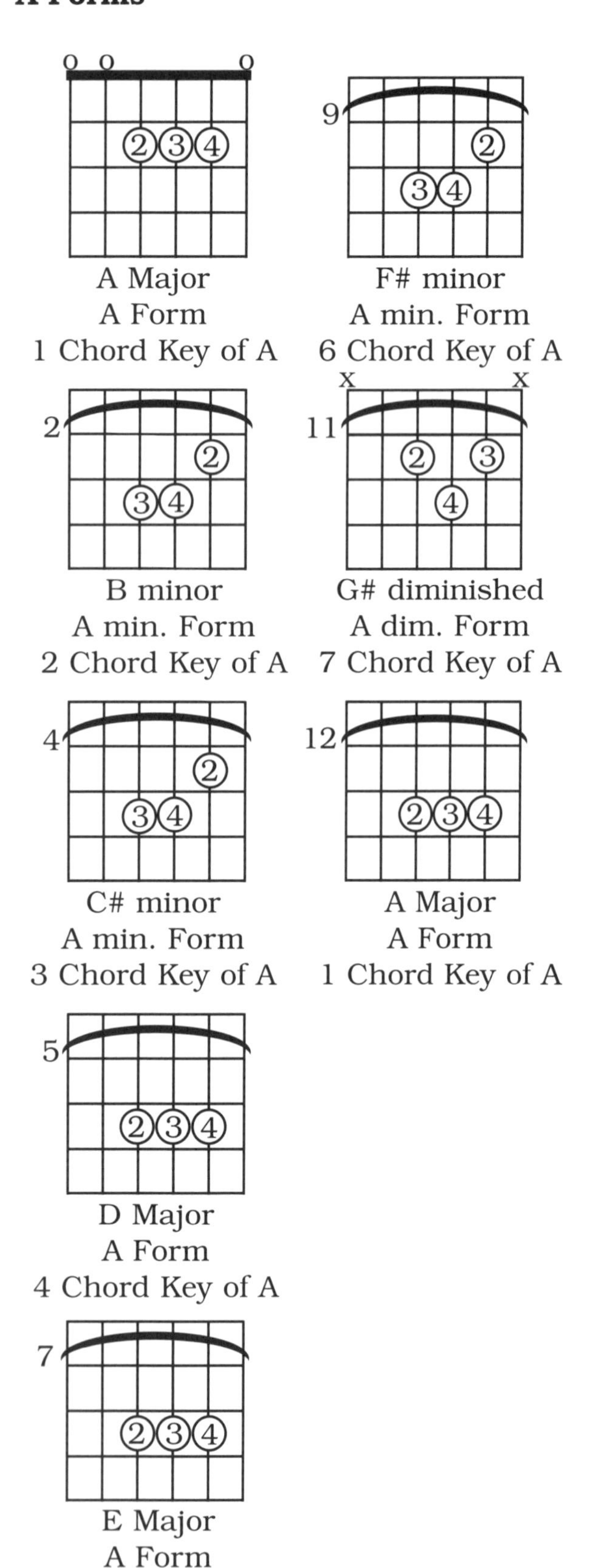

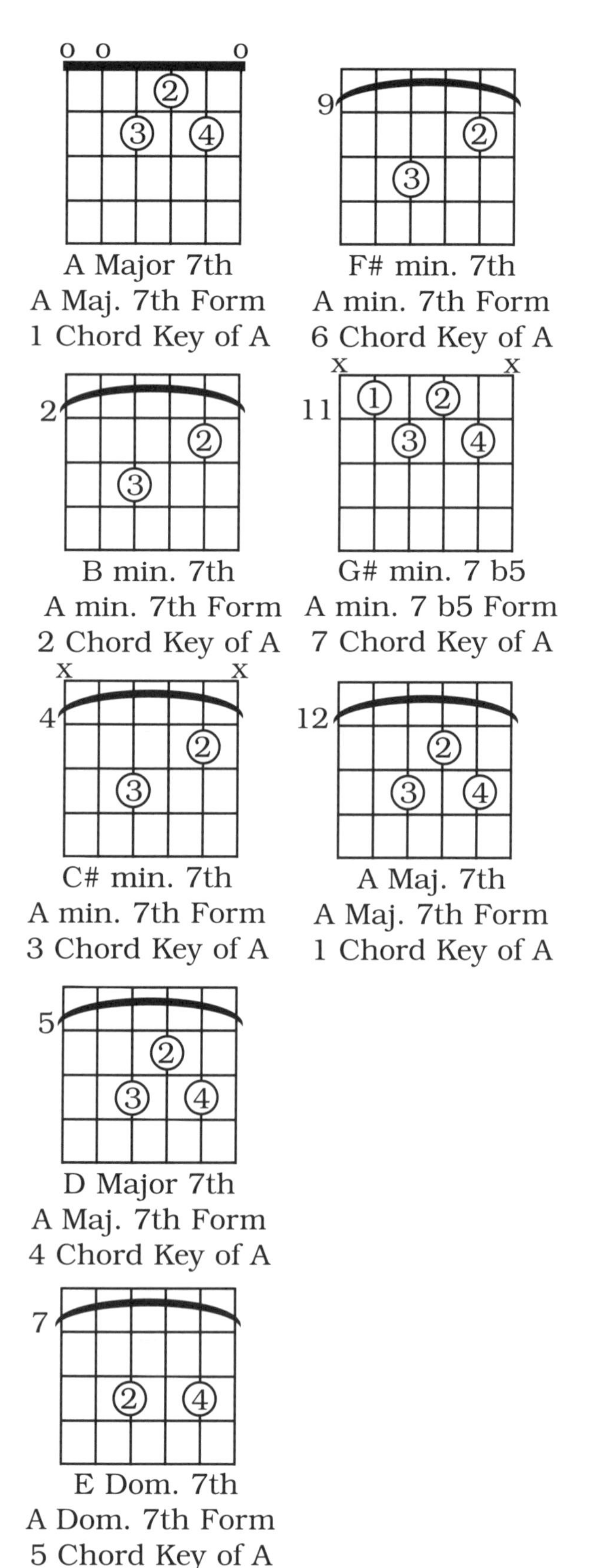

Diatonic Progression - Triads & Sevenths
G Forms

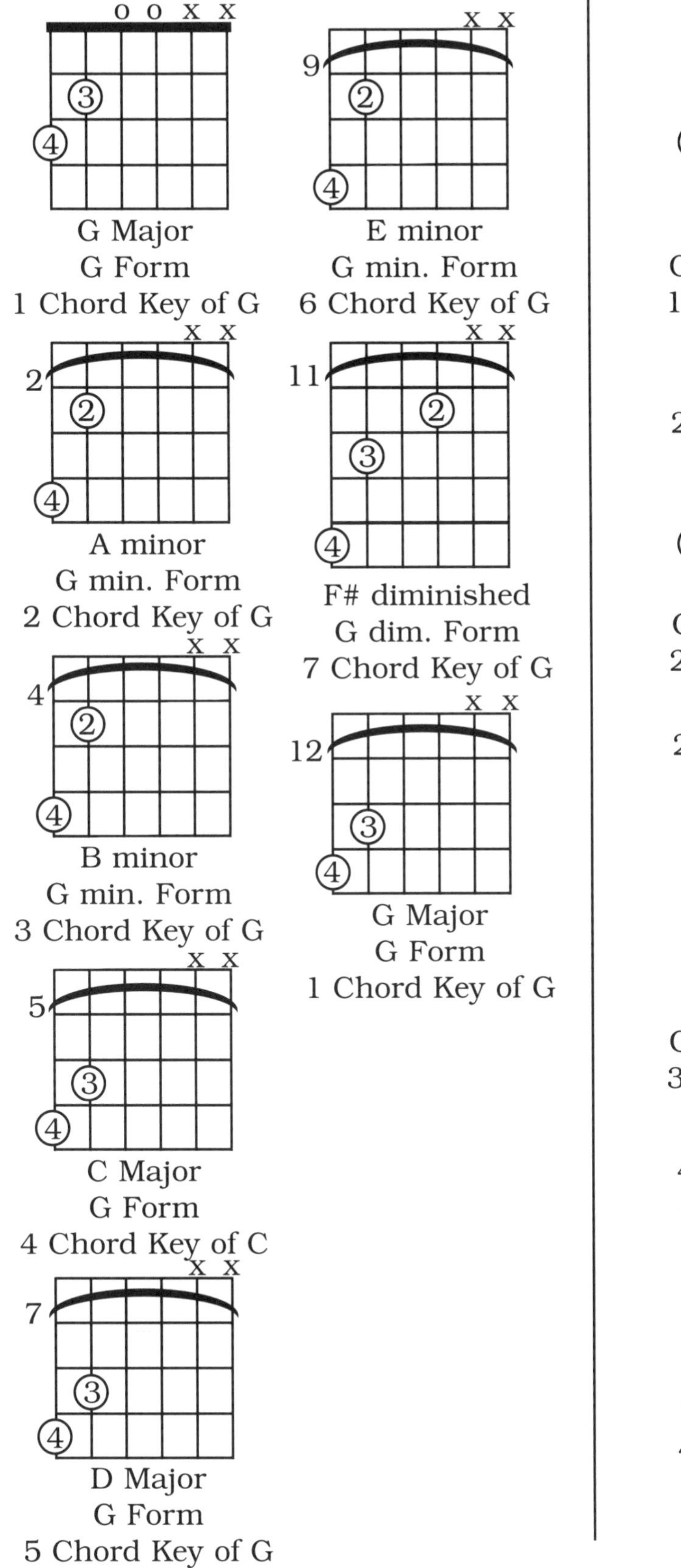

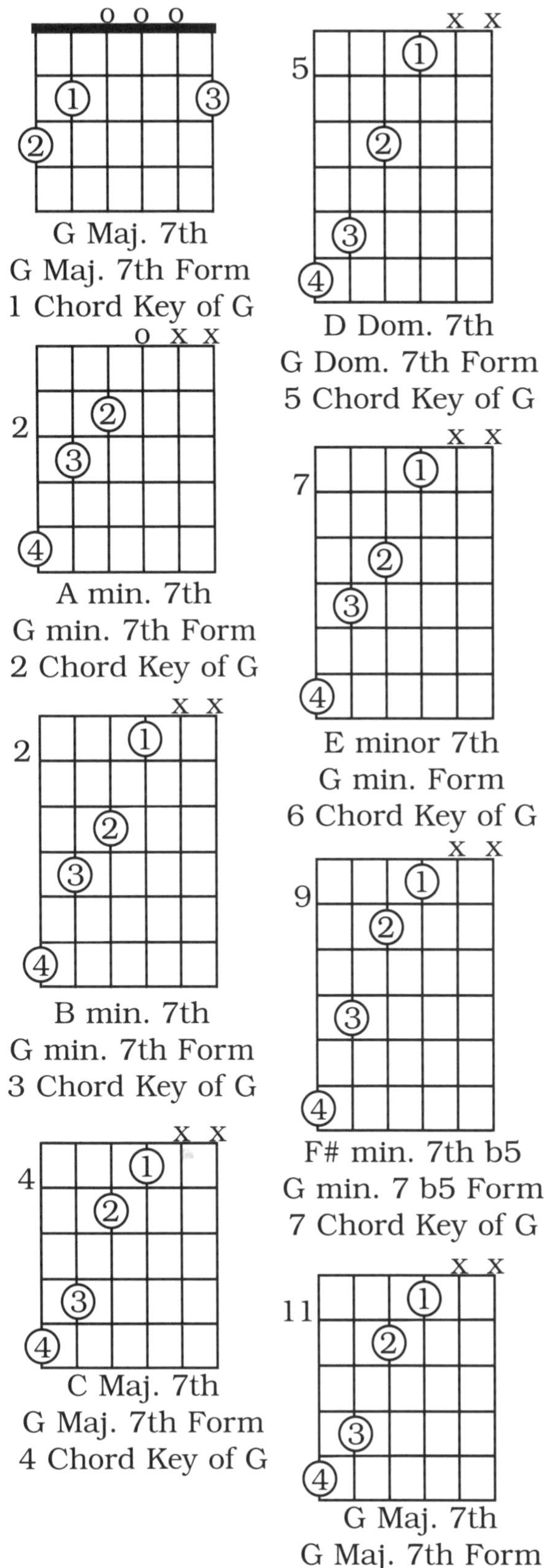

Diatonic Progression - Triads & Sevenths
E Forms

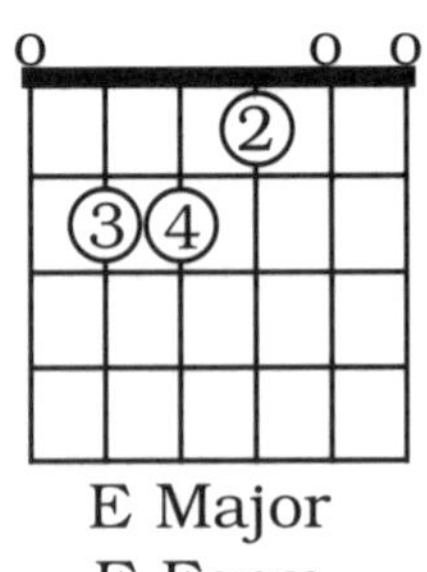

E Major
E Form
1 Chord Key of E

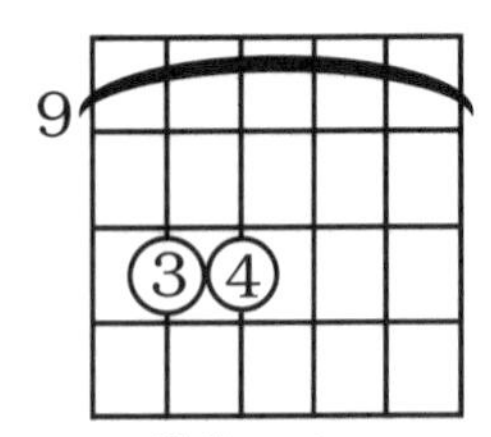

C# minor
E min. Form
6 Chord Key of E

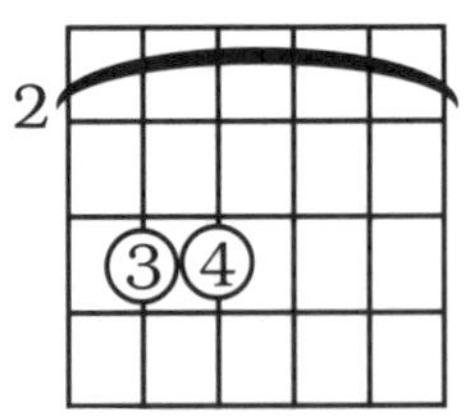

F# minor
E min. Form
2 Chord Key of E

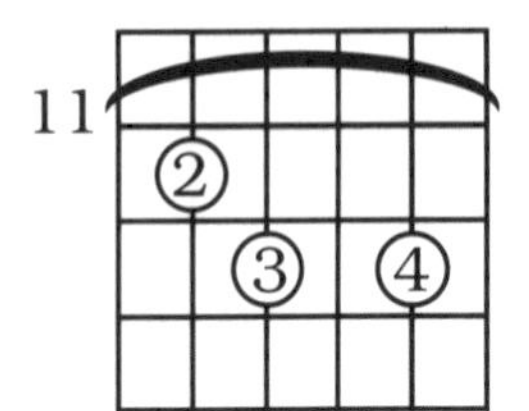

D# diminished
E dim. Form
7 Chord Key of E

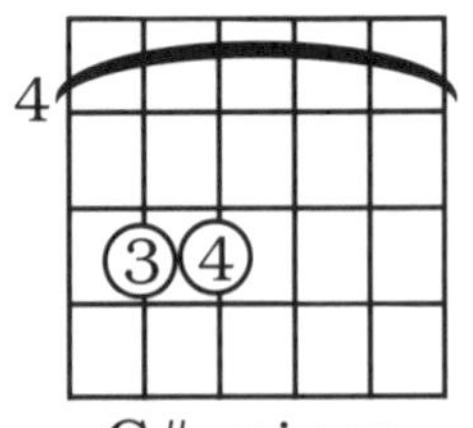

G# minor
E min. Form
3 Chord Key of E

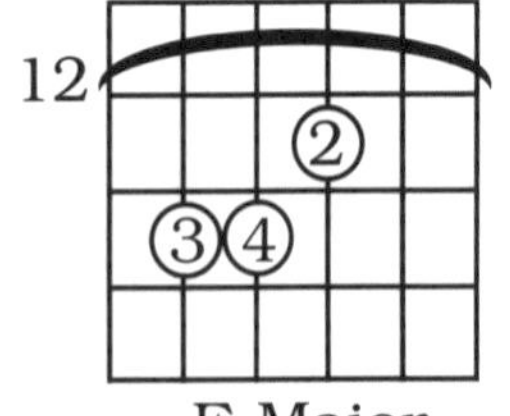

E Major
E Form
1 Chord Key of E

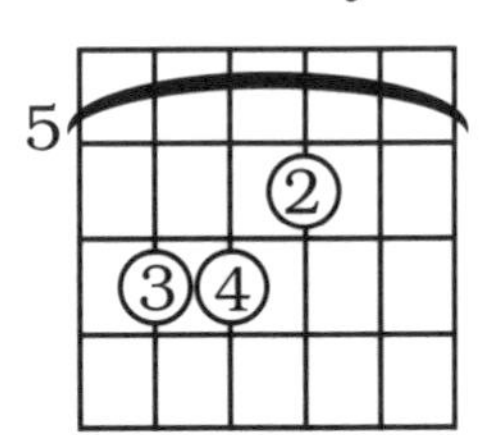

A Major
E Form
4 Chord Key of E

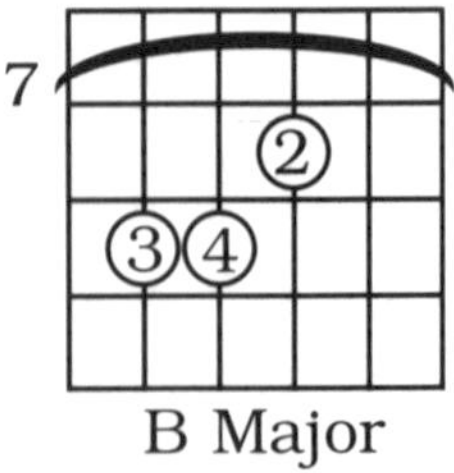

B Major
E Form
5 Chord Key of E

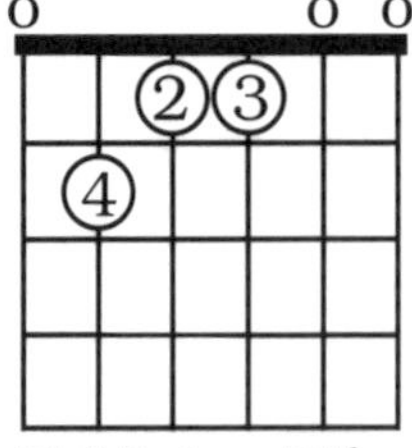

E Major 7th
E Maj. 7th Form
1 Chord Key of E

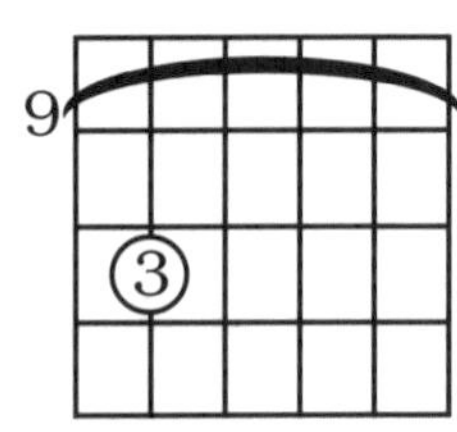

C# min. 7th
E min. 7th Form
6 Chord Key of E

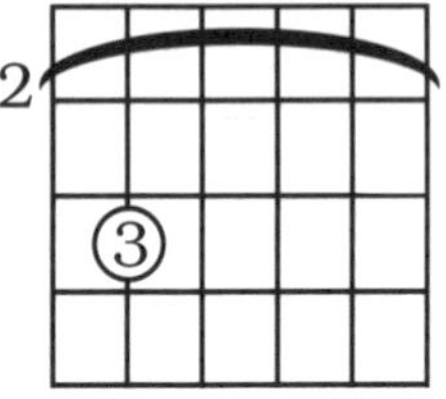

F# min. 7th
E min. 7th Form
2 Chord Key of E

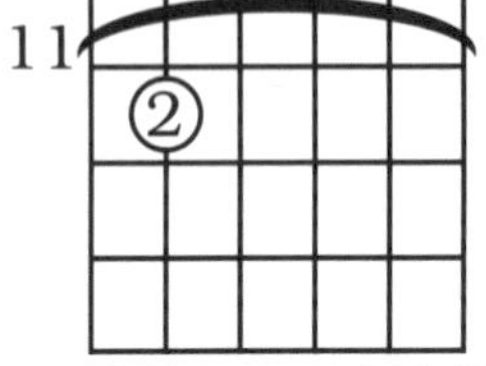

D# min. 7 b5
E min. 7 b5 Form
7 Chord Key of E

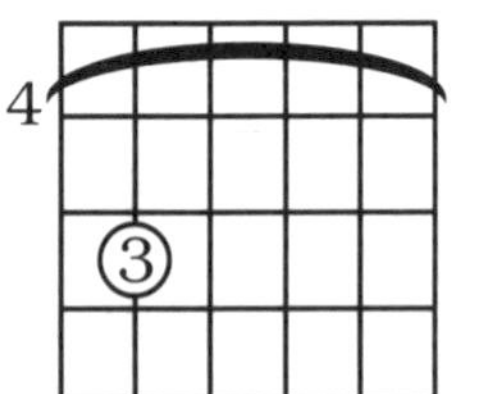

G# min. 7th
E min. 7th Form
3 Chord Key of E

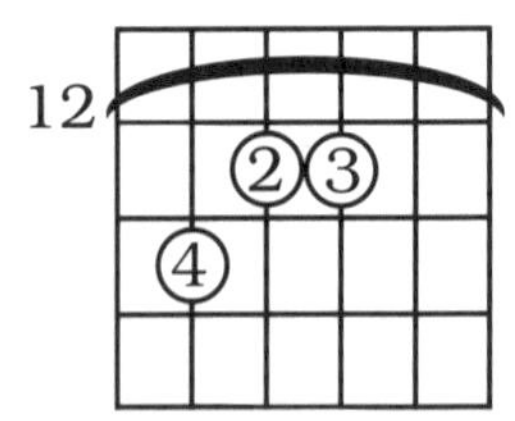

E Maj. 7th
E Maj. 7th Form
1 Chord Key of E

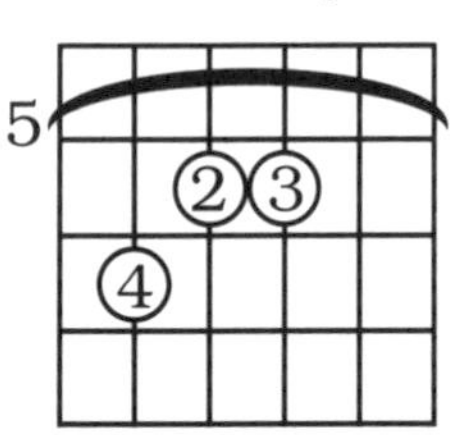

A Major 7th
E Maj. 7th Form
4 Chord Key of E

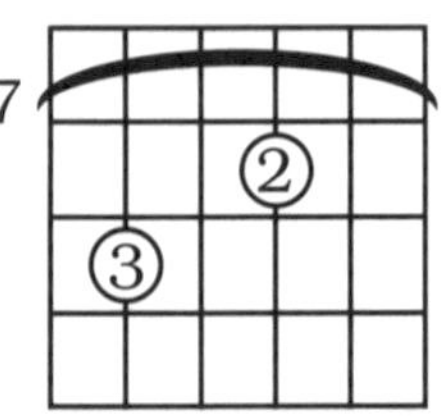

B Dom. 7th
E Dom. 7th Form
5 Chord Key of E

Diatonic Progression - Triads & Sevenths
D Forms

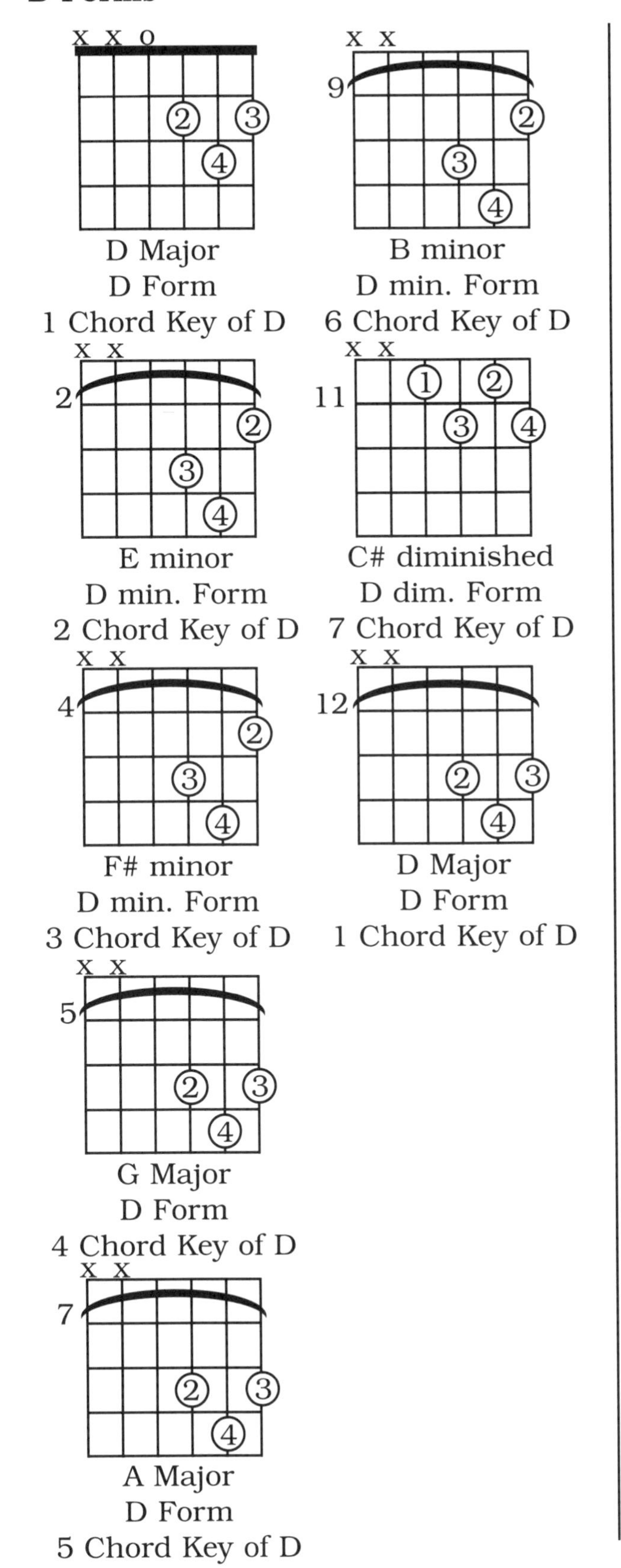

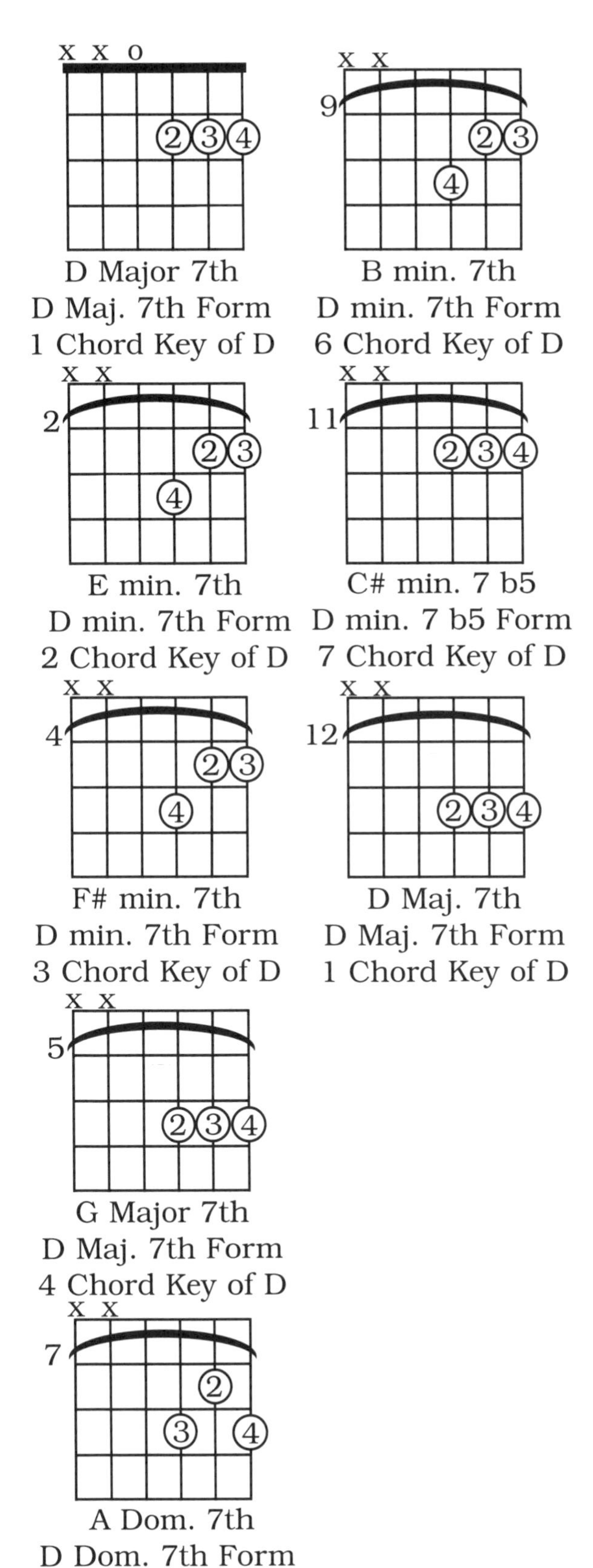

Chord Progression

Progressions are chords *progressing* from one to another in a logical musical sequence. They are the harmonic framework supporting the melodic focus. In order to understand how chord progressions work on the guitar, we'll need to have a working knowledge of keys, and keep a few other balls in the air at once. The requirements will be listed in reverse order (last to first) to show what is operating and why it is necessary.

To execute chords and progressions on the fretboard we need to combine each one's musical formula with a fretboard form as discussed in Vol. II. In general we could play a progression using all open position forms (different forms, same position); we could also use a single form in various positions (same form, different positions); or, most likely, combinations of different forms and positions.

Musically, chords progress in a manner that can be reduced to number values that apply equally to any key or key area. That makes the chords in any key: 1 2 3 4 5 6 and 7 (also written I II III IV V VI and VII). For example a common progression is: 1 6 4 5. The rules for what makes a good progression seem to be the same rules for music in general: whatever sounds good, is good.

To to be able to specify exactly which chord each number represents, we apply both a name and type that identifies each chord within a given key. A chord's **name** is its letter and accidental (when applicable). A chord's **type** is a quality specified by its formula. For example the 1 6 4 5 progression in the key of D is: D Major, B minor, G Major, and A Major; (abbreviated D, Bm, G, and A - since a chord type not otherwise specified is assumed to be Major.) The *type* is Major, the (letter) *name* is D. The type is minor, the name is B; the type is Major and the name is G; etc.

The number of a chord is always a specific type of chord. Using triads: "1" chords are always Major, "2" chords are always minor, "3" chords are minor, "4" chords are Major, "5" chords are Major, "6" chords are minor, and "7" chords are always diminished. Put the other way, the 1, 4, and 5 chords are always Major; the 2, 3, and 6, are always minor; and the 7 chord is always diminished. This is the easiest part since it only changes if you use quatrads (sevenths) or a new tonality or modality. Using seventh chords, the 1 chords are Maj. 7th; 2 chords are min. 7th; 3 chords are min. 7th; 4 chords are Maj. 7th; 5 chords are dom. 7th, 6 chords are minor 7th, 7 chords are min. 7th b5.

To be able to name each chord in a key we first need to know the notes in the key by letter name (and sharp or flat accidentals). Example: The notes (1 2 3 4 5 6 and 7) in the key of D are: D E F# G A B and C#.

To know what letter name the notes in a key are, we need to know the key *signature* of the key. The **signature** is the number of accidentals in the key and which ones they are. For example signature of the key of D is : two sharps - F# and C#. The key signature of the key of Eb is 3 flats - Bb Eb and Ab. To know the key signatures for any key you derive the sharp keys one way and the flat keys another using one kind of counting system for sharp keys, and another for flat keys. The counting system for deriving both sharp and flat key signatures have two parts: Counting in intervals then adding on accidentals in a specific sequence.

Progression - The Chords In A Key

For sharped keys you count in intervals of five to get to each successive key and then add another sharp. Starting with the key of C, the signature is 0 sharps. Five up from C is the key of G, and it has 1 sharp (adds 1). Five up from G is D and it has 2 (adds 1) sharps. Five up from D is A and it (adds 1) has 3 sharps etc.

Sharps are added to each successive key in the following order: FCGDAEB. (That is : F# C# G# D# A# E# and B#). A way to remember this letter sequence is the phrase: Fat Cats Get Dangerous And Eat Birds or just repeat the letters until you know them.

Now combine the addition of each successive sharp with each next key. For example the starting key is always C. C has 0 sharps. Count up five to G and it has one sharp-the first sharp is F# so the key sig. for G is F#. The notes in G are: G A B C D E and F#. Next example: Counting five from the key of G gives us the next key: D. D has two sharps F(at) and C(ats) sharp or F# and C#. The notes in the key of D are: D E F# G A B and C#.

The Flat keys work in a similar manner. First they count in fours instead of fives to each successive key. Starting from C, the next key is F, then Bb, then Eb, and so on. The Flat keys successively add flats in the order: BEADGCF (That is, Bb Eb Ab Db Gb Cb and Fb). A way to remember this one is the stupid phrase: Bill Edwards Always Did Get Cold Feet (worked for me) or just learn the sharps backwards as well.

Now combine the addition of each successive flat with each successive key. For example the starting key is again C. C has 0 flats. Count up four to F and it has one flat - the first flat is Bb so the key sig. for F is Bb. That makes the notes in F: F G A Bb C D and E. Next example: Counting four from the key of F gives us the next key: Bb (remember Bb was added right then). The notes in Bb are: Bb C D Eb F G and B. Next key, Eb, has three flats Bb, Eb, and Ab. The notes in the key of Eb are: Eb F G Ab Bb C and D.

Ok maybe it was more than a few balls to keep in the air. If this is your first exposure to these areas, you're probably either back punching the pause and rewind buttons on your cassette recorder, or staring into space wondering exactly when your nice friendly guitar turned into such a hideous, incomprehensible beast. It isn't over yet. Now we have to go back and do it in the other direction. To understand chord progression we first need the notes of a key to build the chords (in the key) upon. (If you don't yet know how to derive the notes in a key, go to the chapter on keys.) The notes in the key of F are: F G A Bb C D and E. The chords types (if triads) in any key will always be in the same order: Major, minor, minor, Major, Major, minor, and diminished. The chords in any key are given a numerical value (1-7) so they are equivalent in any key. This number also tells us what type of chord it will be:

1 chords are Major	or	Major seventh
2 chords are minor	or	minor seventh
3 chords are minor	or	minor seventh
4 chords are Major	or	Major seventh
5 chords are Major	or	Dominant seventh
6 chords are minor	or	minor seventh
7 chords are diminished	or	minor seventh, flat five

Progression - The Chords In A Key

Combining the number value, chord types and notes of a key gives us the chords in a key. **Continuing with the key of "F" this means the triads and seventh chords in F are:**

1 chord:	F Maj.	or	F Maj. 7
2 chord:	G min.	or	G min. 7
3 chord:	A min.	or	A min. 7
4 chord:	Bb Maj.	or	Bb Maj. 7
5 chord:	C Maj.	or	C Dom. 7
6 chord:	D min.	or	D min. 7
7 chord:	E dim.	or	E min. 7 b5

The triads and sevenths in the key of E are:

1 chord:	E Maj.	or	E Maj. 7
2 chord:	F# min.	or	F# min. 7
3 chord:	G# min.	or	G# min. 7
4 chord:	A Maj.	or	A Maj. 7
5 chord:	B Maj.	or	B Dom. 7
6 chord:	C# min.	or	C# min. 7
7 chord:	D# dim.	or	D# min. 7 b5

The triads and sevenths in the key of C are:

1 chord:	C Maj.	or	C Maj. 7
2 chord:	D min.	or	D min. 7
3 chord:	E min.	or	E min. 7
4 chord:	F Maj.	or	F Maj. 7
5 chord:	G Maj.	or	G Dom. 7
6 chord:	A min.	or	A min. 7
7 chord:	B dim.	or	B min. 7 b5

The triads and sevenths in the key of D are:

1 chord:	D Maj.	or	D Maj. 7
2 chord:	E min.	or	E min. 7
3 chord:	F# min.	or	F# min 7
4 chord:	G Maj.	or	G Maj 7
5 chord:	A Maj.	or	A Dom. 7
6 chord:	B min.	or	B min. 7
7 chord:	C# dim.	or	C# min. 7 b5

The triads and sevenths in the key of Ab are:

1 chord:	Ab Maj.	or	Ab Maj. 7
2 chord:	Bb min.	or	Bb min. 7
3 chord:	C min.	or	C min. 7
4 chord:	Db Maj.	or	Db Maj. 7
5 chord:	Eb Maj.	or	Eb Dom. 7
6 chord:	F min.	or	F min. 7
7 chord:	G dim.	or	G min. 7 b5

Progression - Number Sequences and Chord Type

The use of the triad vs. sevenths (or ninths, elevenths and thirteenths and polychords for that matter) is a matter of style and taste in practice. In rock, the distortion and other effects actually prevent us from distinguishing much in the way of such "color" tones. A metal guitar sound is so heavily saturated with compression and distortion that you can't distinguish much more than basic intervals. In most bluegrass and folk music, the only seventh chord you're likely to hear is the dominant in the five chord, and the rest will be triads. In modern country music you're much more likely to hear quatrads than even a few years ago. In blues, ninth chords are essential to the style. In jazz, the sevenths are considered the basic units, with exotic alterations and extensions a source of harmonic distinction. In popular music, anything goes. More on this in Styles. As individual musicians, each of us has to determine whether we feel the triads or the sevenths are the basic chordal unit in a key.

The numerical value of a chord in a key means we can specify a progression with only a key and a number. For example, the 2 chord in the key of G is A min. (or A min. 7th). A four chord in F is Bb Maj. (or Maj. 7th). A 6 chord in Bb is G min. or Gm7. A seven chord in the key of A is G# dim (or G# min.7b5). A 3 in C# is E#m or E#m7. A 5 in F is C (or C7). And so on. The ability to think and move in increments such as these is fundamental for good musicianship.

A progression of chords is therefore easily reduced to number sequences in a key. For example, the progression: 1 4 1 5 in the key of A is the chords: A D A E, and should be fairly recognizable as the basis for more than a few memorable rhythm guitar parts. Another obvious progression is 1 2 3 4 5. In the key of, say, E this is the chords: E F# min. G# min. A and B. This is also the harmonic basis for numerous songs and depending on how you expressed it rhythmically, should bring a few things to mind. 1 2 5 1 and 1 4 5 1 progressions form the basis for thousands of songs. Now is the time for experimentation and application. By turning this process around, you can reduce progressions you already know to basic elements and even transpose them to other keys without trouble. Play the chords of some songs you know and write down the number sequence of the chord changes. Change the numbers into chords from another key and play the progression again in the new key and you will have transposed the progression.

When we actually apply progressions to the fretboard, we have the option of expressing them in various forms and positions guitarwise. When you played the 1 4 1 5 progression above, which forms did you use? All open forms perhaps. Now use only A forms or C forms and only change positions. Try the progressions using various combinations of forms and positions for feel and sound. Next play the same number sequence transposed to other keys and listen for the similarities and differences.

The fact that certain number chords in a progression are always a certain *type* can work in the other direction as well. For example an A min. chord is either going to be a 2 chord in the key of G, a 3 chord in the key of F or a 6 chord in the key of C. An Eb Maj. 7 will either be a 1 chord in the key of Eb or a 4 chord in the key of Bb. A G Dom. 7 can only be a 5 chord in the key of C. An F min. 7 chord can be a 2 in Eb, a 3 in Db, or a 6 in Ab. A B Maj. can be a 1 in B, a four in F#, or a 5 in E. An A dim. can only be a 7 in Bb (for now). A B min. 7 b5 can only be a 7 in C (for now). And so on. Since certain types of progression are more common than others, then you'll start to see a reduction in the number of possibilities to a manageable number. In fact, even exotic sounding progressions are usually combinations of common ones which have modulated to other keys and back.

Progressions - Chord Function

The combination of brief modulations of key area with altered and extended chords provide a rich harmonic foundation on which to base melodies and melodic ideas. If you think about it, no musical endeavor has to be incomprehensible if we are willing to consider multi layered combinations of basic elements.

If you are into the creative aspects of guitar such as songwriting or arranging, the question sooner or later becomes, "How do chords work together?" or "What chords sound good together?". What follows is an attempt to put questions such as these into perspective.

In an early effort to attribute them with a specific function and placement, the notes and chords in a key were given descriptive names: tonic, supertonic, mediant, subdominant, dominant, submediant, and subtonic (1 2 3 4 5 6 7). Although not all of these terms are actually utilized in modern times, you will still hear three of them used frequently in the context of chord progression. They are the tonic, subdominant and dominant, or 1, 4, and 5 chords. The terms tonic, subdominant, and dominant, refer to the function of the chord in a progression. In any and every key, the 1, 4, and 5 chords are considered the principle chords. They are the chords used most often in music as a basic harmonic background for the vocal, melodic, or improvisational foreground. Many (some say most) rock, country, blues, and folk songs use just the principle chords as the extent of the harmonic content. In jazz, the 1, 2, and 5 chords often serve the same purpose. Songwriters and composers of many genres often embrace this bare bones approach as the least equivocal harmonic material. As a general rule, the most common progression is: tonic, subdominant, dominant, and back to tonic.

But what about the four other chords, the 2, 3, 6, and 7? In progressions, the others will function like either a tonic, subdominant or dominant chord. Over a period of time, the other four names (supertonic, mediant, submediant, and subtonic) have faded in meaning since each of them behave like either a tonic chord, a subdominant chord or a dominant chord in actual usage. This is important so it bears restating. **The 3 and 6 chords function like tonics, the 2 like a subdominant and the 7 like a dominant.**

Again, tonic chords tend to progress to subdominants, subdominants progress to dominants, and dominants progress to tonics. This must be tempered with the understanding that there will usually be a melodic factor that must be taken into consideration. Many (some say most) progressions follow a general sequence of tonic, subdominant, dominant and tonic as a basis for development. The following is a table of some of those possibilities:

T	S	D	T	T	S	D	T	T	S	D	T
1	4	5	1	3	4	5	1	3	4	5	3
1	2	5	1	6	4	5	1	6	4	5	3
1	4	7	1	3	2	5	1	6	4	5	6
1	2	7	1	6	2	5	1	3	2	5	3
1	4	5	3	3	2	7	1	3	2	7	3
1	4	5	6	6	2	7	1	3	4	7	3
1	2	5	3	3	4	7	1	6	2	7	3
1	2	5	6	3	4	5	6	6	4	7	3

Progressions

Using the previous number sequences, pick some keys and forms and play through the progressions using new fretboard combinations. In other words if you are used to playing the open chords, use forms in other positions and vice versa. The first thing you should notice is that some of these progressions have a sense of finality to them especially if they end in a 1 chord. The term for this repose is cadence. A **cadence** is a progression that gives a feeling of resting - something like hitting home plate. Naturally there are about a zillion different types of cadences with some interesting names to learn, but we'll just mention a few of them here. The 5 - 1, or authentic cadence is the most definite and the most common. The 4 - 1, or plagal cadence is common to church music (Ah-men). When a progression ends in other than a 1, it is termed deceptive, the most common being 5 - 6.

What follows are a collection of four bar progressions (including cadences) all of which are in the key of **D Major**. They have been notated in slash sheet format. For learning purposes, they have additional markings that indicate each chord's numerical value and function within the progression. T=Tonic; S=Subdominant; and D=Dominant.

The first group are 2-5 variations. The 2-5 is one of the most widely used two chord progressions in popular and many other styles of music. Here's two strategies to derive the maximum enjoyment from this entire section. Play through the progressions and find the ones you like, then 1) teach the chords to a friend and make them play it over and over while you practice your lead playing, or 2) add a melody and lyrics, make a hit song, retire, and play guitar all day.

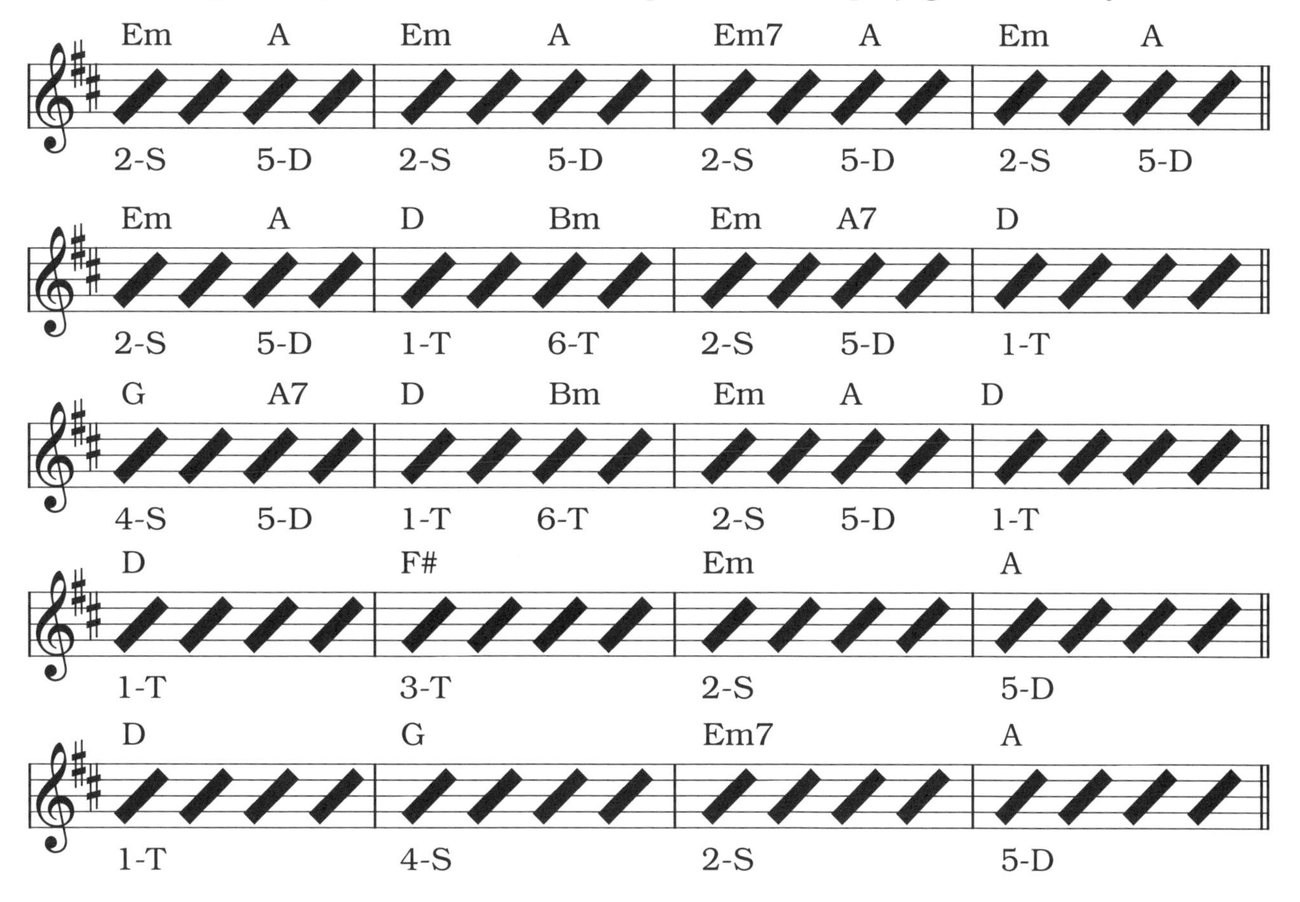

Progressions

More four bar progressions in the key of D Major with numeric value and function added.

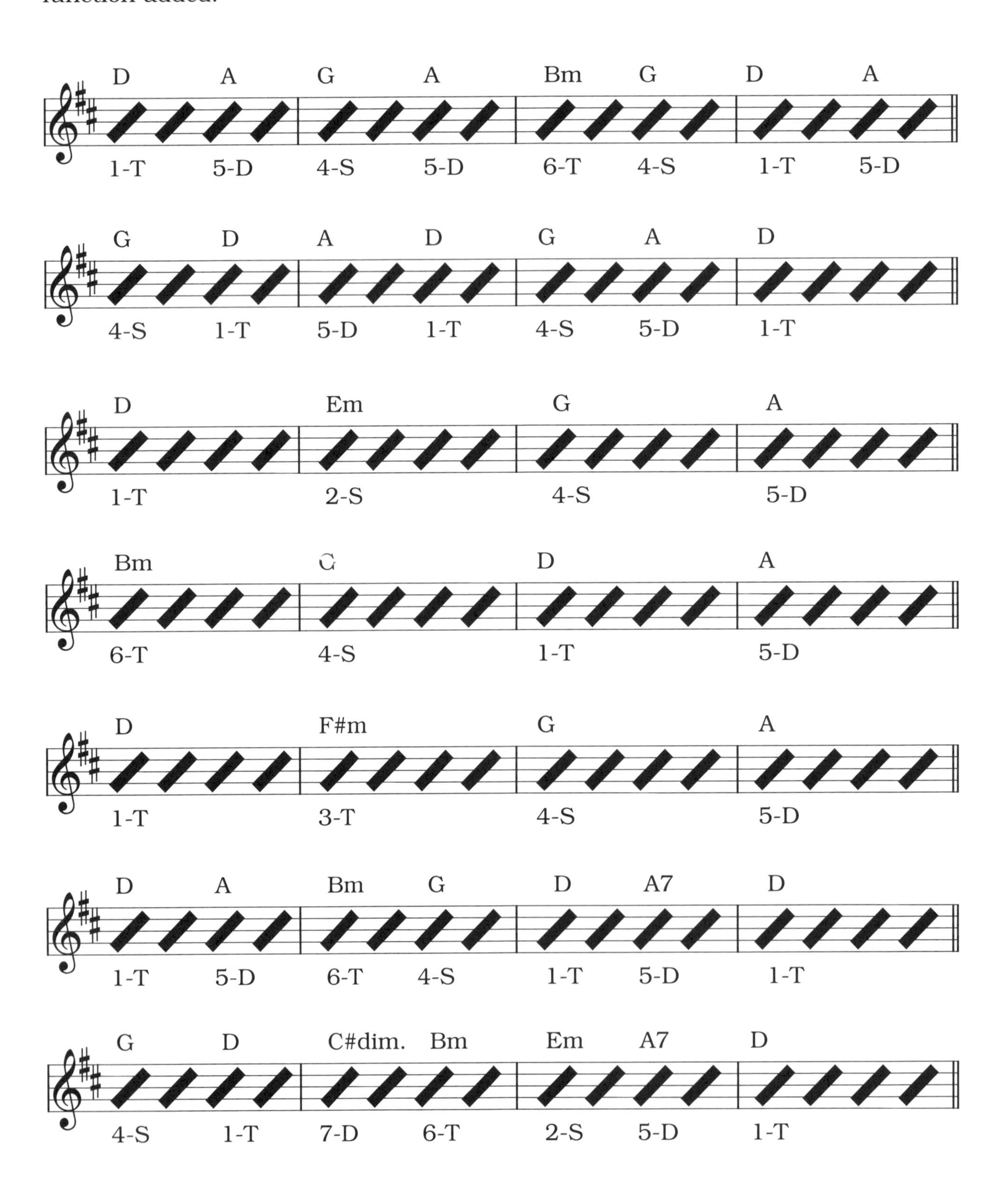

Progressions - Minor Keys

The way diatonic progression works with minor keys is a little different than with Major keys. Building the chords on the natural minor degrees does not produce much in the way of chord function. For the minor keys to work in a manner similar to Majors, we must build the chords off the harmonic minor degrees instead of the natural minor. The addition of the sharped seventh degree creates chord function where before there was none. As before we'll determine the key signature to learn the notes in the key and build the chords on each degree in the key.

In the key of D minor, the key signature is Bb, making the notes in the key: D E F G A Bb and C. This is the same key signature (and notes) as the key of F Major, and the term for this relationship is relative. D minor is the relative minor of F Maj., and F Maj. is the relative major of D min. Every major key has a relative minor (and vice versa) which is an interval of a minor third below it. Knowing the relative is the easiest way to determine the key signature for minor keys. Then add the sharped seventh degree to make it harmonic minor. The triads and quatrads which will occur on these degrees in order are as follows.

1 chords:	minor	or	minor #7th
2 chords:	diminished	or	minor 7th b5
3 chords:	augmented	or	Major 7th #5
4 chords:	minor	or	minor 7th
5 chords:	Major	or	dominant 7th
6 chords:	Major	or	Major 7th
7 chords:	diminished	or	diminished 7th

Adding the sharped seventh degree or the harmonic minor gives us the notes: D E F G A Bb and C#. The chords in D harmonic minor (and their spellings) are now going to be:

1 chord: D min.	Spelled:	D F A	or	D min. #7	Spelled:	D F A C#
2 chord: E dim.	Spelled:	E G Bb	or	E min. 7 b5	Spelled:	E G Bb D
3 chord: F aug.	Spelled:	F A C#	or	F Maj.7 #5	Spelled:	F A C# E
4 chord: G min.	Spelled:	G Bb D	or	G min. 7th	Spelled:	G Bb D F
5 chord: A Maj.	Spelled:	A C# E	or	A dom. 7th	Spelled:	A C# E G
6 chord: Bb Maj.	Spelled:	Bb D F	or	Bb Maj. 7th	Spelled:	Bb D F A
7 chord: C# dim.	Spelled:	C# E G	or	C# dim. 7th	Spelled:	C# E G Bb

The next key we'll do this in is E harmonic minor. The key signature for E minor is the same as for G Major, so the notes in E natural minor are E F# G A B C and D. The addition of the sharped 7th degree produces the notes: E F# G A B C and D#.

The chords (and their spellings) in E harmonic minor are:

1 chord: E min.	Spelled:	E G B	or	E min. #7	Spelled:	E G B D#
2 chord: F# dim.	Spelled:	F# A C	or	F# min. 7 b5	Spelled:	F# A C E
3 chord: G aug.	Spelled:	G B D#	or	G Maj.7 #5	Spelled:	G B D# F#
4 chord: A min.	Spelled:	A C E	or	A min. 7th	Spelled:	A C E G
5 chord: B Maj.	Spelled:	B D# F#	or	B dom. 7th	Spelled:	B D# F# A
6 chord: C Maj.	Spelled:	C E G	or	C Maj. 7th	Spelled:	C E G B
7 chord: D# dim.	Spelled:	D# F# A	or	D# dim. 7th	Spelled:	D# F# A C

Progressions - Minor Keys

The next key is C harmonic minor. The relative major of C minor is Eb (up a minor third), so the key signature for both keys is Bb, Eb, & Ab. Adding the #7 of the harmonic minor makes the notes in C harmonic minor: C D Eb F G Ab and B . The chords in C harmonic minor and their spellings are:

1 chord: C min.	Spelled:	C Eb G	or	C min. #7	Spelled:	C Eb G B
2 chord: D dim.	Spelled:	D F Ab	or	D min. 7 b5	Spelled:	D F Ab C
3 chord: Eb aug.	Spelled:	Eb G B	or	Eb Maj.7 #5	Spelled:	Eb G B G
4 chord: F min.	Spelled:	F Ab C	or	F min. 7th	Spelled:	F Ab C Eb
5 chord: G Maj.	Spelled:	G B D	or	G dom. 7th	Spelled:	G B D F
6 chord: Ab Maj.	Spelled:	Ab C Eb	or	Ab Maj. 7th	Spelled:	Ab C Eb G
7 chord: B dim.	Spelled:	B D F	or	B dim. 7th	Spelled:	B D F Ab

The next key we'll do this in is F harmonic minor. The relative major of F is Ab (up a minor third), so the key signature for both is Bb Eb Ab and Db. Adding the #7 of the harmonic minor makes the notes in F harmonic minor: F G Ab Bb C Db and E . The chords and their spellings in F harmonic minor are:

1 chord: F min.	Spelled:	F Ab C	or	F min. #7	Spelled:	F Ab C E
2 chord: G dim.	Spelled:	G Bb Db	or	G min. 7 b5	Spelled:	G Bb Db F
3 chord: Ab aug.	Spelled:	Ab C E	or	Ab Maj.7 #5	Spelled:	Ab C E G
4 chord: Bb min.	Spelled:	Bb Db F	or	Bb min. 7th	Spelled:	Bb Db F Ab
5 chord: C Maj.	Spelled:	C E G	or	C dom. 7th	Spelled:	C E G Bb
6 chord: Db Maj.	Spelled:	Db F Ab	or	Db Maj. 7th	Spelled:	Db F Ab G
7 chord: E dim.	Spelled:	E G Bb	or	E dim. 7th	Spelled:	E G Bb Db

The next key is A harmonic minor. The relative major of A minor is C (up a minor third), so the key signature for both keys is no accidentals. Adding the #7 of the harmonic minor makes the notes in A harmonic minor: A B C D E F and G# . The chords in A harmonic minor and their spellings are:

1 chord: A min.	Spelled:	A C E	or	A min. #7	Spelled:	A C E G#
2 chord: B dim.	Spelled:	B C F	or	B min. 7 b5	Spelled:	B D F A
3 chord: C aug.	Spelled:	C E G#	or	C Maj.7 #5	Spelled:	C E G# B
4 chord: D min.	Spelled:	D F A	or	D min. 7th	Spelled:	D F A C
5 chord: E Maj.	Spelled:	E G# B	or	E dom. 7th	Spelled:	E G# B D
6 chord: F Maj.	Spelled:	F A C	or	F Maj. 7th	Spelled:	F A C E
7 chord: G# dim.	Spelled:	G# B D	or	G# dim. 7th	Spelled:	G# B D F

The last key we'll do this in is G harmonic minor. The relative major of G is Bb (up a minor third), so the key signature for both is Bb and Eb. Adding the #7 of the harmonic minor makes the notes in G harmonic minor: G A Bb C D Eb and F#. The chords and their spellings in G harmonic minor are:

1 chord: G min.	Spelled:	G Bb D	or	G min. #7	Spelled:	G Bb D F#
2 chord: A dim.	Spelled:	A C Eb	or	G min. 7 b5	Spelled:	A C Eb G
3 chord: Bb aug.	Spelled:	Bb D F#	or	Bb Maj.7 #5	Spelled:	Bb D F# A
4 chord: C min.	Spelled:	C Eb G	or	C min. 7th	Spelled:	C Eb G Bb
5 chord: D Maj.	Spelled:	D F# A	or	D dom. 7th	Spelled:	D F# A G
6 chord: Eb Maj.	Spelled:	Eb G Bb	or	Eb Maj. 7th	Spelled:	Eb G Bb D
7 chord: F# dim.	Spelled:	F# A C	or	F# dim. 7th	Spelled:	F# A C Eb

Progressions - Minor Key Functions

With minor keys, the same general philosophy applies as with majors in that whatever sounds good, is good. The same, somewhat less general order of functions also applies in that there are Tonic, Subdominant, and Dominant functioning chords that tend to progress in the order: T S D and T. Here again, the 1, 3, and 6 chords are tonics; the 2 and 4 chords are subdominant; and the 5 and 7 are dominant. Here again, progressions which produce a feeling of rest or repose are termed cadences.

The triads and quatrads in D harmonic minor are:

D min.	or	D min. #7
E dim.	or	E min. 7b5
F aug.	or	F Maj. 7th #5
G min.	or	G min.7th
A Maj.	or	A Dom. 7th
Bb Maj.	or	Bb Maj. 7th
C# dim.	or	C# dim. 7th

What follows are some four bar progressions in the key of D minor. The 5-1 progression seems to be the most common two chord progression in the minor tonality.

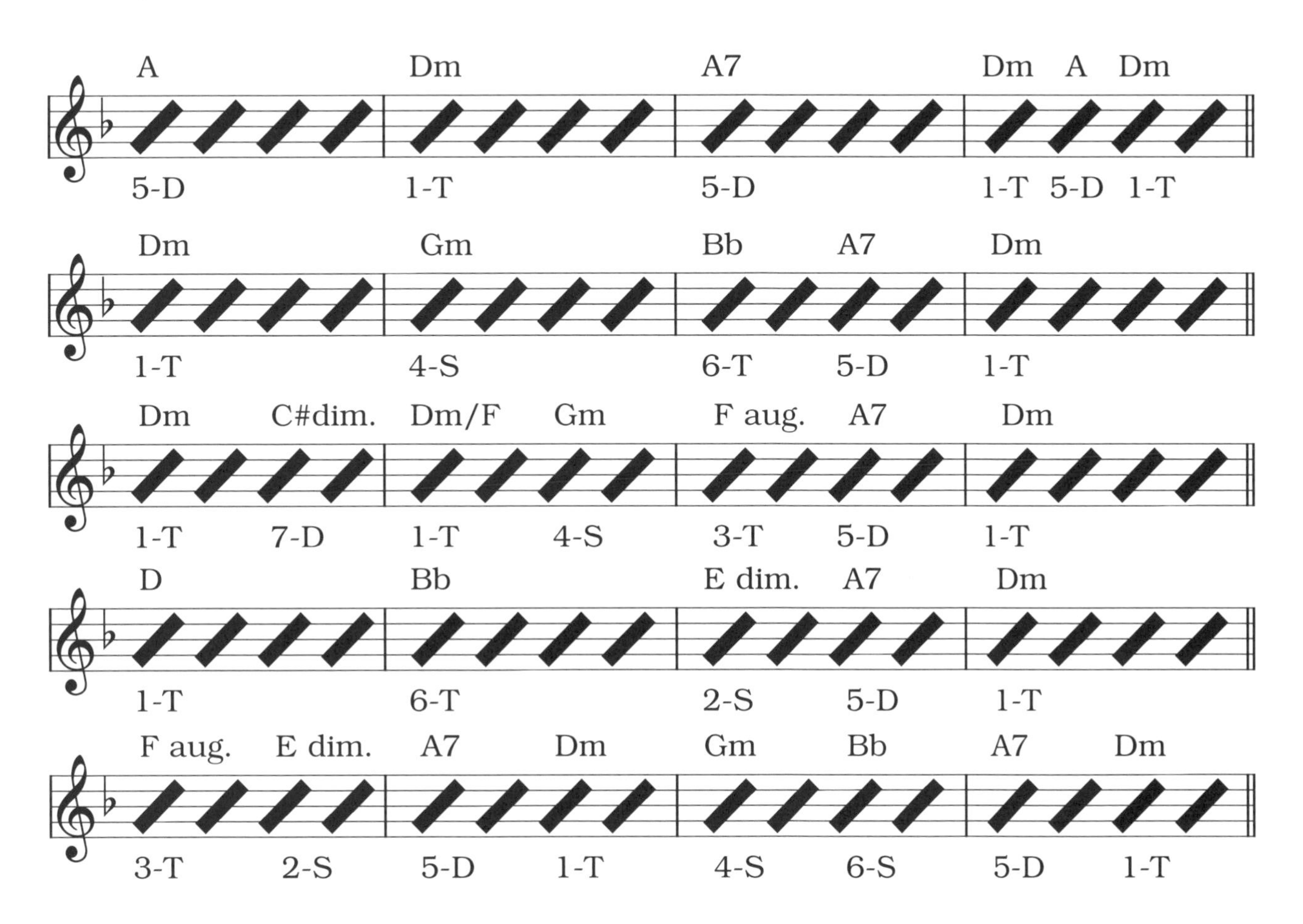

Progressions - Modulation

A certain amount of experimentation will demonstrate that the limitation of the chords to one key makes harmonic progression a little on the predictable side. What's called for are ways to access other chords and key areas in an orderly manner. The term for changing key areas is **modulation**. The methods for modulation we will be discussing are secondary dominants, diminished sevenths, function shifting, tonality shifting, and chromaticism.

The first method of moving beyond the boundaries of the key is termed secondary dominants. **Secondary dominants** are dominants of chords other than the tonic in the key. The concept behind secondary dominance is the idea of temporarily using a chord not of the key that is a dominant of a chord that is in the key. The pull of the fifth is the strongest tension and resolution of all two-chord progressions, and permits us to travel outside our key by one chord easily and harmoniously. For example: The key of C Major has the chords C Dm Em F G Am and B dim. The primary dominant is the G chord and we describe it musically as the 5 of 1 (V of I) or just the 5 chord. The first secondary dominant is the 5 of 2, or A Major since the 5 of Dm is A, and dominants are Major (for triads). The next secondary dominant is the 5 of 3, or B Major. The next one would be the 5 of 4, but using triads, that is our tonic again, so we'll skip it for now. The 5 of 5 is the D Major chord. The 5 of 6 is the E Major and the 5 of 7 is F#. This gives us five secondary dominant chords with which we can temporarily leave the confines of the key. Secondary dominants can be written 5 of 2, 5/2, V/II, etc. In the function part of the example below, S/D is an abbreviation for secondary dominant.

The (two chord) secondary dominant progressions in the key of C are:

5/2:	A Maj.	to	D min.
5/3:	B Maj.	to	E min.
5/5:	D Maj.	to	G Maj.
5/6:	E Maj.	to	A min.
5/7:	F# Maj.	to	B dim.

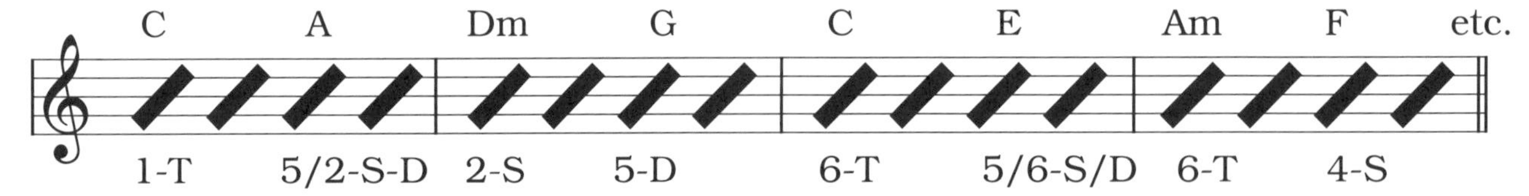

The (two chord) secondary dominant progressions in the key of G are:

5/2:	E Maj.	to	A min.
5/3:	F# Maj.	to	B min.
5/5:	A Maj.	to	D Maj.
5/6:	B Maj.	to	E min.
5/7:	C# Maj.	to	F# dim.

The (two chord) secondary dominant progressions in the key of Bb are:

5/2:	G Maj.	to	C min.
5/3:	A Maj.	to	D min.
5/5:	C Maj.	to	F Maj.
5/6:	D Maj.	to	G min.
5/7:	E Maj.	to	A dim.

Progressions - Modulation

Take some time and write out the secondary dominants in the keys you find yourself playing in the most. It may help to simplify things if you remember that the order of notes in fifths is B E A D G C G F Bb Eb Ab Db Gb Cb and Fb.

Diminished seventh chords provide an interesting means of both changing key areas and substituting for the dominant chord. With diminished chords, however, it is important to be able to think enharmonically. **Enharmonic** means the same tone has different names. Here's how diminished substitutions work. An "A" diminished seventh chord has the notes A C Eb and Gb. It can be expressed three other ways in inversion: C Eb Gb A; Eb Gb A C; and Gb A C Eb. If we flat the root tone of each inversion, these are the chords that are produced: Ab7th (Ab C Eb Gb); B7th (B Eb Gb A) - (B7th B D# F# A enharmonically); D7th (D Gb A C) - (D F# A C enharmonically); and F7th (F A C Eb). This means that just one diminished seventh chord can be be resolved to the 1 chords of Ab 7th, B7th, D 7th and F 7th. The symmetry of the diminished seventh chord results in only three completely different ones possible, as follows.

The four 2-chord progressions built from the (A C Eb Gb) diminished chord are:

A dim.7	substitutes for (Ab dom.7th)	and progresses to	Db Maj.
C dim. 7	substitutes for (B dom. 7th)	and progresses to	E Maj.
Eb dim. 7	substitutes for (D dom. 7th)	and progresses to	G Maj.
Gb dim. 7	substitutes for (F dom. 7th)	and progresses to	Bb Maj.

The four 2-chord progressions built from the (G Bb Db Fb) diminished chord are:

G dim.7	substitutes for (F# dom.7th)	and progresses to B Maj.	
Bb dim. 7	substitutes for (A dom. 7th)	and progresses to	D Maj.
Db dim. 7	substitutes for (C dom. 7th)	and progresses to	F Maj.
Fb dim. 7	substitutes for (Eb dom. 7th)	and progresses to	Ab Maj.

The four 2-chord progressions built from the (B D F Ab) diminished chord are:

B dim.7	substitutes for (Bb dom.7th)	and progresses to	Eb Maj.
D dim. 7	substitutes for (Db dom. 7th)	and progresses to	Gb Maj.
F dim. 7	substitutes for (E dom. 7th)	and progresses to	A Maj.
Ab dim. 7	substitutes for (G dom. 7th)	and progresses to	C Maj.

Naturally, the diminished sevenths do not have to resolve to a Major chord type. They can progress to minors and other types of chords. Below are a couple of progressions using this type of substitution. More later.

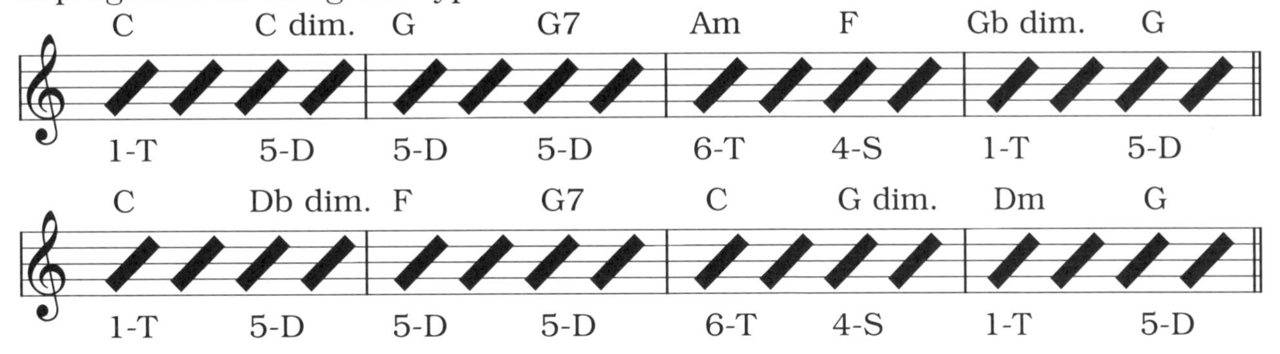

Progressions - Modulation

The term **function shifting** pertains to treating a chord (which has a specific tonic, subdominant or dominant function) as one of the other two functions (other than secondary dominants). In a major key, any minor triad you encounter within the key is going to be either the 2 (subdominant), 3 (tonic), or 6 (tonic) chord in that key. If you shift the function of a 2 chord, you will treat it like one of the tonic chords and vice versa.

Any major triad you encounter within a key will either be a 1 (tonic) chord, 4 (subdominant) chord, or a 5 (dominant) chord. If you shift the function of a 1 chord, you will treat it like either a subdominant or dominant chord. Shifting the function of the 4 chord means treating it like a dominant or tonic. Shifting the function of a tonic chord means changing it to subdominant or dominant, and so on.

In the first example, the Am would clearly be a tonic (6 chord) in the key of C, but the function shifted to subdominant (2 chord) in the key of G.

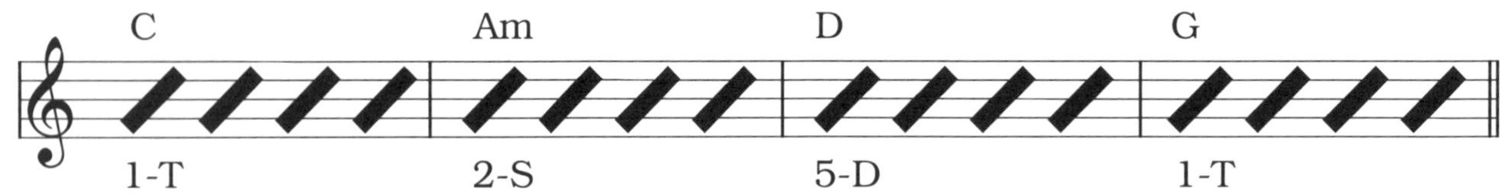

In the next example, the Em becomes a subdominant in the key of E instead of a tonic in the key of C.

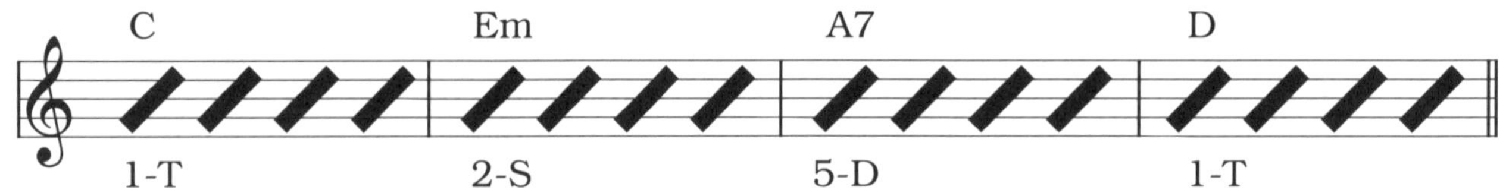

Tonality shifting is a term for changing the character of a chord from one type to another. This means you can leave the key temporarily by changing a major chord to a minor (and vice versa) and then treat it as if it were a 2, 3, or 6 chord of another key.

In the example below, the first shift is when the C tonic changes to a dominant in the key of F. When the F changes to F min., it becomes a subdominant in the key of Eb.

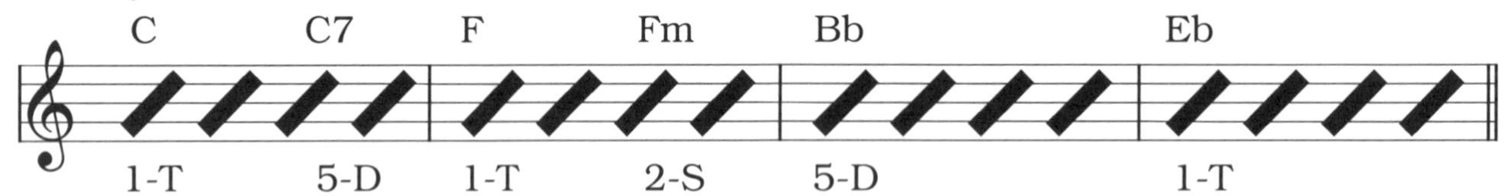

In the following example, the first shift is when the F tonic changes to a dominant in the key of Bb. When the Bb changes to Bb min., its function can't be established until a chord follows.

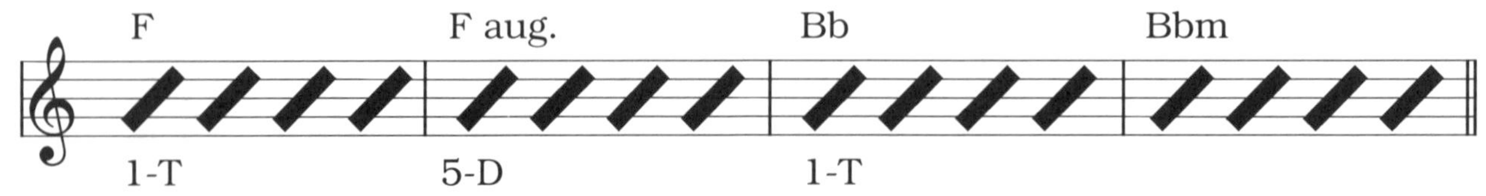

Progressions - Modulation

The last method of modulation we'll discuss covers a great deal of harmonic motion. It is termed chromaticism. **Chromaticism** is the use of half step increments as scale or key degrees instead of the usual combinations of whole steps and half steps. Major, minor and other chords played in half step increments are common to almost every music style. Try to keep these all purpose alternatives in mind when developing ideas. They will be useful in a variety of situations.

In the example below, the triplet chords F F# and G produce a smooth chromatic transition to the G# chord in the second measure. The G# chord can be considered a new tonic or possibly a chromatic dominant of C since it is raised one half step above G.

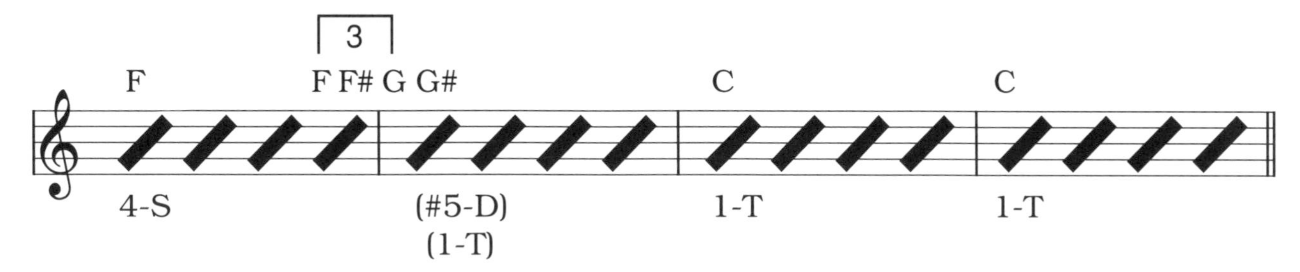

Below the motion from the E to F and A to A# are both examples of chromaticism.

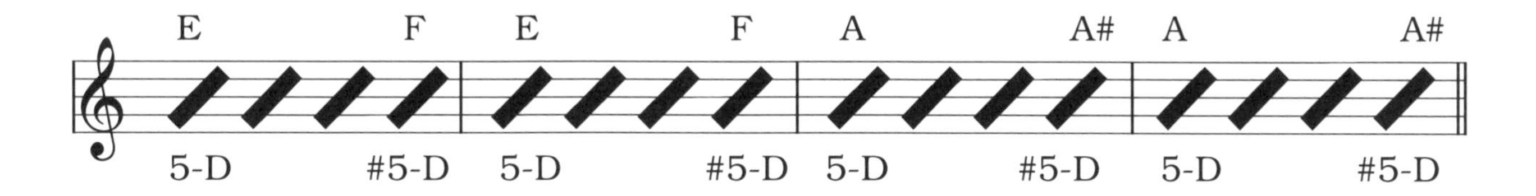

The last section deals with alternative methods of progression in modern and popular music. The first one is the concept of non-harmonic guitar oriented progressions dubbed *sonic shapes.* With sonic shapes, the tonal characteristics of chords in sequence takes a back seat to the guitar pattern for the purpose of uncovering new sounds independent of traditional harmonic organization. With sonic shapes, anything goes. Sonic shapes are patterns repeated in several positions on the fretboard. Noted jazz guitarist, Howard Roberts, used to write a column for Guitar Player magazine, and spoke frequently on this subject. If you're interested, check out some of their back issues.

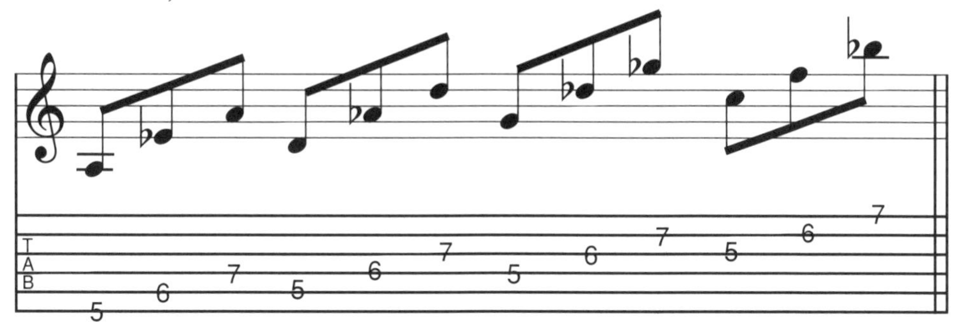

Progressions - Alternative Methods

The last alternative method for chord progression has been a mainstay of the pop, rock, and metal styles for many years. From the early metal of "Iron Man" to mainstream rock like "Smoke On The Water", to MTV's theme music, this type of progression is a modern songwriter's mainstay. It is the idea of building (usually) major chords upon pentatonic scale tones. For example, in the key of A pentatonic minor, the notes are: A C D E and G. The progression then would include the chords A Maj. C Maj. D Maj. E Maj. and G Maj. You can add the ubiquitous b5 degree (the so-called blue note) to the scale and include that chord as well.

With the exception of the tonic, the functions of each chord in sequence is somewhat unclear, so rather than try to attach a logic similar to the diatonic chords, we'll just leave it up to each person's judgement as to which chords tend to go where. The rhythmic parts are all but missing, so each player will have to fill in those blanks for now.

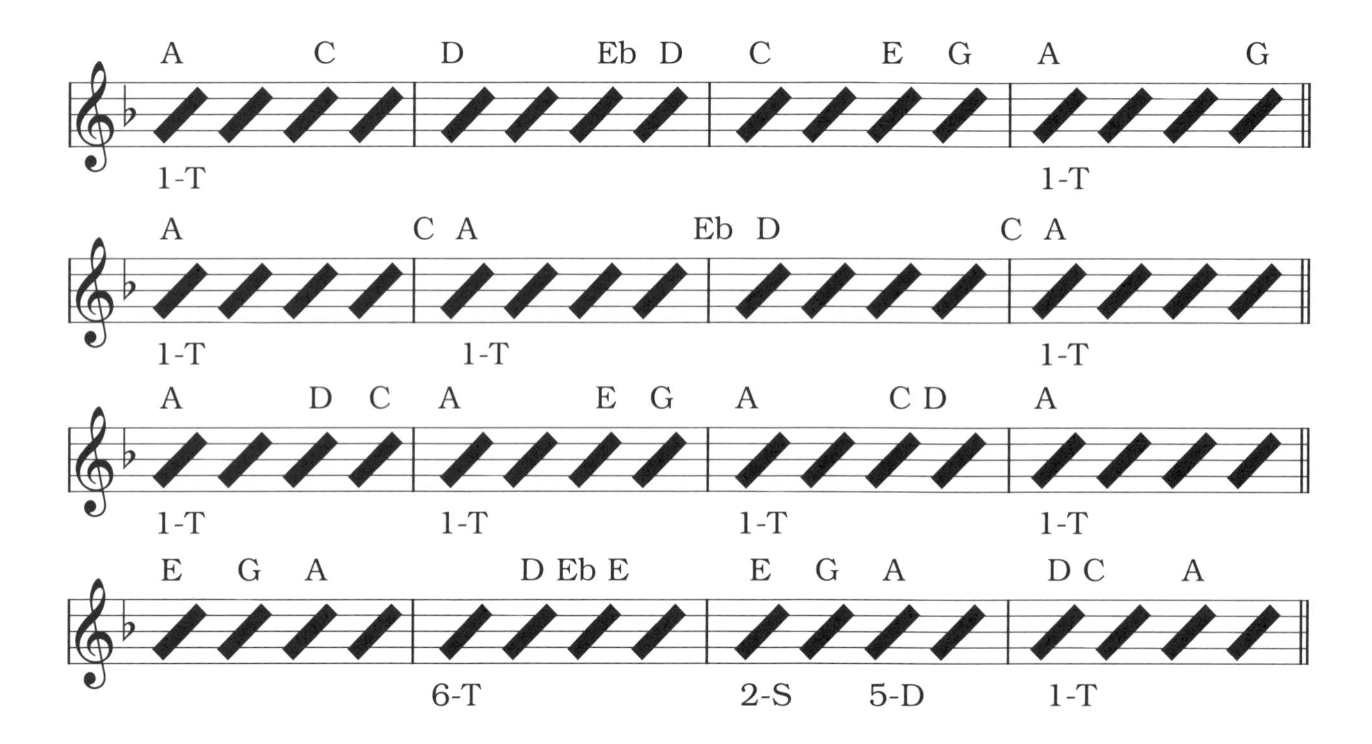

It is hoped that this system provides not just familiar progressions, but also a lot of possibilities for creative experimentation. At least there are sensible alternatives to stabbing in the dark for things that might work then trying to remember what sounded good and never knowing why. The methods presented offer a number of possibilities for chords in sequence. By combining varying, and experimenting, you should be able to use them to analyze and understand other people's music and more importantly, develop some ideas of your own.

Rhythms & Progressions Combined

In this section, we combine rhythm and progressions to produce a musical synergy, suggesting more than the sum of its parts. The first progression is based on the two-five in the key of C and it should bring to mind at least two or three pop songs. The harmonic structure begins with the progression 2 5 1 4 in the key of C, then the Bb behaves like a chromatic (sharp) 5 chord in Dm only to resolve to a 5/5 (E). The E is the dominant of the Am and the change to the A major makes it a dominant of the Dm and the cycle starts again.

The right hand strumming pattern is easy but not too sing-song sounding. Watch for the variation or rhythmic *turn around* in the last measure.

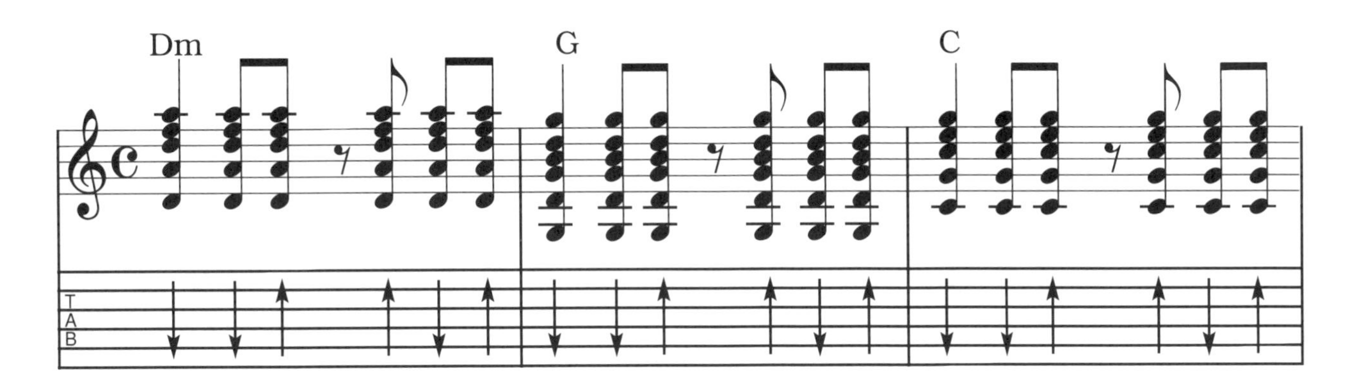

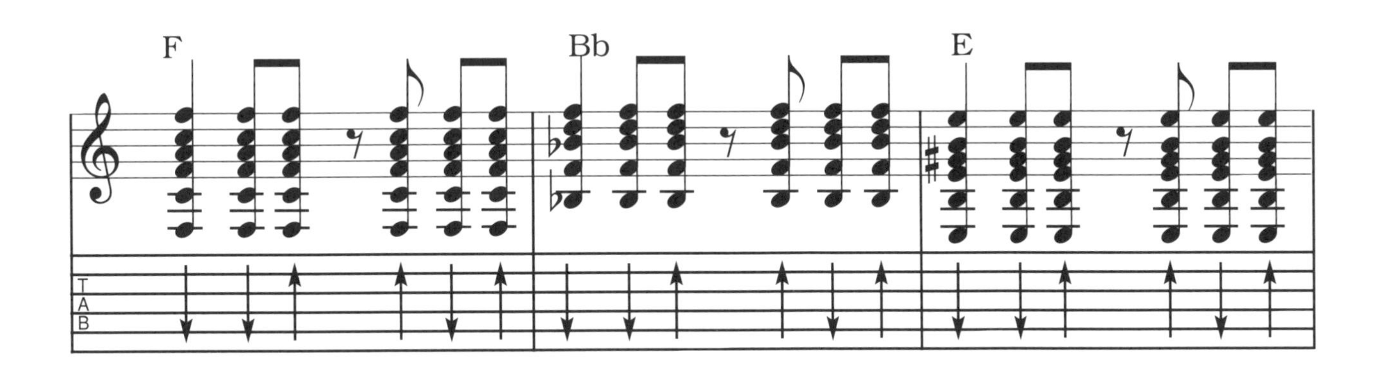

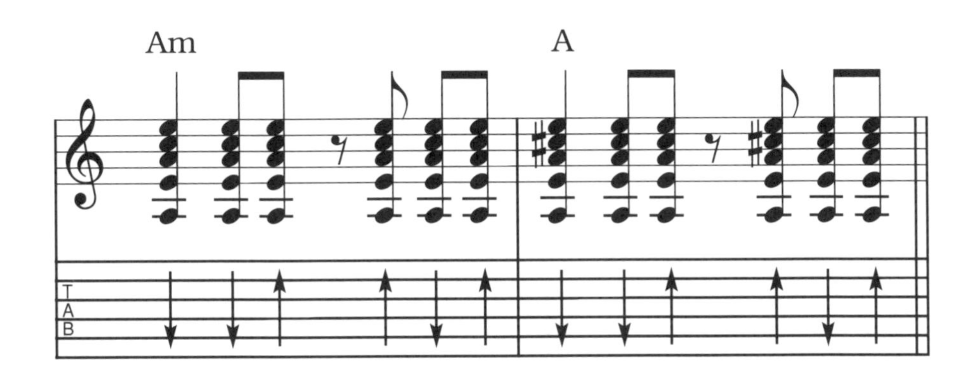

Rhythms & Progressions Combined

The next rhythm features simple bass lines with the strumming pattern in a country or county rock style rhythm. The key is E minor and the harmonic structure of the progression is 1 3 4 6 5. Tonic to tonic (1-3), then subdominant to chromatic dominant (4-6), then to dominant (5).

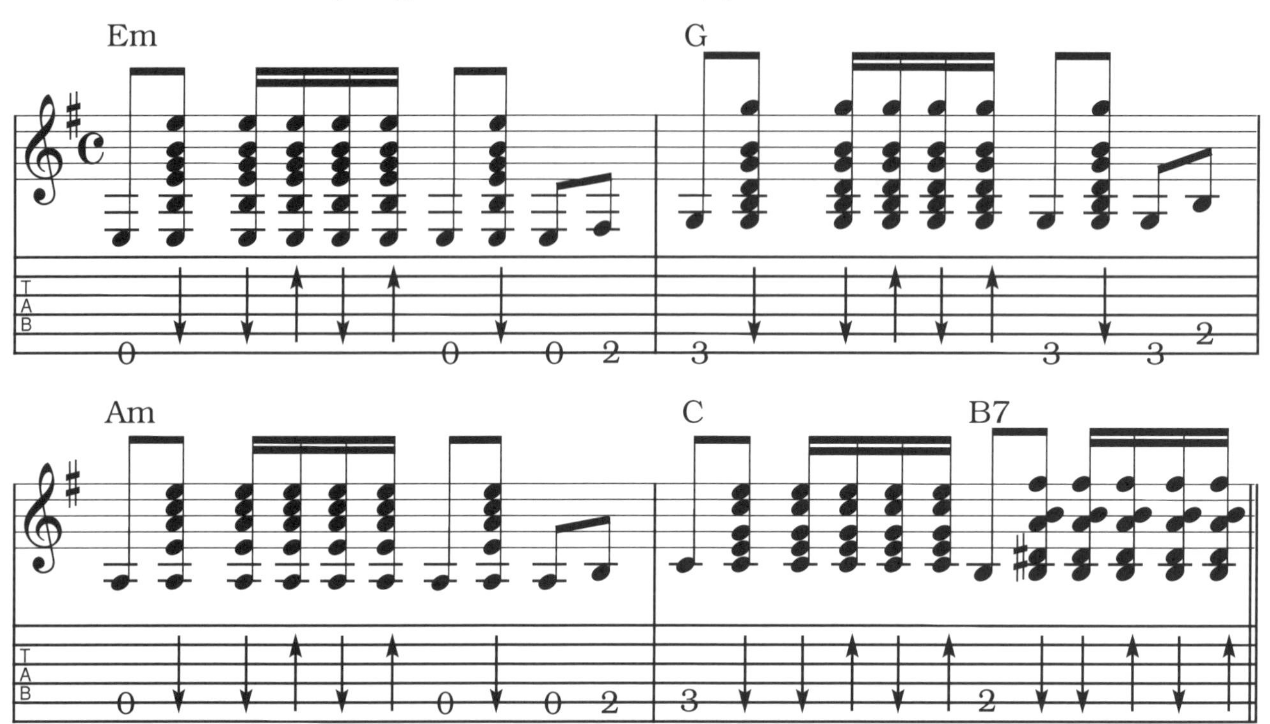

Below is a variation in a similar style using triplets and strong upstrokes.

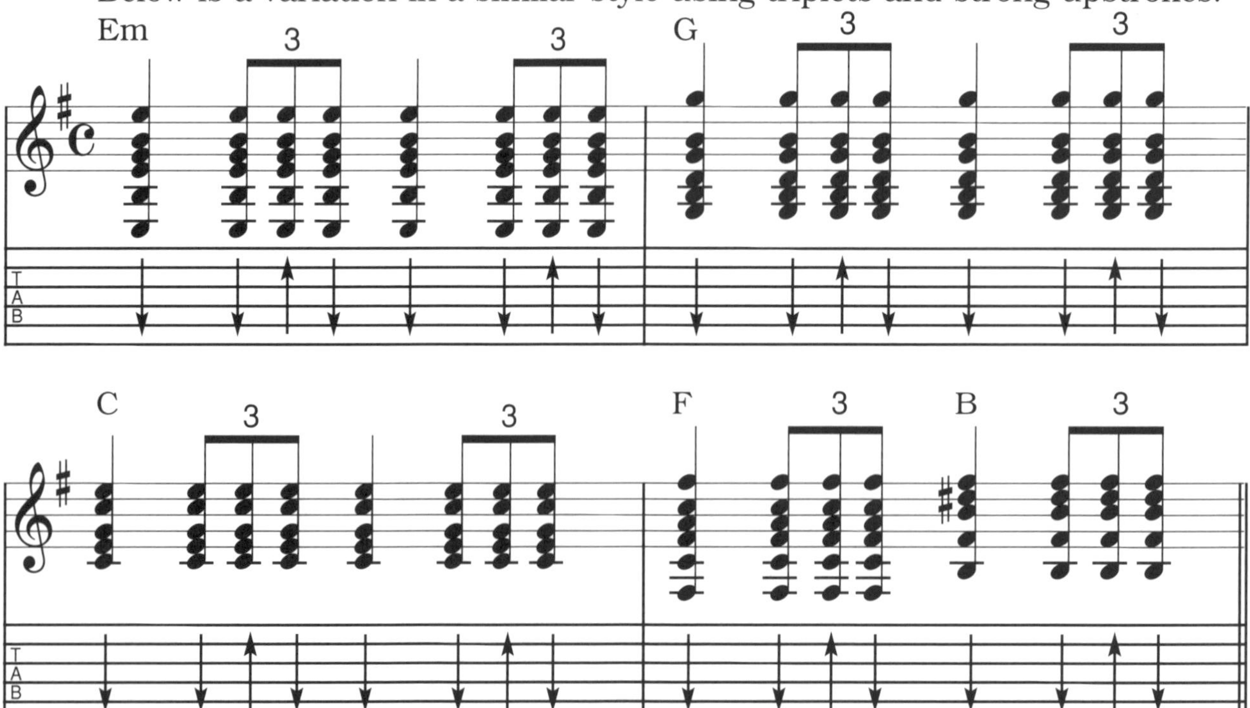

Rhythms & Progressions Combined

The next exercise is a basic rock and roll progression in A. If given a chance, most guitarists will avoid the standard notation when there is an easier alternative. In this exercise, the chord designations (all open position forms) only tell a small part of the story and so you'll have to actually read the notation to play the rhythm. The harmonic structure is all 1 4 5 stuff, so to keep it from getting too boring, we've added some other elements. It is continued on the next page.

Rhythms & Progressions Combined

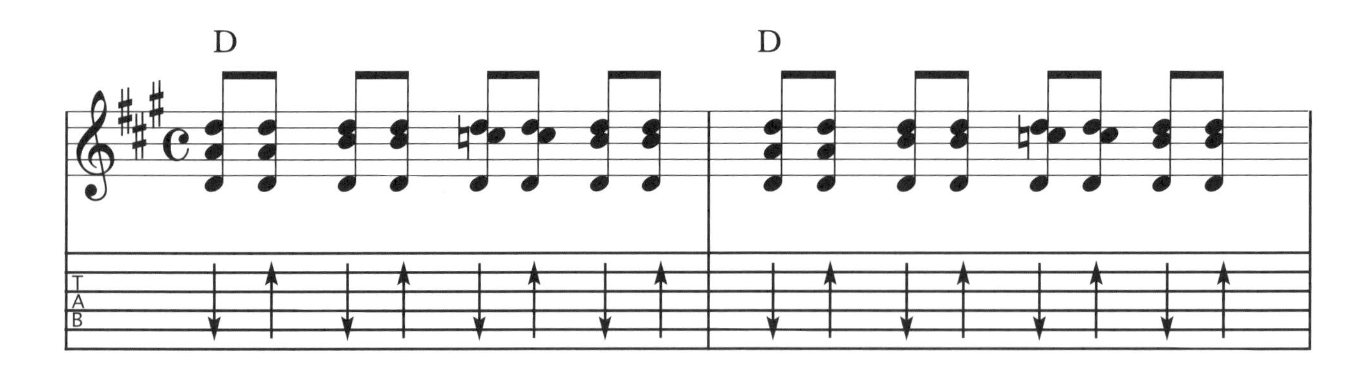

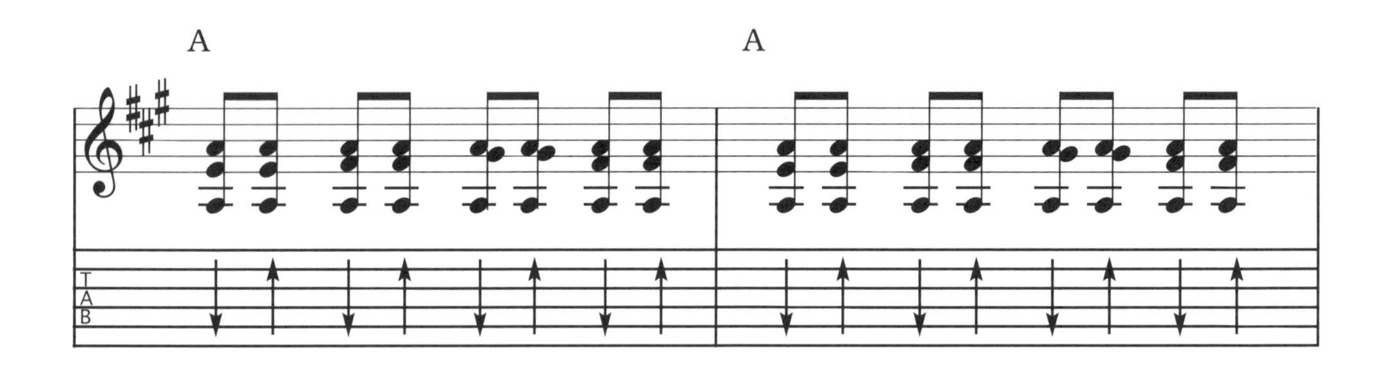

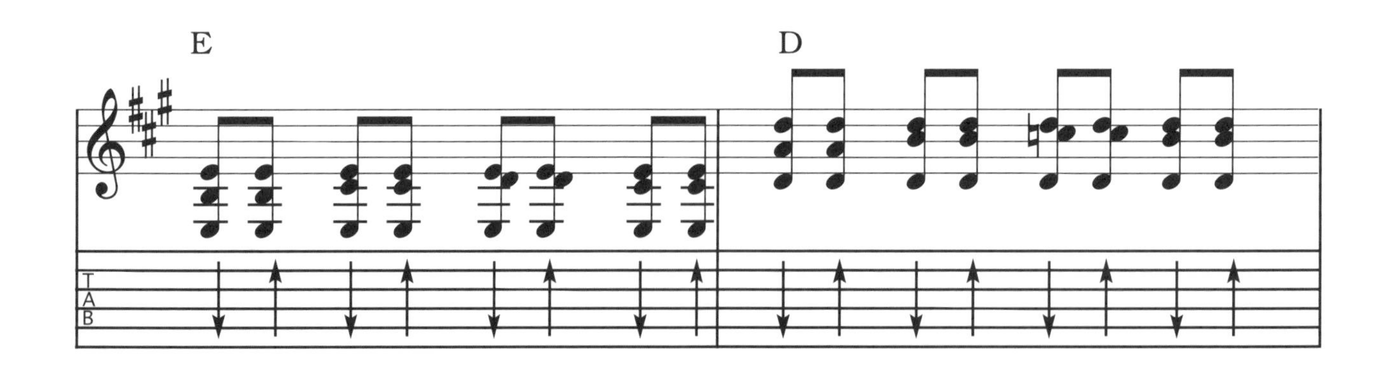

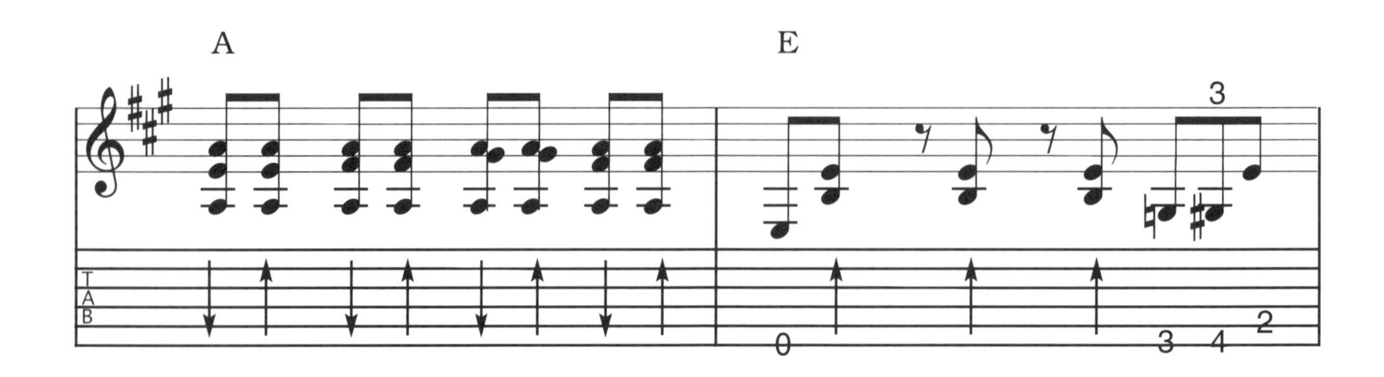

Rhythms & Progressions Combined

The next rhythm is a typical flamenco progression in B minor, and features the rasgado technique on the second beat of each measure. With the exception of the rasgado, this is the same strumming pattern used in the first exercise. The difference in the chord progression alone changes the feel as well as the style.

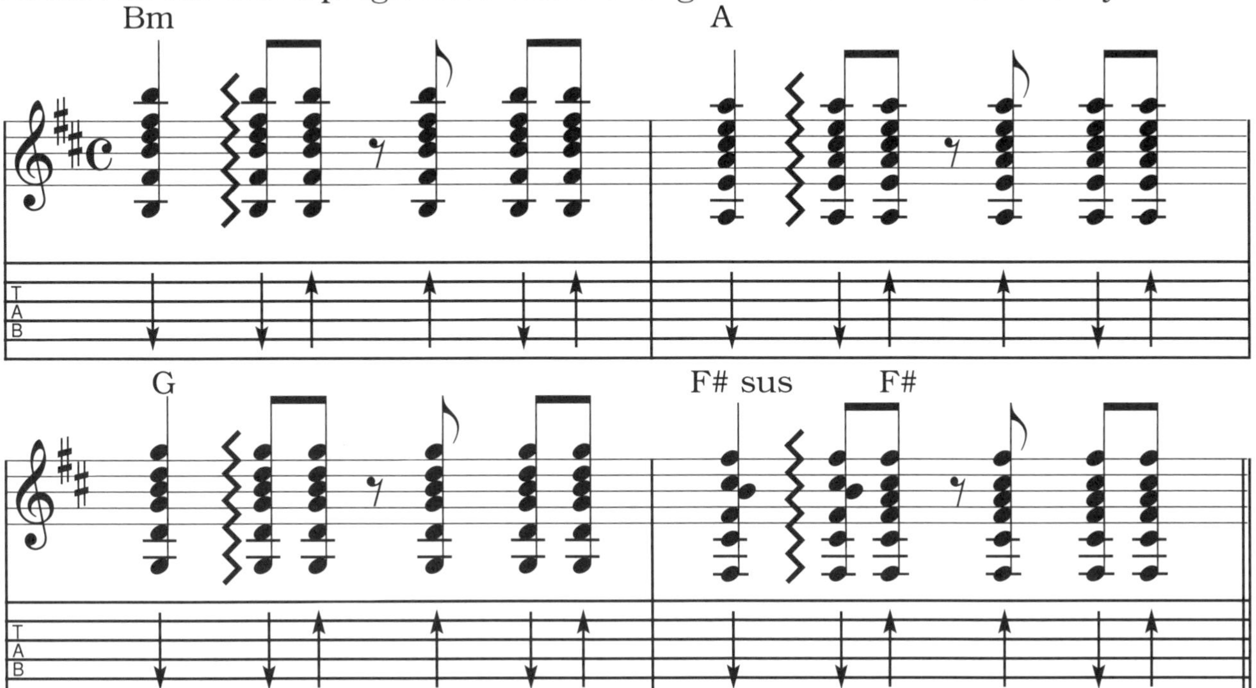

Next is a typical bluegrass style rhythm part. Bluegrass groups tend to rely on the steady bass lines as found in the example below. These two lines are the "A" part, with the "B" part on the following page.

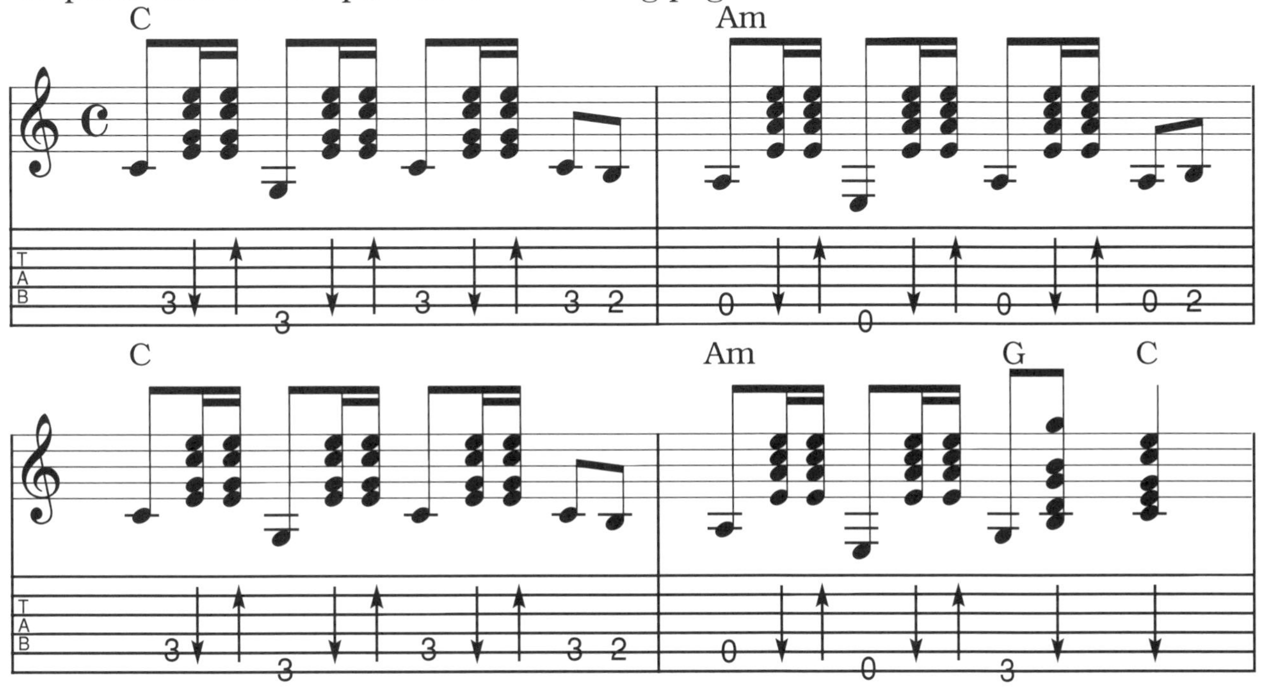

Rhythms & Progressions Combined

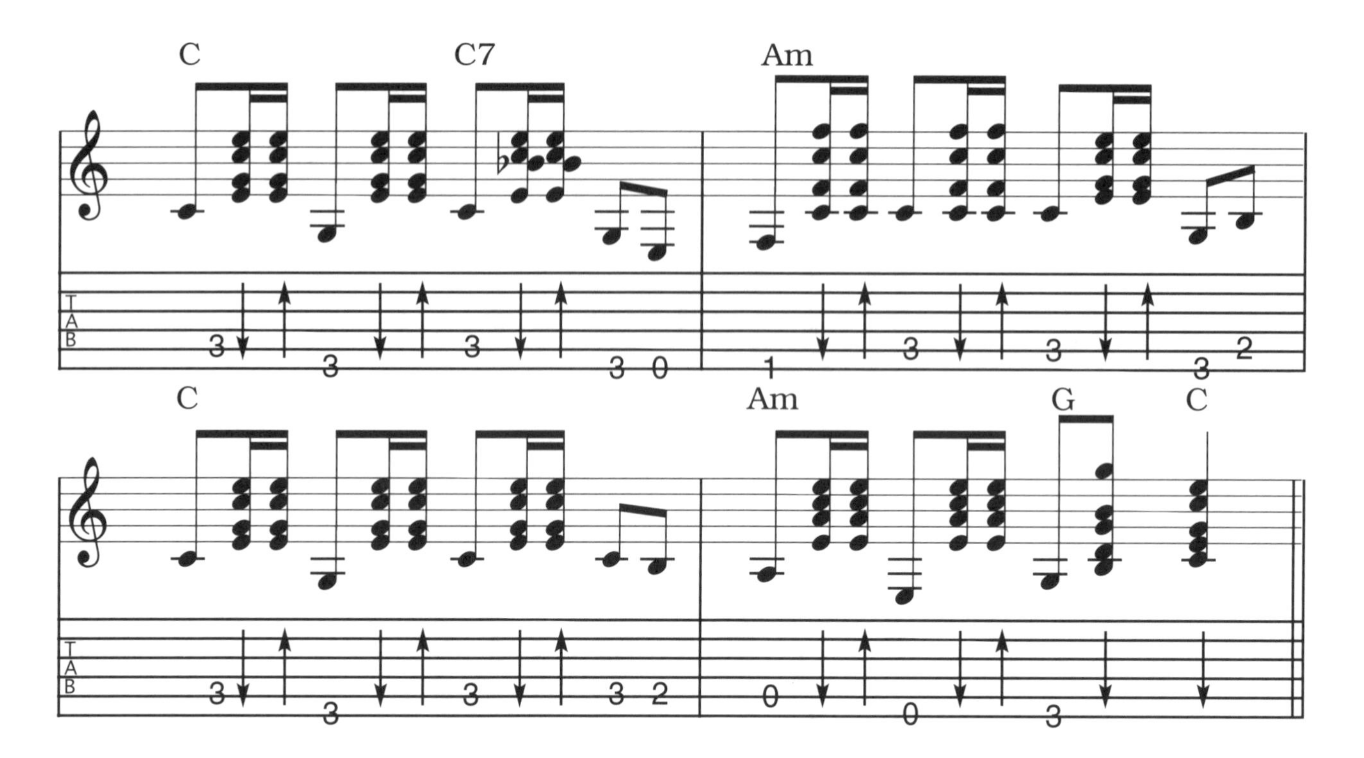

If you're playing these progressions just once or twice through and then moving on, you're missing out on an important element of the learning equation. You should be experimenting with these simple frameworks and developing them further. Expand on them. There is much to be gained by the process of constantly changing and rearranging what you've learned and trying to improve and broaden the material. This is the essence of improvisation: altering certain components of the music without losing the key elements which define both the specific piece and the style in general.

The next section is devoted to one of our three full length **etudes,** or study pieces. "Francesca" is featured in the second video in the series, and focuses on arpeggios and challenging rhythms in the flamenco style. Typically an etude will focus on one particular technique, but each of these compositions was developed to also double as a performance piece of varying levels of difficulty.

Francesca

Bill Edwards

Rit.
To Coda

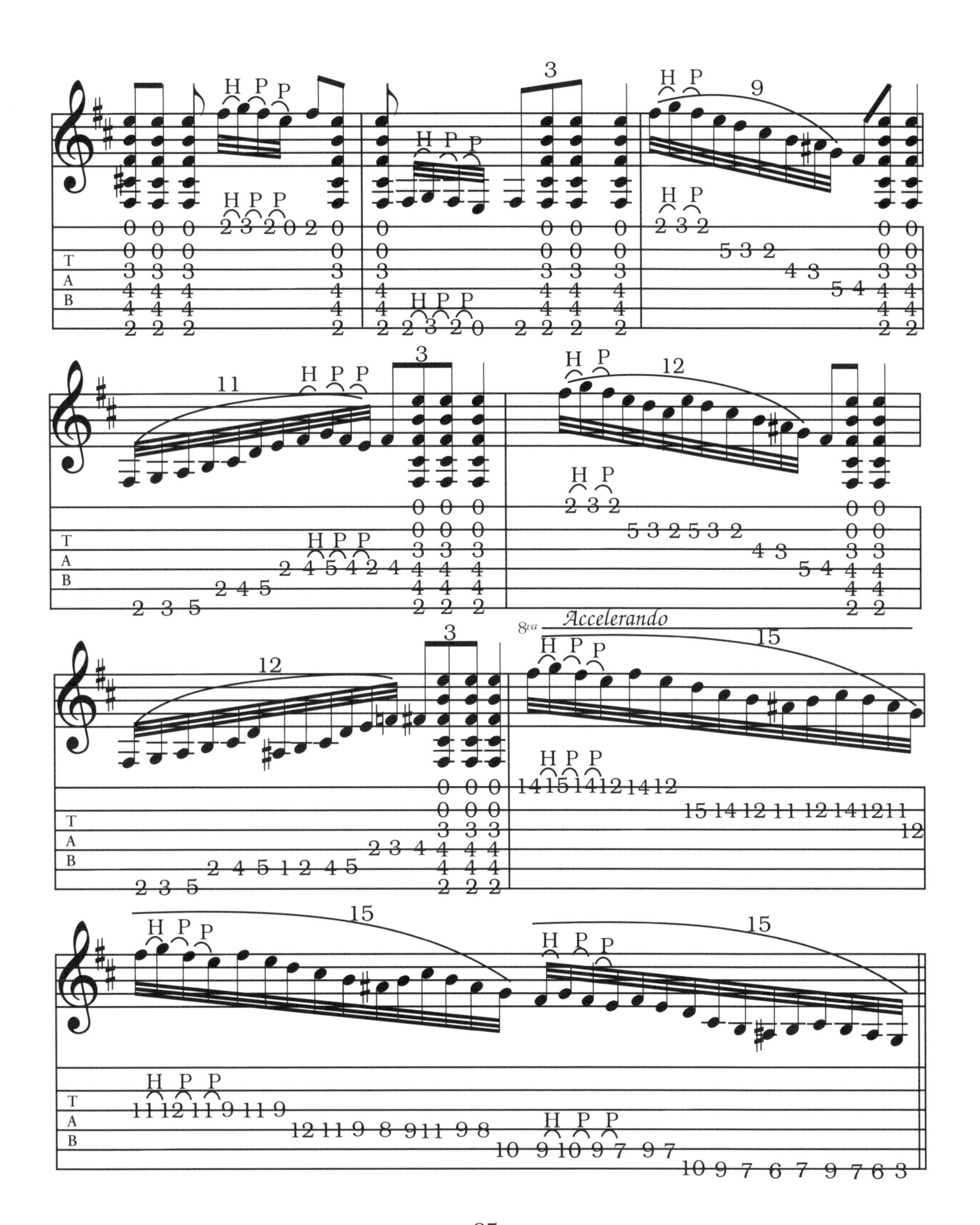
8va
Accelerando

Ritardando
Accelerando
Ritardando

Accelerando
Ritardando
T
A
B

Rit.
Simile

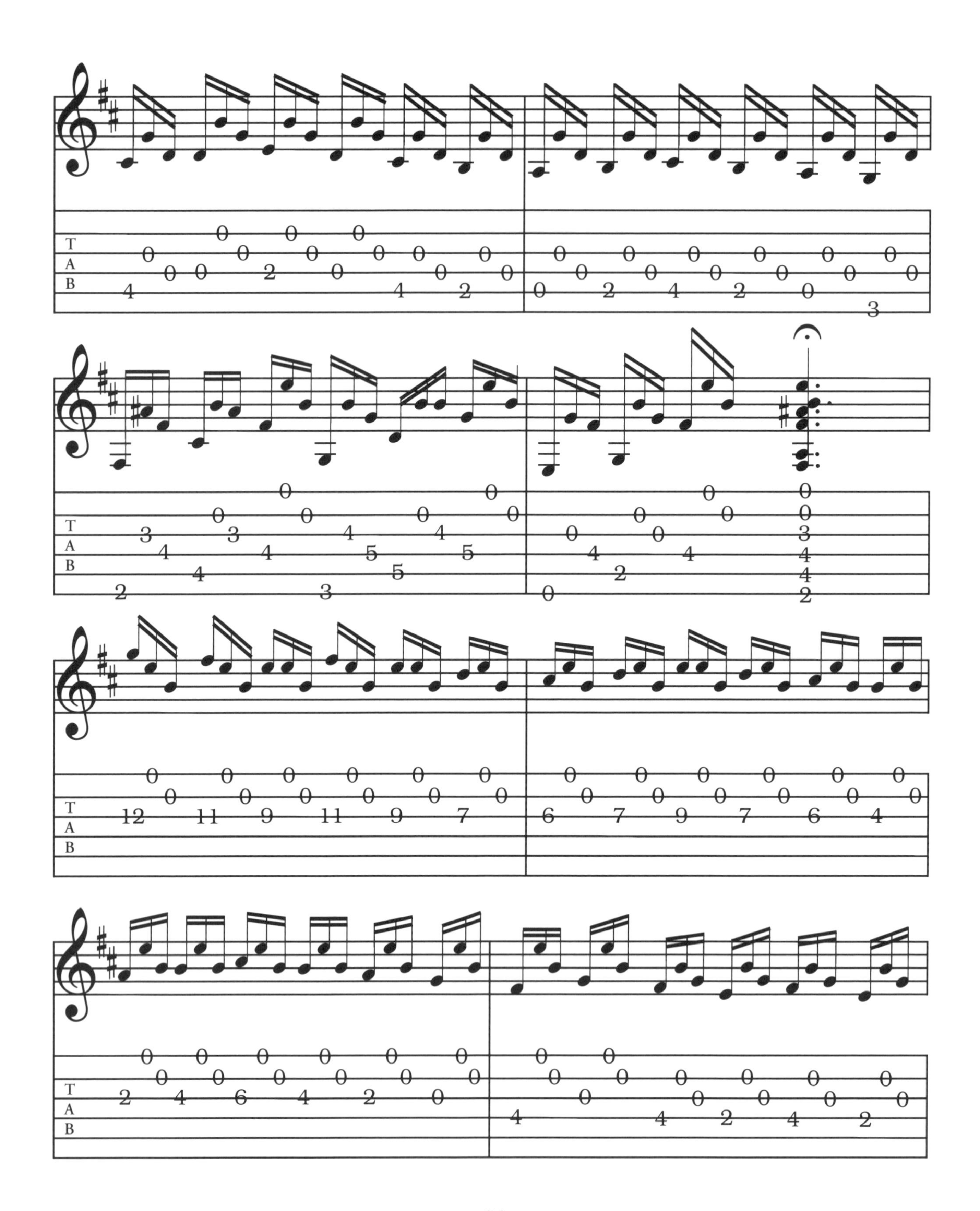

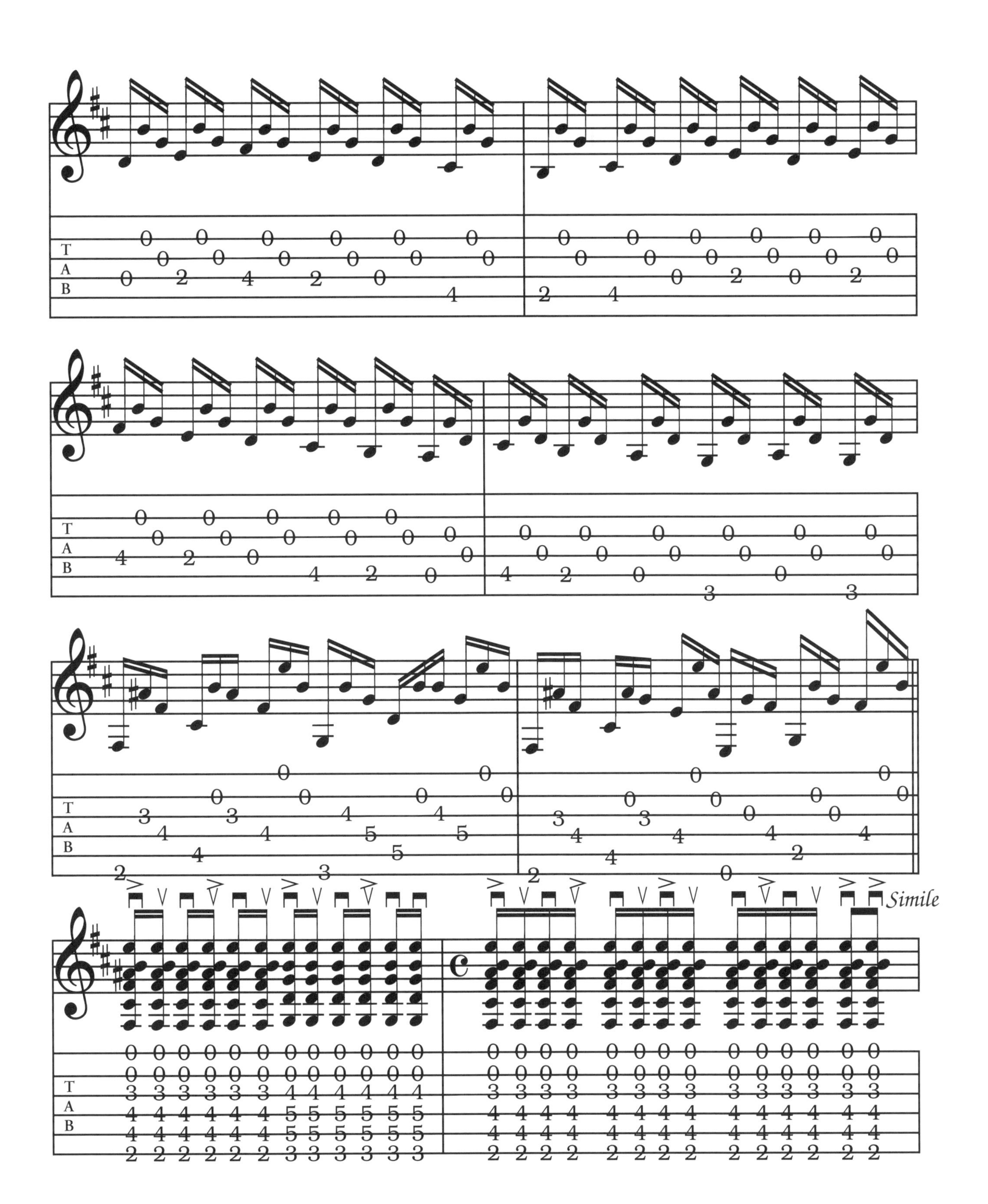
Simile

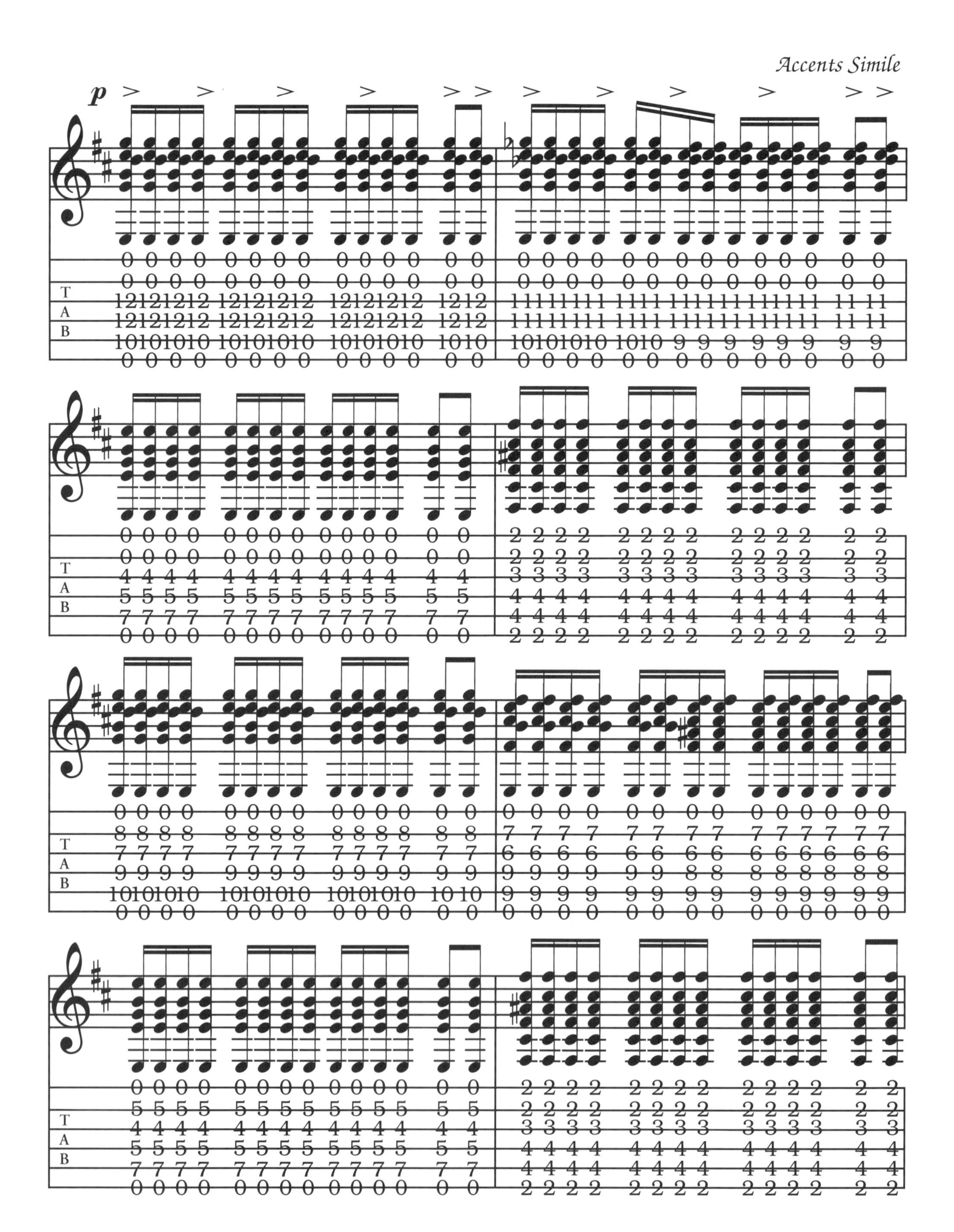
Accents Simile
p

Crescendo

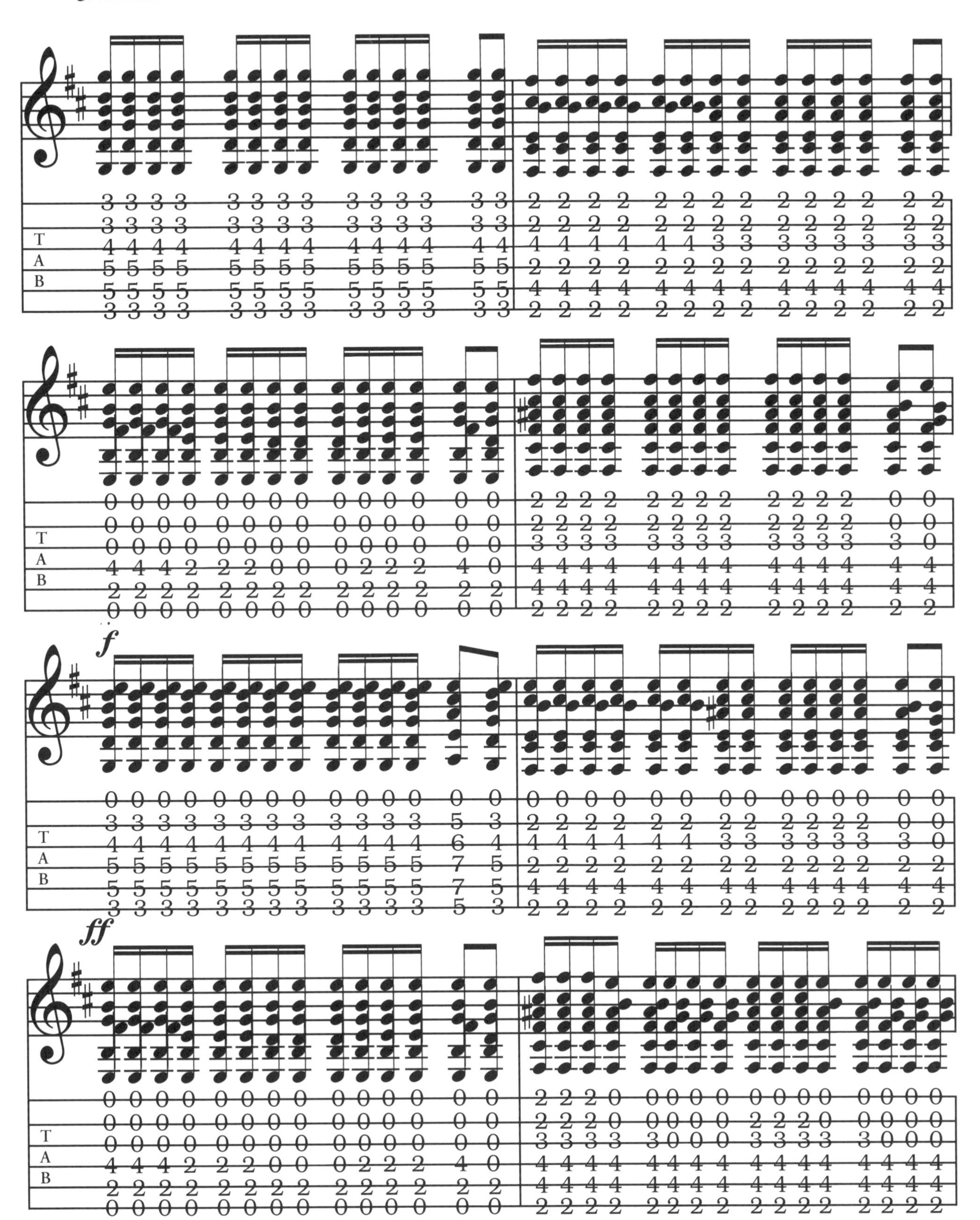

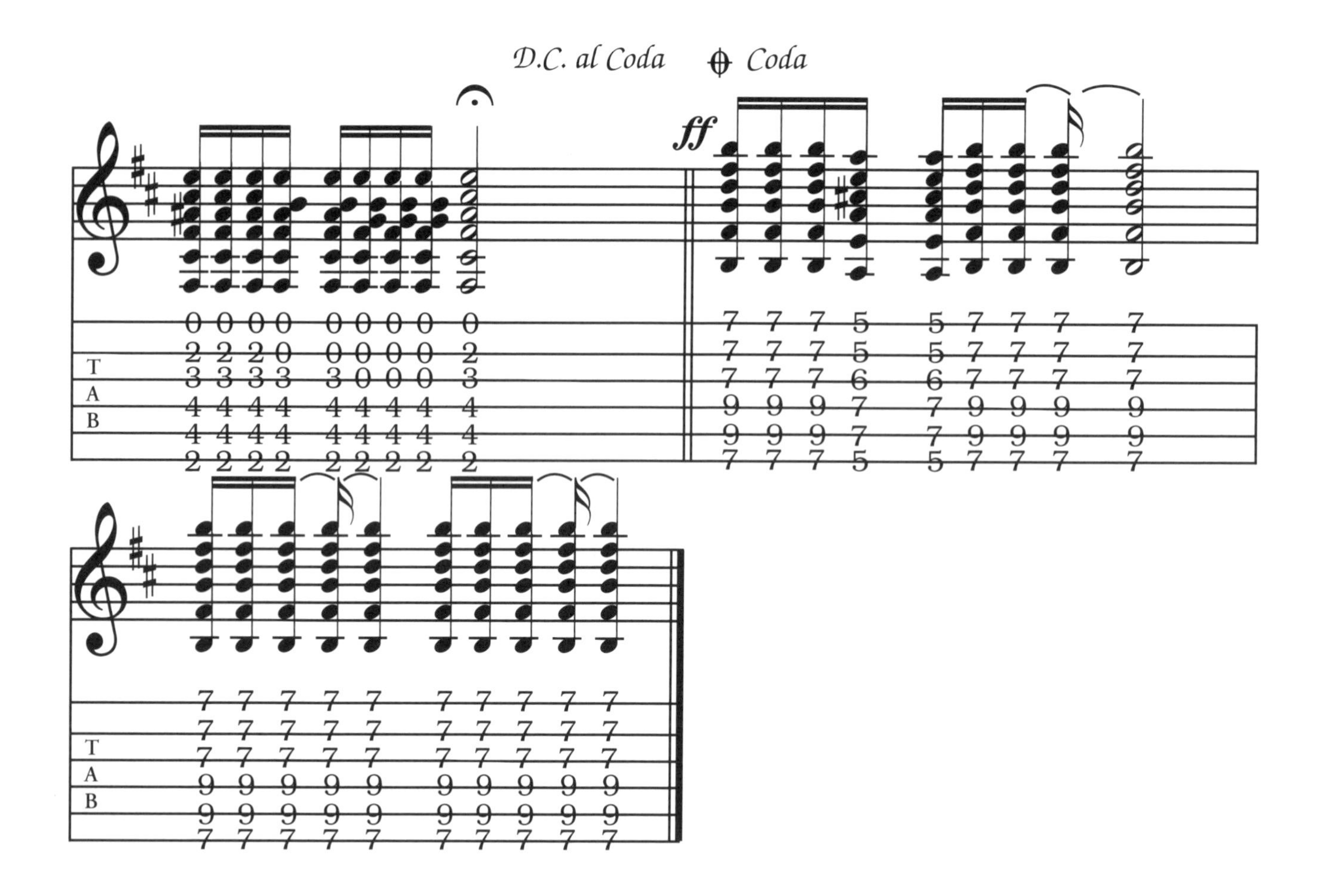
D.C. al Coda
Coda
ff
T
A
B
T
A
B

Lead Playing

In the "Introduction to Lead Playing" section of Vol. II, we broached the subject by making an analogy to verbal communication, where the basic unit of exchange was the phrase, in the same sense as the basic unit of verbal communication is the sentence. (It might not be a bad idea to review that section as a foundation and basic philosophy for what follows here.) The object is to provide a more structured approach to improvisation than simply finding the right scale to play against the right chord or chords. Good lead playing accomplishes more than just playing appropriate scale tones against a progression, in that the player makes musical statements much the same way we speak in word groups with pauses that separate one idea from the next. As both the correct choice of words and the way they are used is essential to being understood, so the correct choice of melodic and rhythmic material and how they are expressed is fundamental to good lead playing. The vehicle for both is the phrase, and the purpose in both cases is to say something worth listening to.

The terms riff, lick, phrase, lead, solo, leitmotiv, motive, theme, subject, melody, etc., are all terms for musical statements consisting of tones in sequence expressed coherently. As groups they can be longer or shorter, and have more or less significance to the composition as a whole. For example a turnaround is shorter and less important than a song's melody but both are cut from the same cloth in terms of the material that goes into them. In more traditional terms, a theme or subject is larger and more significant than a motive. In common usage, a riff and a lick are considered the same thing - phrases - but leads and solos are usually collections of riffs and licks.

Whereas a musical phrase would be the equivalent of a verbal sentence, there can be larger sections that would be considered paragraphs or even essays. Often a lead is built around a few basic ideas that have been joined together and then restated, expanded, and developed to produce a more interesting and substantial whole. If you have an overall idea of what you are trying to accomplish or say in a solo, you can more effectively communicate by building your phrases based upon basic ideas.

What makes up a guitar phrase? The elements of a typical guitar phrase are: note selection, rhythmic expression, intervallic direction, iterations, and articulation techniques. Note selection pertains to a key area(s) and can be thought of as a tone pool where we draw from a selection of available resources for a specific purpose such as style or effect. This tonal orientation lends a fundamental character that prevails over the entire lead. The rhythmic expression is the combination of durations, tempo, etc., that contributes to the feel of the phrase. Intervallic direction is termed motion in traditional music theory, and pertains here to both the note by note raising or lowering of pitch, as well as the overall direction of the phrase and its sections. Iterations, or note sequences, are repeating series of tones in sequence. The term iteration is intended to convey repetition on not just one, but many levels often occurring simultaneously, such as numeric, intervallic, and sectional sequences and their repeating structures. The articulation techniques are the slurs, string tricks, etc., that are so much a part of guitar playing that they are often taken for granted or overlooked. In fact, the significance of hammer-ons, pull-offs, bends, etc., to phrase structure is such that I'd be willing to venture that it isn't likely that a lead has ever been played where they didn't figure in somehow. On the other hand, there have been times when the technique per se, has become the focus of the solo to the point that everything else is relegated to secondary status. Are you old enough to remember when right hand tapping became the big thing?

Lead Playing

What changes scales into musical phrases? The process that turns raw scales into usable riffs and licks is how they are expressed rhythmically, iteratively, and melodically. In the section on rhythmic phrasing, we examine the non-tonal characteristics of notes in sequence. In the section on iterative phrasing, we explore the repetition of note sequences in terms of various intervallic and numerical values. What do melodic phrases have that rhythmic and iterative ones don't? In a word - character. They have more personality and memorability in the form of rhythmic and tonal qualities in a synergistic combination. Iterations of note sequences contribute to phrasing, but as a kind of filler. Articulation techniques contribute also, giving them uniquely guitaristic qualities, as well. The melodic character of a phrase is more a matter of how things work as a whole, and how we relate to them as people. When it works, the whole becomes more than the sum of the parts.

Contrary to popular belief, the role of the solo in a song is not to demonstrate the technical proficiency of the lead guitarist. Self promotion notwithstanding, I believe it is to enhance the song and give it a secondary focus of interest. Having an outstanding technical command of the instrument, however, means you are going to be able to do things that you might not be able to do otherwise. The point is that the solo exists to create another level of interest. In other words, do something interesting, unusual, and unpredictable. The things we haven't heard before are what most of us listen for. Ah, what the hey. If all else fails just play faster than the other guy.

Since we've already examined the raw tonal groupings in Volume II, our exploration into phrasing will begin with primarily rhythmic statements, and progress to iterative and melodic statements.

Rhythmic Phrasing

This section deals with the rhythmic aspects of phrasing. Just as the rhythm of a composition contributes greatly to the music's feel, the rhythmic character of a phrase lend it defining qualities as well. The importance of this area of endeavor lies in the fact that it is relatively neglected and often taken for granted. When constructing solos, guitarists tend to become absorbed in the technical, tonal, and pattern related demands, with less regard for the rhythmic aspects of phrasing. In this section we will produce phrases with minimal materials in order to concentrate on the rhythmic nature of single notes in sequence. The steady beat of a metronome, or better still, a drum machine will make this section more accessible and enjoyable. If these aren't readily available, tapping your foot can be better than nothing at all. Be creative. I read an account by a personal friend of Beethoven's, who walked into the great man's rented room once to find him pounding on the walls with both hands trying to work out a rhythm, so, um, don't hesitate to try something off the wall. Ever seen Bobby McFerrin?

Below are examples of two familiar themes from different backgrounds that you should be able to identify without the benefit of their tonal elements. They've been notated on the open E string for the sake of simplicity, but if the monotone gets in the way, you can play them as muted chords instead. If the rhythmic notation used below is hard to follow, then go to the sections on Notation Formats and Rhythm and work on some foundational stuff for a while.

The first one's a giveaway, and the second one should be pretty obvious, too. Below are the same rhythms with the tones added for clarity. By the way, they're both arranged as single string presentations in the key of E harmonic minor.

Evidence of their intrinsically rhythmical nature exists in the fact that they are among the first, uh, rap tunes in history. The thing to try to get a handle on is what exactly makes these two phrases as rhythmically coherent as they are. How did they become, among other things, universal door knocks? Try to think of examples in the styles you like, of phrases that emphasize rhythmic character and examine why they work so well. Rhythmic definition and simplicity will usually be factors when one becomes widely recognized and accepted.

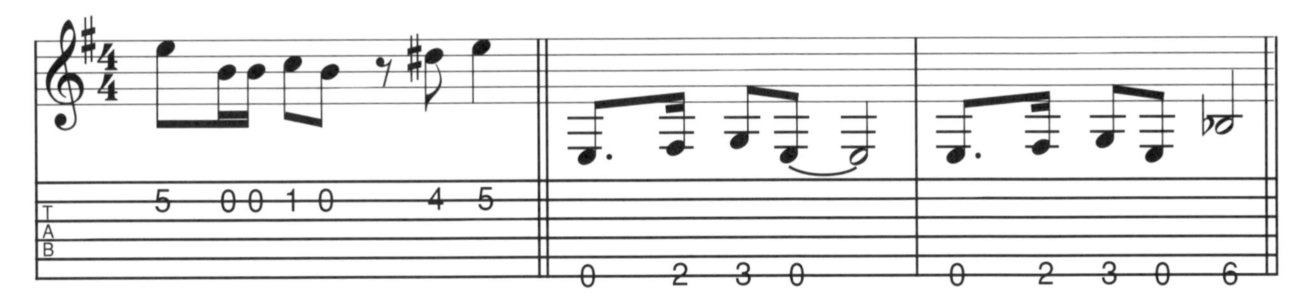

Rhythmic Phrasing

What constitutes rhythmic definition? Within a composition there are a number of repetitive rhythmic characteristics. The most basic is the beat. The beat underlies all other rhythmic phenomena. The accented count of a group of beats gives a numerical value to the group known as meter. If the first of every three beats is accented, then it is said to be a three. If the first of every four beats is accented, then we will hear four beats per measure of time, and so on. For establishing relative values of durations within these groups, a value is given to each beat. This value is in the form of a type of note which gets a beat, such as a quarter note or eighth note. Overlying this rhythmic framework of beats, measures and durational values, our rhythmic phrasing is to be formed. What gives a phrase its definition is its cohesiveness and relevance. Rhythmic cohesion means that the durations making up the phrase hold together as a set with continuity. Relevance pertains to how well people will respond to it and whether they are likely to perceive it as a valid statement.

Rhythmic phrasing refers to the way the solo is played independent of pitch and other considerations. This reduces our focus to mainly the beat, and the combinations of durations. For phrasing purposes, it might be helpful to think of this as "the rhythm of the lead". This works for two reasons. First, the way each phrase is expressed on the single string level is really a microcosm of what happens on the rhythm playing level with all six strings. The larger strokes of rhythm playing are miniaturized down to one string where the tonal and rhythmic character varies more often, but the same principle is in effect. Second, it boils things down to just beats and durations. If you acquire the discipline to always play in definite rhythmic statements, half of all the possible mistakes you could make in lead playing stand to be eliminated. Half pertains to the definition of music as pitch and time relationships. In more positive terms, the advantage is that you will be playing more musically as a matter of course. As guitarists we tend to dismiss rhythmic issues as beginner stuff, and it is easy to lose sight of its significance in the area of lead playing. From a practical standpoint, playing rhythmically is a prerequisite to playing musically.

When improvising, try to mentally put the rhythm of each phrase out in front of the patterns, notes selection, articulations, etc., and concentrate on the part that gets taken for granted. The overall goal is to make statements that have rhythmic and tonal coherence in a way the makes them both more effective as a whole. The problem is that we tend to put our focus on the tonal aspects much the same way we automatically look at our left hand instead of our right whenever we are learning something new. The idea is redirect our focus to see right hand as the all important rhythm maker. When the technical aspects of lead playing become less of an obstacle, the hard part becomes a matter of taste in the form of restraint. In other words, we have to discipline ourselves to try not to blurt out too many notes at one time.

Rhythm is how you say what you say in a lead. The tones are like the words, but the rhythm is the delivery including the emphasis and the expressiveness. This aspect of lead playing stands to contribute to your overall progress as much as any other. We'll start our approach by experimenting with simple rhythmic statements and then combine and vary. Since the beat is the unit of currency in rhythm, the beat groupings, or measures, will be the guide to the length of our statements. The first step is to establish how many measures or parts of measures a phrase is to have. By starting with small phrases, we can establish definition and build up to larger and more impressive ones as we go.

Rhythmic Phrasing

Next we'll present some two bar repeatable rhythm patterns that we can vary and layer in order to develop something of interest. First practice the basic rhythms until they are easy at about M.M. ♩-100. For obvious reasons, only the first figure has been notated in tablature.

Rhythmic Phrasing

Although there isn't anything to write home about, each of the previous examples has what would pass for rhythmic definition. Each two-measure phrase holds together and can be related to by us as listeners. If we try to put any more constraints on what constitutes definition, then we risk putting limitations on what can be a rhythmic statement. In fact too many things actually work to try to put much more spin on it. Outstanding examples of rhythmic definition are drummer Steve Gadd's snare drum intro to Paul Simons' song "Fifty Ways To Leave Your Lover", Queens' "We Will Rock You," and the old General Cinema coming attractions hihat shuffle. Another distinct and haunting rhythm is the military snare roll associated with a condemned man ascending the gallows.

We speak and write in phrases without even giving it much thought. It didn't come naturally at first, but by now we aren't even conscious of the process. Eloquent orators pace their delivery in calculated rhythms. Persuasive lawyers are trained to use precise pauses until the effects of significant statements have registered on their juries with maximum impact. Same thing applies here. If we are able to develop the rhythmic habit early, then later we will only have to concern ourselves with combinations and variations of rhythmic and other material.

In the following exercises, various tonal materials have been added to further develop the seven rhythmic phrases.

Rhythmic Phrasing

Hopefully, what becomes progressively more apparent is that the rhythmic character acts mainly as *support* for the stylistic character of the phrase. Although we often associate pure rhythms with attention getting and specific events or compositions, the stylistic intent of rhythmic phrases is often unclear until tonal materials or other elements are included. In other words, the tonal material lends essential defining qualities for what we perceive as the style of the music. The tempo of the rhythm sets the stage for one essential distinction, however, and that is whether it is to be fast or slow, and as Alice's Queen of Hearts observed: "That's very important!"

Iterative Phrasing

In between playing the basic tonal elements and playing melodic phrases are the fields of rhythm and iteration. Rhythm, in general is everything that pertains to the duration of notes relative to one another. In a specific sense, it is metrical in that its values are denoted by a temporal unit called a beat. Iterations differ from rhythms in that they are somewhat independent of an overall rhythm and its beats. The music's beat will stay the same for extended periods, usually the length of the composition, but the iterative character of a phrase can change quickly and often. The concept of iterations as an aspect of phrasing is simpler than the words make it seem. Iterative phrases are based on repetitive numerical sequences such as found in the technical development exercises but on a note by note basis regardless of the number of notes per string played. The term iterative is used instead of repetitive to suggest levels of repetition, in terms of both multiple repetitions, and different types of repetitions. Notes can be played in groups of sequences that repeat independent of an overall beat.

To put it differently, rhythm can be considered repetitions of the beat, whereas iteration is repetitions of note sequences.

Notes can be grouped in successive number combinations that iterate (repeat) at specific intervals (of time, number, and pitch). This makes them easy to relate to for a variety of reasons. The most common iterations are fours, threes, twos and ones. Fives are not uncommon, but tend to be perceived as combinations of threes and twos; sixes and eights are very common but can also be heard as double threes and double fours; sevens are usually are interpreted as threes combined with fours. We tend to hear the lowest common denominators in terms of iterations, and like beats, we relate best to fours, threes, and twos depending on the tempo of the piece.

In the technical development exercises we limited the character of the studies to a number of notes per string in order to concentrate on the right and left hand synchronization. In this section we apply the repetitive note sequences to specific tonal material such as scales and arpeggios to produce a kind of musical intermediary between the raw tonal elements and melodic phrases. Iterations are more than just intervals, scales, and arpeggios, but less than melodic phrases. They can be considered a kind of tonal filler that all composers and improvisers use to one extent or another. Overuse of iterative phrasing gives the music a predictable character the same way that overusing a given articulation technique, such as tapping, does. They both tend to get old fast so don't rely on them to be more than they really are. On the other hand, nothing will improve your improvisation skills as rapidly as expanding your thinking patterns to include iterative phrasing as opposed to rerunning all those grooves you've worn into your neck out of habit.

In the examples that follow, we've tried to provide a sampling of different combinations of fretboard forms, tonal elements, and repetitive sequences. Again, these are examples only, for purposes of illustrating concepts at work. You've only really learned this section when you can use these methods to produce your own iterative phrasing with an understanding of the guitar form(s), the tonal material(s), and the repetition sequence(s).

Each iteration is described in the same order of presentation as the Fretboard Logic series itself: the appropriate fretboard orientation first, its musical orientation second, and the sequential nature of the iteration third.

Iterative Phrasing - Fours

The first iteration sequence uses the E diatonic scale form in the 8th position and is a C Major scale. It is a series of ascending fours (four scale tones), repeating in ascending ones (single scale tone increments).

The second iteration of fours also uses a the E diatonic scale form, but is an A minor scale. In this series, each four note segment descends three scale tones, returns to the first, and then repeats one scale tone lower.

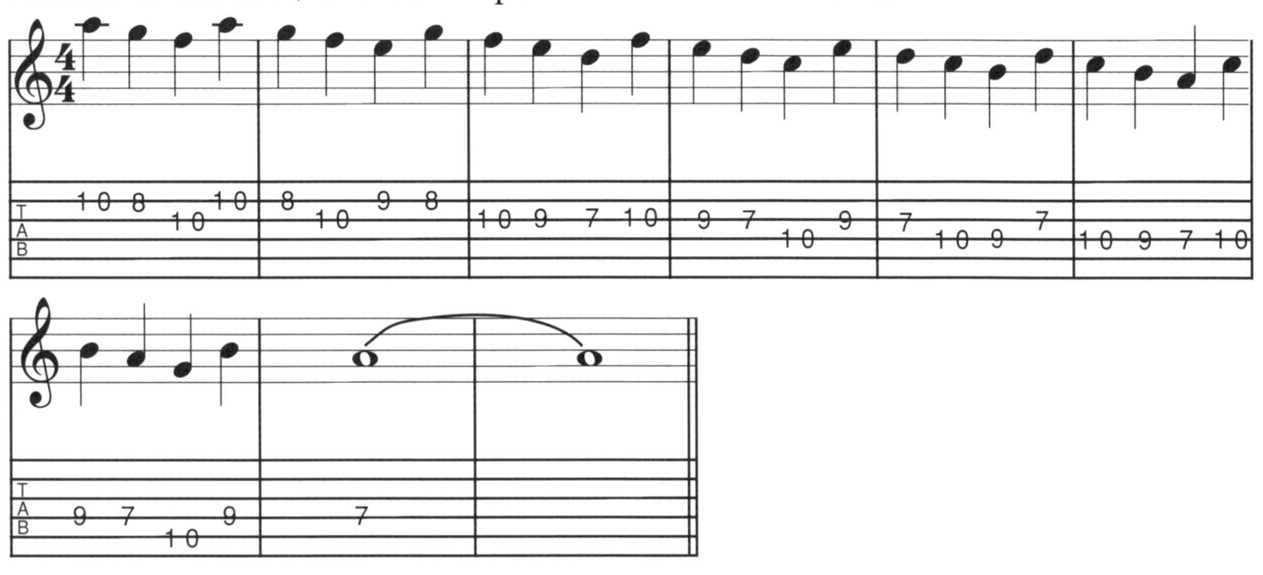

Iterative Phrasing - Fours

The third example is based on Lead Pattern 1, and is a C pentatonic Major scale. It is a series of descending fours, repeating in descending ones (single scale tone increments).

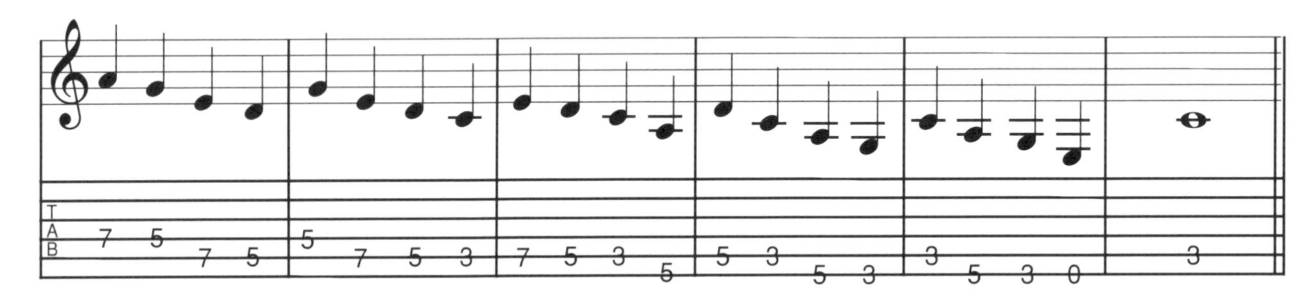

The third example is based on Lead Pattern 1, and is a C pentatonic Major scale. It is a series of descending fours, repeating in descending ones (single scale tone increments). The fourth iteration is based upon a single string, A harmonic minor scale. It is a series of descending fours, plus a drone (basso ostinato) in the form of an open first string. The series repeats in descending ones (again, single scale tone increments), which changes direction after the second sequence. It is continued on the next page.

Iterative Phrasing - Threes

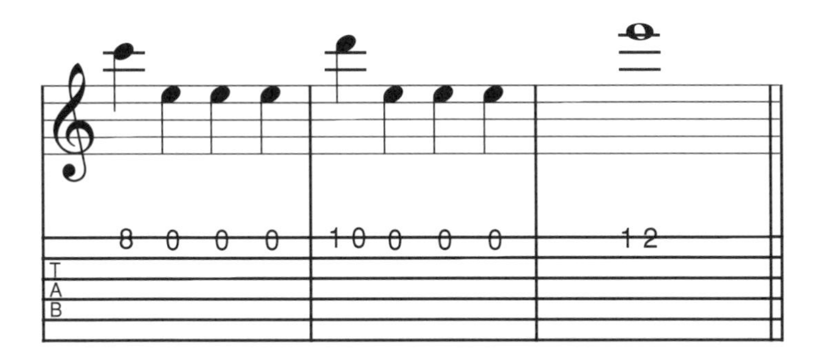

The next iteration is an arpeggio based on the A min. form in the 7th position, making it an E min. arpeggio. The sequences are descending threes that increment in ones (single chord tones).

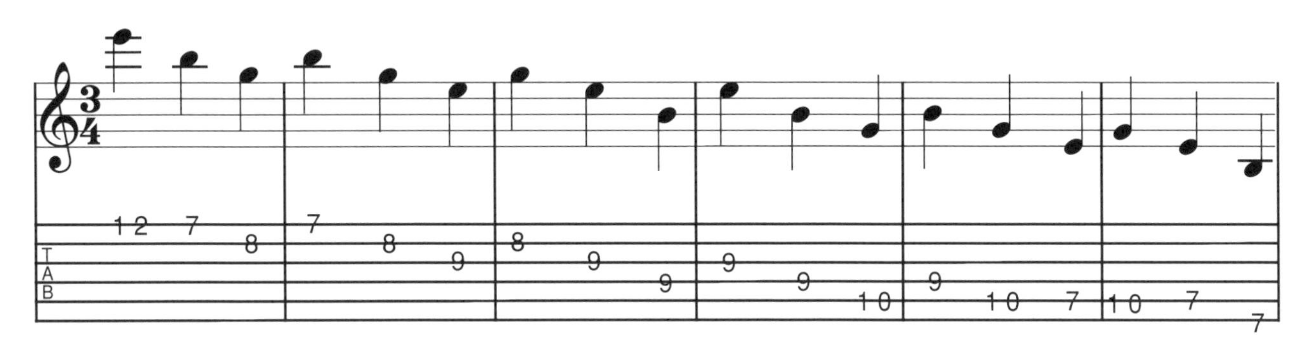

The next three is another arpeggio based on the extended diminished lead pattern from the open position, making it a G dim. arpeggio. The sequences are descending ones that return and then increment in ascending ones. It is continued on the next page.

Iterative Phrasing - Threes

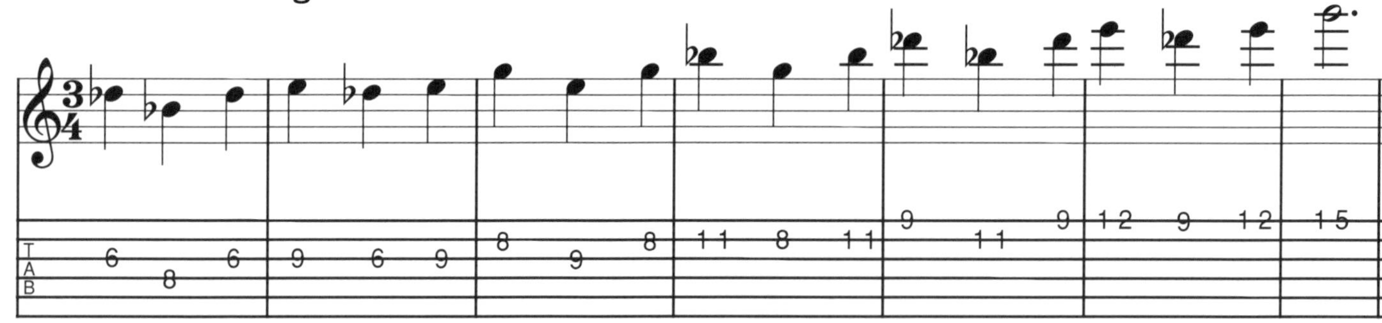

In the following example, the sequence verges on the melodic, because it isn't as continuously iterative as any of the preceding phrases. By adding a third dimension of repeats, it ceases to be perceived as strictly repetitive. It is a single string series of threes, with a tonal orientation of A phrygian. Were it strictly iterative, the sequence would be: up a scale tone then back, descending in ones. However, the first two measures repeat in a larger phrase sense, and then double up in the last four measures. Play this phrase both ways, as written and as continuous iteration of threes and compare them to get a feel for the added dimension.

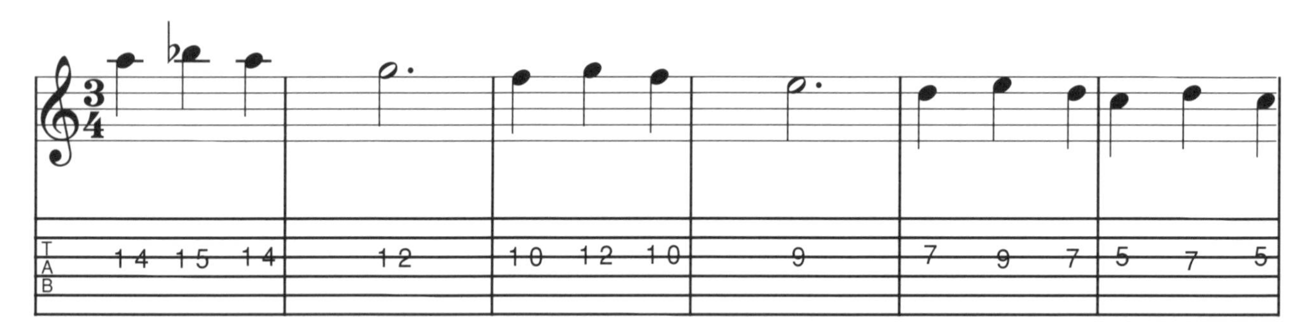

Below is a three based on an E min. chord form in the 12th position, producing an E minor arpeggio. It is descending threes and ones.

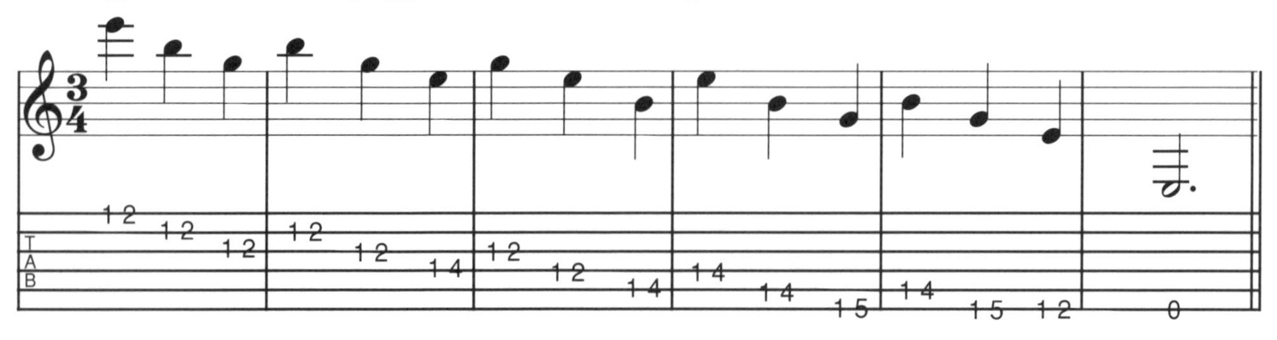

Iterative Phrasing - Twos

The first two is derived from the D pentatonic scale form in the second position, and is tonally oriented to an E Major pentatonic scale. This is simply a repetition of selected notes in sequence, and verges on being a rhythmic phrase.

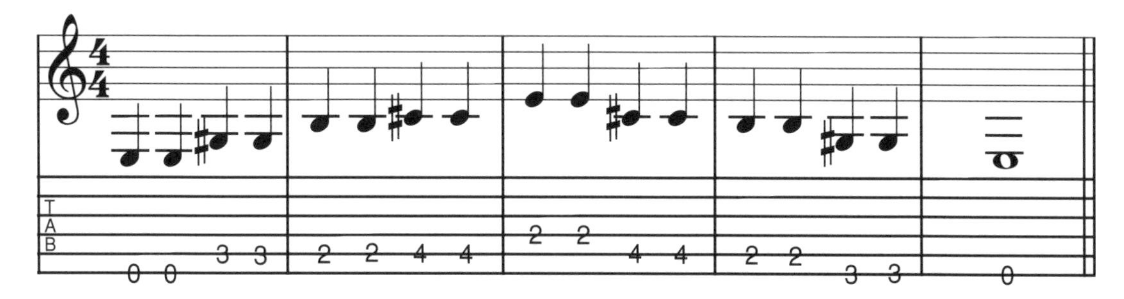

The next two is derived from the C diatonic scale form, and is tonally oriented toward the B Phrygian mode. The repetitive sequence is down two scale tones, descending in single scale tone increments.

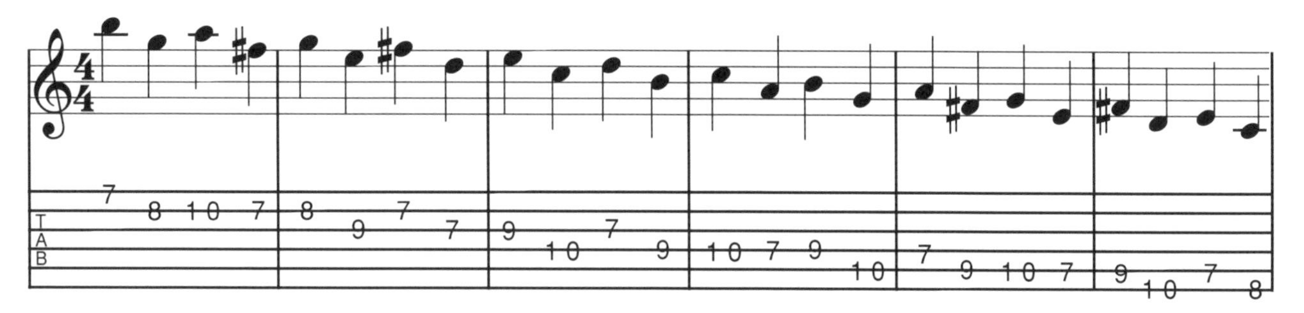

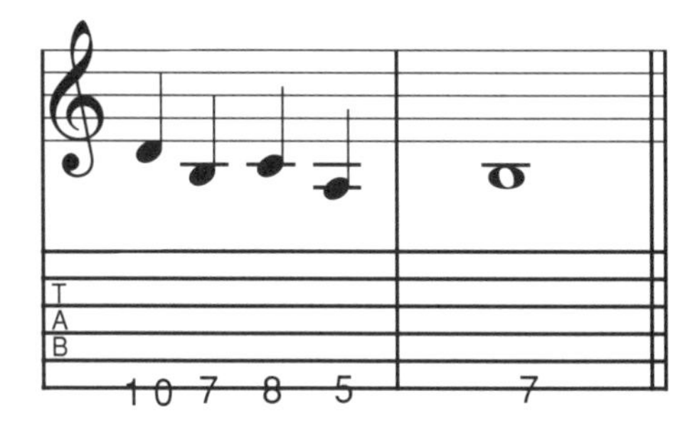

The last iterative two comes from Harmonic Minor Lead Pattern II, and is tonally oriented toward the C harmonic minor scale. The repetitive sequence is down one scale tone, ascending in two scale tone increments.

Iterative Phrasing - Sixes & Eights

The next iterative phrase is a simple six played out on the first and second strings starting from the seventh position. It uses a portion of the C, A, and G diatonic scale forms, plus a whole tone section between the C and A. The tonal orientation is a little harder to specify. The first six notes have a somewhat modal sound somewhere between locrian and mixolydian, with each six note group ascending a tone and having no specific tone center in much the same way. However, the ending notes of each six in sequence are the last four notes in a G Major diatonic scale, so it appears to be more Major than anything else. Its easier to just call it partly atonal and pass it off as different, yet familiar.

Next is an eight which utilizes E chord forms in the seventh, fifth, third and second positions. The key area is B minor, and since the tonal material is quite specific, can be considered a chord progression as much as an iterative phrase. The chords in progression are B min., A Maj., G Maj. F# Sus., and F# Dom. 7th. It continues on the following page.

Iterative Phrasing - Eights

Ok. That's enough examples to get the idea of iteration in phrasing across. Again, the examples are meant only as a stepping off place to motivate you to start applying the concept to your own playing and recognizing it in others. As with most of the material and methods in Vol. III, the variations and combinations are practically limitless, and you are encouraged to experiment and develop your own ideas in this area. If you start to hear this type of phrasing in guitar music you are either just learning or already familiar with, (and see it in a new light) then we've both done our jobs. Go ahead and take it one step further now. Improvise using ideas in a similar and intentional manner. For this approach to work, you have to do more - way more - than just play the examples. That's the bad news. The good news is if you see what's going on, then it stops being guesswork and starts being fun (re-creation) in a very short time.

The more experienced readers have already noticed that the iterative phrases have not been properly notated with respect to key or time signatures. This was done to emphasize the repetitive nature of the phrases independent of rhythm in particular. Another thing you may have noticed is that the examples are less than spectacular from a musical standpoint. Given a choice between an example that is clear and unambiguous, and one that is zoomie and incomprehensible, I'll always go with the former. After all, what is advanced playing if not layered combinations of the basics? Heck, what's advanced anything if not interesting combinations of basics? Anyway you'll get to hear some zoomier stuff in later works. By then, if all goes according to plan, you'll be able to recognize things you used to couldn't recognize, including poor sentence structure.

Melodic Phrasing

Scales are groups of notes taken from a key consecutively, and are related by a character derived in a physical sense from their whole step-half step structure, and in a perceptual sense by how we relate to them physiologically and to an extent, culturally. Arpeggios are similar to scales in that they are derived from a key in a consecutive manner and are expressed as successive tones. The overall result of a particular step structure or note selection can be a kind of happy, lighthearted sound, a sad, serious sound, or numerous stylistic, social, even religious connotations. The metaphor of communication via speaking or writing is ideally suited to convey the difference between scales and arpeggios as basic music elements and musical phrases. Either way, the idea is to say something worth listening to. This means we must organize the available tones into rhythmic, melodic and necessarily guitaristic statements.

Phrases occur when related notes, usually the notes in a key area, are structured into coherent segments. These segments usually take form in tonal, rhythmic and iterative organizations. A melodic phrase differs from a rhythmic or iterative phrase by having more discernible relevance to us as human beings. A rhythmic phrase has an emphasis on rhythmic rather than tonal or repetitive character. An iterative phrase relies on numerical, sequential, and intervallic repetition(s) rather than a rhythmic character. A melodic phrase combines the qualities of both rhythmically and sequentially grouped tones in a manner such that we as listeners are able to relate to them in a way that is more than the sum of the parts. With melodic phrasing, the quality of the phrase can be measured by its memorableness, and the emotional and social impact it has on us as individuals and societies.

One hallmark of a melodic phrase of lasting quality has always been simplicity. The history of music is filled with examples of simple expressions of pitch and time in combinations that soar high above the humble materials of which they were made. A few examples of sparse and simple themes that have become indelible in our memories are first eight notes of Beethoven's Fifth Symphony, the first four notes of the "Dragnet" theme, the first six notes of "We Will Rock You" by Queen and the first six notes of "The Star Spangled Banner". Don't equate complexity with quality. Overly complex melodic ideas can alienate your listener and make the beauty harder to find.

Melodic quality, like all beauty, is in the eye of the beholder. A melody that brings tears to one person's eyes can be reviled as pathetic schmaltz by another. With that in mind, our intention here is to approach melodic phrasing as phrasing with an emphasis on tonal coherence rather than intrinsic value. The key to that coherence will be dividing tones into those which are played in passing, and those which are targets to be led up to. Target notes have more tonal significance that passing notes within the context of the phrase. Target notes, like key notes, center the tones and create tonal orientation. In general, target notes are more likely to be chord tones than not. Furthermore, in the context of the phrase, some chord tones will have more significance as target notes than others. The concept of intervallic direction, aka melodic motion, pertains to the individual tone by tone changes. Direction implies that if the next tone played is different, it can only be above or below the previous tone. It will also be a specific intervallic distance above or below. Groups of intervals account for a melodic phrase's tonal content, and a group of tones can have a general direction as well.

Melodic Phrasing

The intervallic distance of all scale tones in sequence is seconds - major seconds or minor seconds. When you reduce it to these terms, the reason that diatonic scale tones played in succession can sound boring becomes apparent. If they lack interest in and of themselves its because it is the same motion and the same one or two directional intervals over and over. Pentatonic scales have seconds and thirds but less tonal variety. The intervallic distance of all triadic arpeggios in sequence is thirds and fourths. Seventh arpeggios in sequence consist solely of thirds and seconds. Having at least twice the inherent intervallic content means that arpeggios played tone by tone will have that much more interest. Our strategy for melodic phrasing will be to think in terms not so much of the individual motion of each interval, but rather in scale and arpeggio segments.

We'll present melodic statements derived from scale material, arpeggio material, and combinations of both. You may find if you learn to look at it this way, that some of the most melodic tone sequences are combinations of both scale and arpeggio segments. Later on we will combine these types of phrases with iterative and rhythmic ones, and add on technical articulations, intervals, etc. You get the idea. The following phrases are derived from scale material only. Either record the progression or have someone play it while you play the phrases.

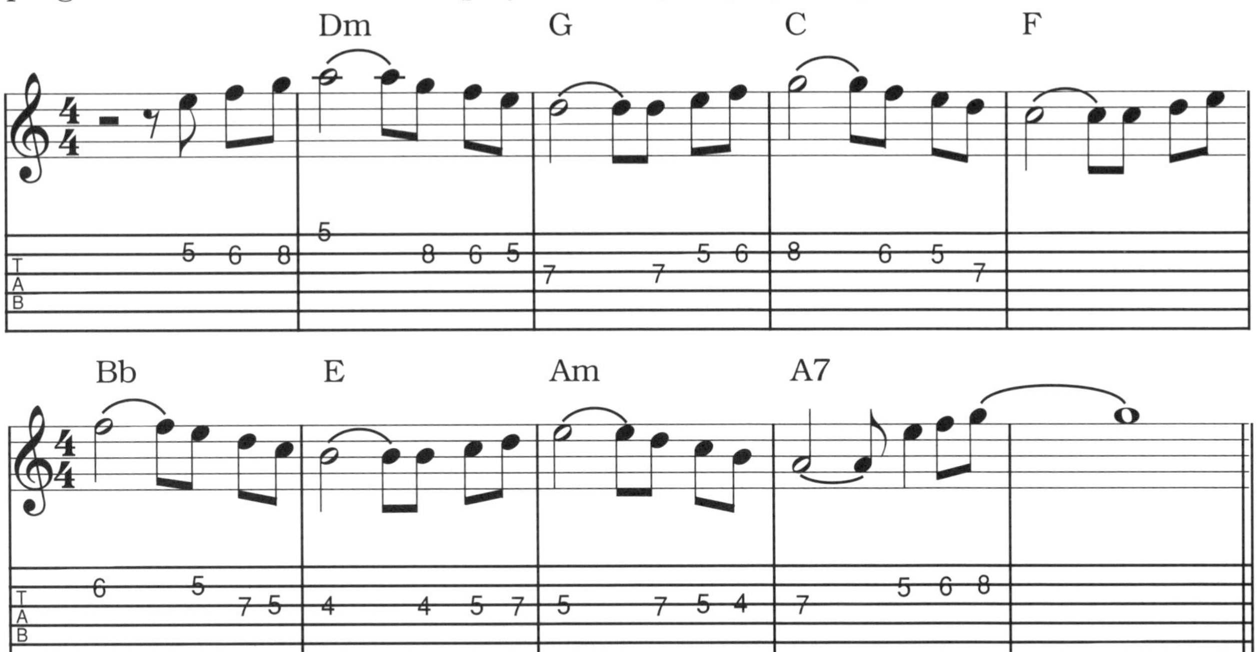

The phrase was written for the purpose of distinguishing between a few things. The scale form guitarwise is G dia. form, 5th position. The scale material is consecutive seconds but the rhythm of the phrases is the same. Each phrase's motion, or intervallic direction, alternates up and down. Circle the target notes. Each half note is a target note and a chord tone (arpeggio note) occurring with every chord change. In the second measure, the "A" target note is the five of the Dm chord. In the third measure, the D is the five of G. In the fourth measure, the G is the five of C; the C in the fifth measure is the five of F, and so on until the last measure where the target note is the tonic. The notes in between the target notes are passing tones.

Melodic Phrasing

In the example below, we've used only arpeggios for our melodic material with the same rhythmic phrasing as before. The distinction between passing tones and target notes is harder to discern because every passing tone is also a chord tone. In other words, just being a chord tone doesn't make a target note. Part of what makes a note a target, is the rhythmic organization of the notes leading up to it.

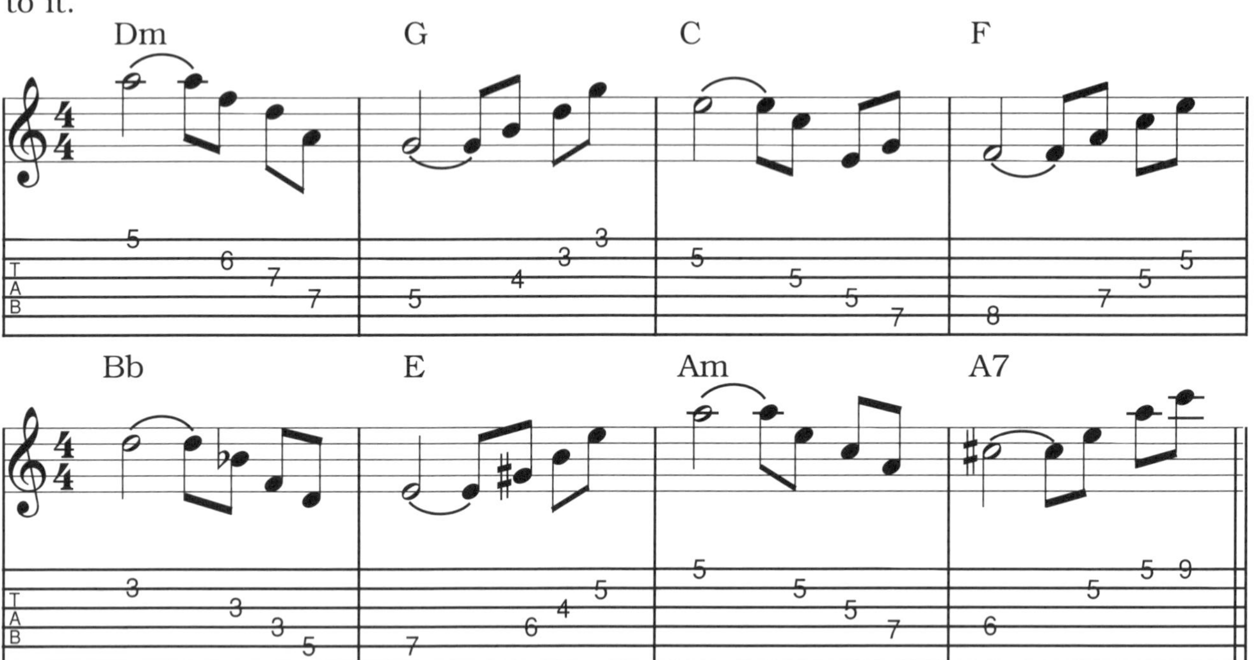

In the next example, we've kept the rhythmic structure and combined scale tones and arpeggios to produce a better mix of melodic materials.

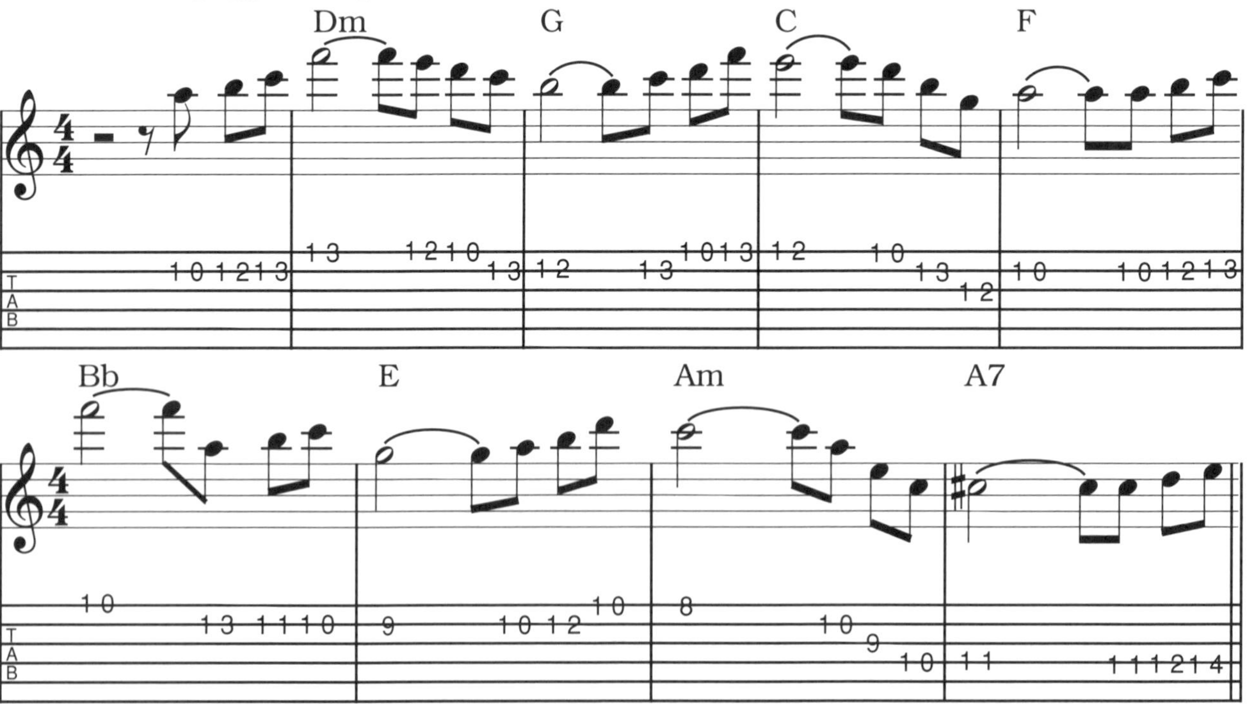

Melodic Phrasing

By keeping the rhythmic and directional aspects the same for each exercise, the differences between scalar and arpeggiated melodic material should become more evident. When combined, the intervals of scales and arpeggios provide the most options for intervallic motion in melody. Two benefits of visualizing the raw melodic material via scales and arpeggios is that we can use the patterns that already exist on the fretboard, and we don't have to think through each individual interval, making it possible to get past the raw materials to the finished product faster.

One of the objects of this section is to try to get you to think like a vocalist instead of a guitarist. If you can sing your lead and are happy with the way it sounds, then it is probably going to hold up as a melodic effort. As guitarists, we routinely overplay, both to demonstrate our abilities and as a way to have as much say as possible in the music. It has been said many times that its what you *don't* play that counts. Playing melodically is one of the best ways to get past the guitar to the music.

The next section is devoted to the next study piece from the videos, "Tearin' Up The Pea Patch." It is a fast-paced, scale-oriented ditty in the country fusion style known as "chicken pickin." It was developed as a kitchen sink project to demonstrate that when constructing a lead, a lot seemingly disparate tonal material can work in combination although in this case with tongue located in cheek. Among other things, The Patch features chromatic scales, whole and half tone scales, blues major and minor, plus rhythmic, iterative and melodic phrasing. All of this was thrown together to some extent in order to combat the simplistic mindset which limits a guitarist's thinking to the tired old refrain of "What scales go with what chords?"

Any literati types out there figure out where the title came from? Here's a hint: it involves a lovable rascal who spent time in hoosegow for embezzling from the bank where he worked. Email me if you figure it out.

Tearin' Up the Pea Patch

Bill Edwards

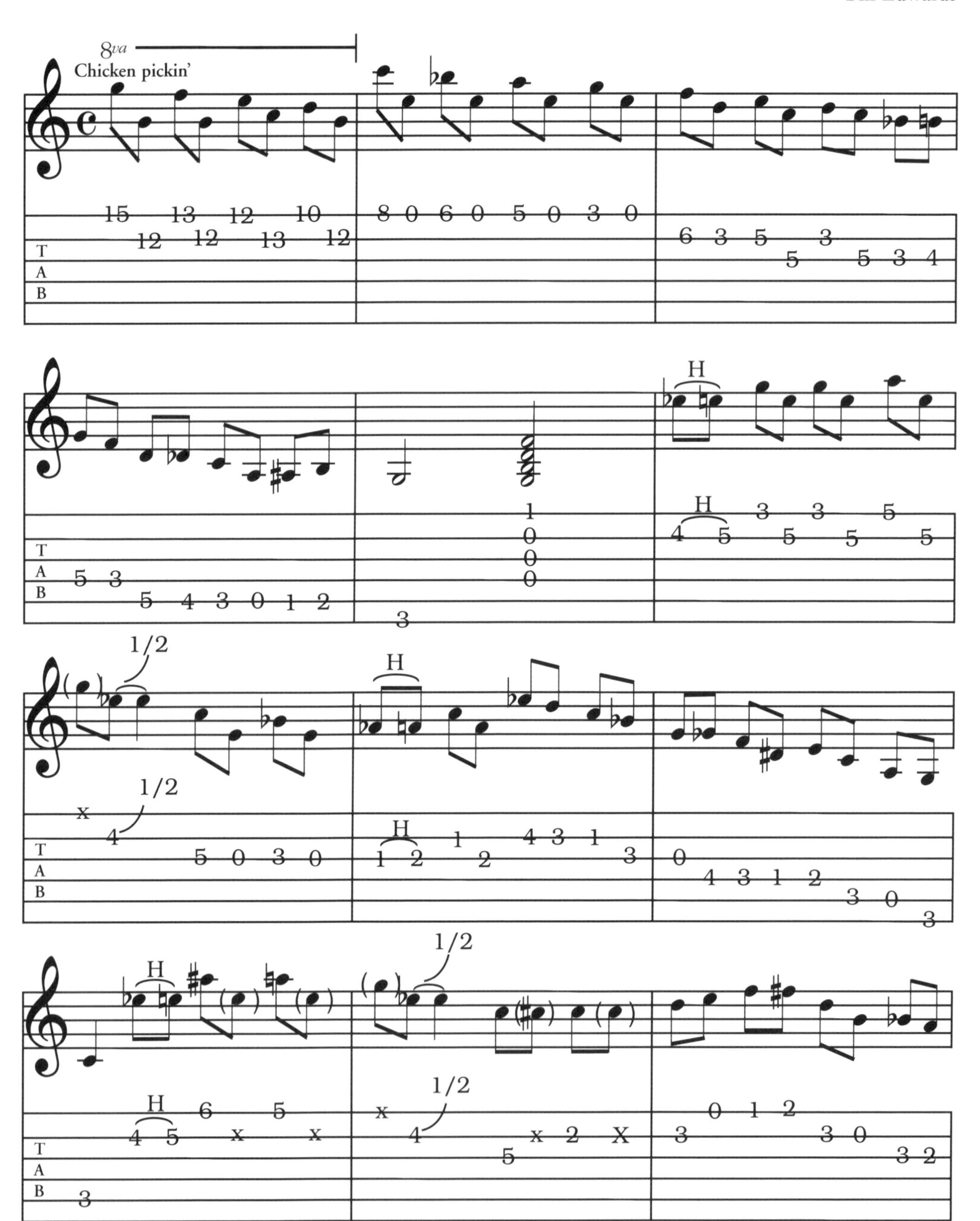

H
1/2
T
A
B
x

T
A
B
H
1/2
x
S

1/2
1/2

H
1/2
T
A
B
H
H
H
1/2

T
A
B
P
S

H
P
P
H
H
P
P
P

H P P P
1/2
S
T
A
B
8va

8va
1/2
H
X
16
T
A
B
17 X 15 X
13 14
13
14
15 13
17 15
16 13
14 12
14 11
8va
12 15
13 16
14 17
16 19
15 17 15
18 17 15
17 16
14
17 15 14
17 15 14
15
8
8
9
10
8
8
9
8
8
7
8
7
8
7
8
6
1/4
8 9
6
9
6
9 10
7
10 11
8
11
8
10
8
10
8
11
8

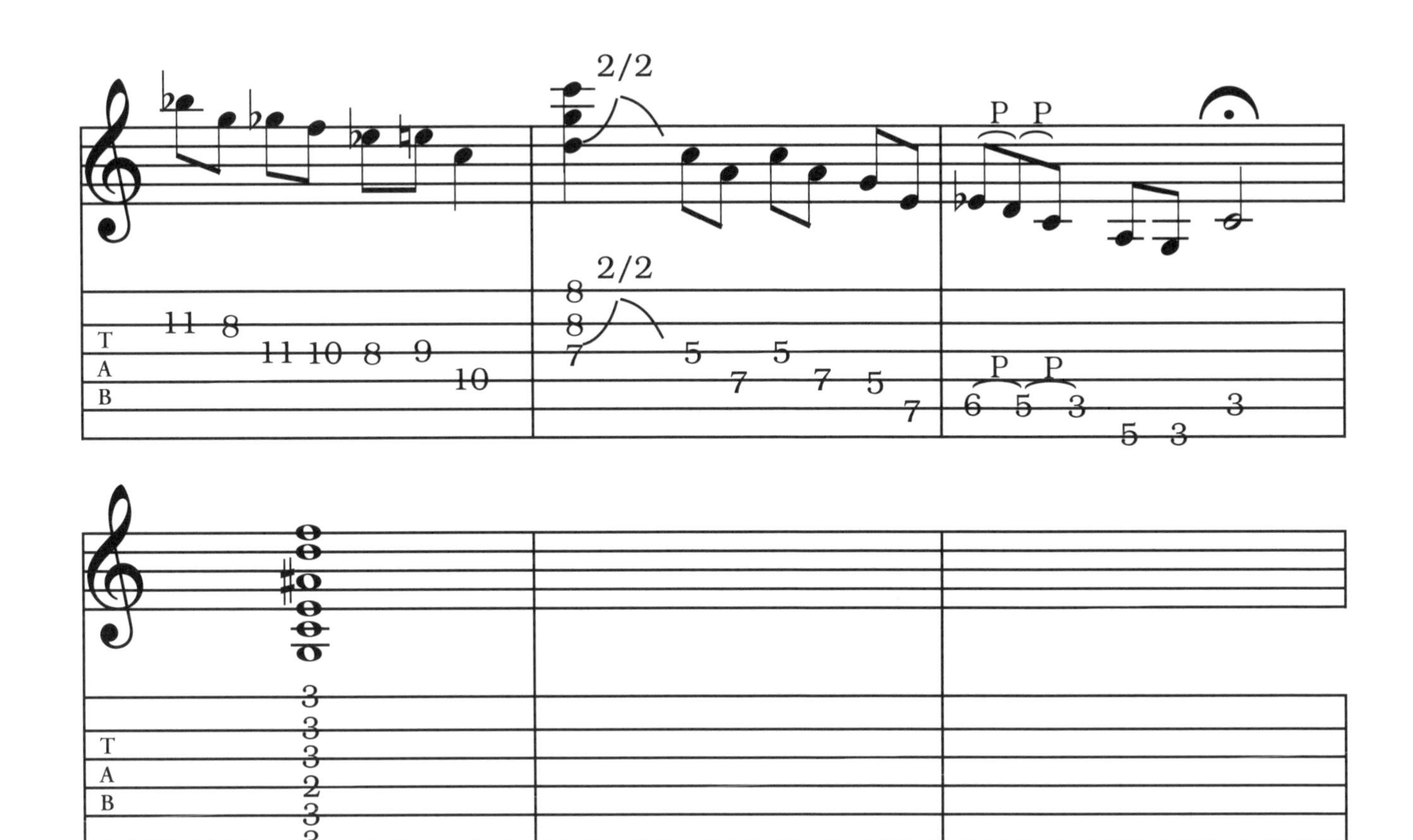
2/2
P P
T
A
B
2/2
P P
T
A
B

Styles

The different styles of music throughout history have been a reflection of the great musicians who not only pioneered new ideas and methods, but were also standouts among their peers in a cultural sense as well. As much as forging new musical standards, they permeated the cultural strata of the times, conditions, and locales in which they lived. In this way, these musical trend setters have been able to affect entire societies either as representatives of the norm, or in conspicuous opposition to it.

This cultural facet of music styles is often more essential than the very quality of the music itself. What else would explain why the arguably superior music of the 18th and 19th centuries fails to compete commercially with popular styles such as rap, rock, country, and so on? Why are so many symphony orchestras, with their highly skilled and dedicated musicians, dependent on grants and private funding while the often unskilled and musically illiterate are able to sell albums by the millions? The answer lies in what you could call "culture clubs." Rap, for example, is about as unsophisticated as music can get. Tonal materials are virtually nonexistent and the lyrics are usually uttered in a monotone sing-song and practically inaudible. But rap, like all styles of music, has the ability to speak to people on a level that identifies and defines them culturally as much as stylistically. Our capacity to understand and relate to the different styles of music varies not only from society to society but also along personal growth curves throughout our lives.

Music's power to influence is sometimes profound. In many religions, the services alternate frequently between musical and non-musical sections because the nature of the music, including the participatory music, evokes deep feelings in what may have been an otherwise decidedly unreligious experience. In militaries throughout history, music has been used similarly to promote feelings of national pride and cohesiveness, even among disparate factions. Musicians have the potential to harness an almost unlimited power to influence the way people feel. This influence will, by necessity, take root within a stylistic and cultural milieu. Music styles are context sensitive and we tend to perceive them the same as our peer groups agewise and otherwise. In other words, typical rock music will likely be perceived three different ways by a young child, a teenager, and a senior citizen. The same is true for classical, jazz, country, rap, and other styles.

As stated in the introduction in Vol. II, it is necessary to distinguish between what is meant by guitar styles and music styles. A guitar style usually pertains to an overall technical approach to the instrument such as flatpicking, chord melody arrangement, chord comping, fingerpicking, etc. Musical style relates to the musical and cultural characteristics of what is being played. Playing a specific type of guitar, such as classical, acoustic, electric etc., also has a tendency to dictate certain stylistic directions from the standpoint of technique, cultural influences and even attitude. For example, nylon string guitarists generally use a technique referred to as classical technique meaning the player plucks the strings with the fingers of the right hand often using fingernails to produce variations in tone. The style of music termed classical is derived primarily from period in music history. Guitar and music styles imply other more subtle dichotomies as well. We all know classical guitar players who look upon electric and acoustic guitar players as distant and somewhat excusable cousins. This section will discuss stylistic issues in terms of guitar, music, and culturally related aspects.

Styles

When a person takes up the guitar, he or she generally starts out by learning chords. For various reasons, guitarists tend to gravitate toward one of three common approaches to chords. The first approach is to play multiple chord forms in a single (open) position, and the second is to use a single form in multiple positions. The third approach would be multiple forms in multiple positions. Each of these formats also happens to be associated with different styles of music.

The first approach to chords, multiple forms in the open position, is generally associated with folk style, country, bluegrass and pop music. It is considered by most teachers to be the fastest and easiest way to get a student playing. The standard route is to get a book of songs by an artist or group the student is familiar with and practice the changes until it sounds passable and then play along with the teacher, the recording, or a friend.

The second approach, playing usually the E or A form in multiple positions, is associated with rock, metal, and popular music. When this approach is combined with the distortion effect, the chords are referred to as power chords, and it is considered a "heavier" sound.

The third approach, using multiple forms in multiple positions, is connected with the all of the above styles, plus classical, (including baroque and romantic) jazz, flamenco, and the numerous fusions of different styles. A fusion is when characteristics of two or more styles are combined to produce a type of music that is distinct from either of the original styles. Examples of fusion are country-rock, jazz-grass (aka "Dawg" music), classical-metal, rockabilly, etc. The guitar piece "Classical Gas" by Mason Williams, is a fusion of bossa nova rhythms and classical harmonies. The piece "Mood For A Day" by Steve Howe, is a fusion of both classical and flamenco influences.

"Oh, I listen to all kinds of music. In 'Waynes World' I especially liked the part where they're riding around in the car listening to *opera*."

Tipper Gore, Former First Vice-Lady
and founder of PMRC, a special interest group which
successfully lobbied for mandatory record labeling -
upon being asked what type of music she listens to.

Styles

There isn't any music that was created in a total vacuum. Every style grew out of the music that preceded it. Even what is now considered distinctly American music grew as hybrids and variations of music brought by immigrants from other countries. Irish, Scottish, Celtic, etc., tunes were blended and varied to become what we now know as American folk and bluegrass. These styles evolved further to become country music. What were once termed negro spirituals, the seeds of which sailed from Africa to germinate in southern soil, evolved into the blues and continues to thrive as a deeply emotional style of music. The blues and country both contributed to what was to become rock and roll, and so on. In each style there is a combination of factors which contribute to its character and distinguish it from preceding styles. The next step is to discuss a few styles in terms of the guitaristic and musical components that make it what it is.

The characterizations for the different styles are derived from the Menu headings. The specifications for the different styles are generalized and not to be considered as chiseled in stone. Over a period of time changes have occurred to alter our perceptions of what makes a style the way it is. When you examine a given artist you can get much more specific, and accurate specifications can be obtained when analyzing an individual composition.

Styles - Baroque Classical and Romantic

The classifications for music written prior to the 20th century are separated by the life spans of the preeminent musicians of the era as much as by stylistic characteristics. As a matter of practicality, we will only discuss these styles in terms of the great masters of the day.

To most amateurs and non musicians, classical music is pretty much everything outside of popular music. In the realm of strict musicology, though, the term has a more specific meaning. Classical music actually refers to the music of Haydn, Mozart, Beethoven, and to some extent, Schubert. Their combined lifetimes represent a period of music dating from about 1750 to about 1820, so this time frame is termed the classical period in music history. The period preceding classicism was called the baroque period and the period immediately following, the romantic. The term classical was later applied because the music of these masters was deemed of a high class or rank and many authorities feel this level of musical accomplishment has never been surpassed. Classical music is characterized by its relative objectivity, formalism, simplicity, and interestingly, its emotional restraint.

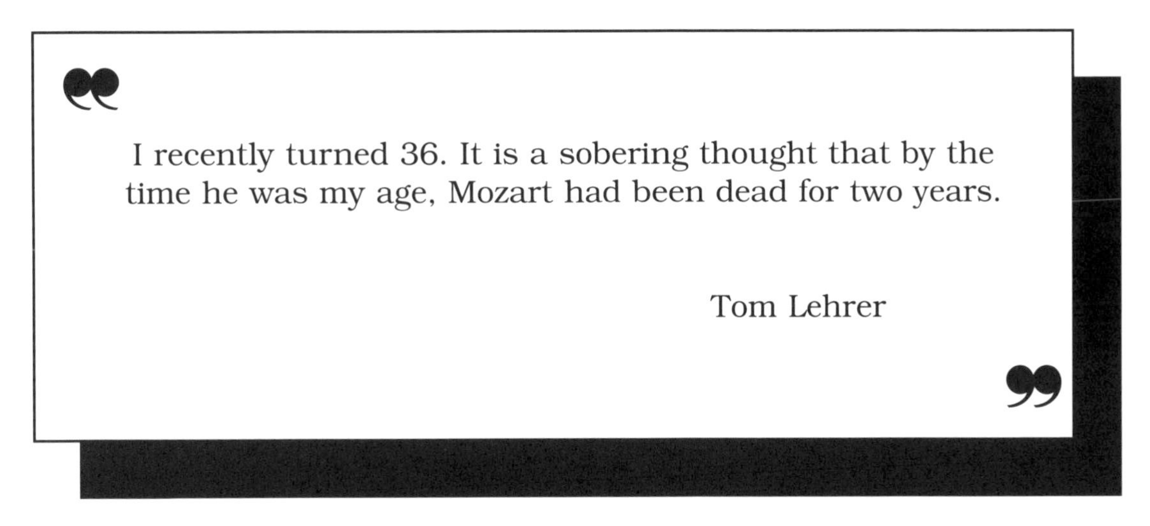

The term baroque, in contrast, refers in general to a style of overly ornamental architecture and a painting style as well as music. The word comes from the Portuguese "barroco" for an irregularly shaped pearl, and literally means grotesque or in poor taste. (Of course. Who would want a tasteless and grotesque painting by that baroque painter Rembrandt?) Needless to say, it is used in music as a purely chronological term. The music of J.S. Bach is of this period and stands among the worlds greatest musical achievements. The period spans from about 1550 to 1759, and here again, represent the lifespans of Cavalieri to Handel. Other notables of the baroque period include Caccini, Vivaldi, Scarlatti, Buxtehude, Pachelbel, Telemann, Couperin, Rameau, Purcell, and Handel. Many musicians refer to the works of the Baroque period as classical music, anyway. Adherence to the various musical forms developed in this period (formalism), and took precedence over the more subjective elements such as emotional content. Among the vocal forms introduced during this period were the opera, oratorio and cantata, aria and recitative. Among the instrumental forms spawned were the fugue, concerto, sonata, suite, prelude, passacaglia, chaccone, tocatta and rondeau.

Styles - Baroque Classical and Romantic

The romantic period followed the classical and spanned from 1820 to about 1920 or the lifetime's of Weber to Sibelius. Romantic music can be characterized by an emphasis on emotional elements as opposed to a stricter adherence to form. The emphasis changed, paraphrasing Monteverdi, to "Let Emotion be the master, not the servant of music." The term derives from the Romanesque period of the middle ages which was popularized in the 19th century in the writings of Scott, Wackenroder, Tieck and Novalis. These authors, in search of themes, returned to the knights of old with their ladies in waiting, heroic kings, and pious monks. They longed for a fantastic, imaginative, and picturesque quality that spoke to the most fundamental human conditions of joy, despair, honor, deceit, love, and hatred. The music of this period became a more conscious reflection of the passions of the composers and the societies in which they lived. Among the romantic composers are Berlioz, Mendelssohn, Schumann, Chopin, Liszt, Wagner, Bruckner, Brahms, Tchaikovsky, Dvorak, Mahler, MacDowell and Strauss.

Styles - Blues

The roots of traditional blues can be traced back to the music of early black Americans. Brought to this country as slaves to work in the fields, they would communicate to one another by means of hollering back and forth over great distances. These field hollers evolved into a highly imaginative form of vocalization that was rhythmic and tonal on the surface, and emotional and spiritual underneath. As most slaves weren't allowed the benefits of an education and so could neither read nor write, their songs were passed down to successive generations in much the same way that epic poems of ancient times were told and retold by master storytellers. The music eventually divided into two fairly distinct forms. One was a form of worship and prayer which was to become known as gospel music, and the other was a form of lament which was to become the blues. Nowadays "the blues" or feeling blue is synonymous with loneliness and any nonspecific, dissatisfaction, unhappiness, or sorrow.

The blues was a distinctly southern style, with Mississippi, Tennessee, and Louisiana as major centers of early development. Among the notable twentieth century blues artists are W.C. Handy, considered by many to be the father of the blues, Gertrude "Ma" Rainey, Robert Johnson, Blind Lemon Jefferson, Son House, John Lee Hooker, Mississippi John Hurt, Rev. Gary Davis, Count Basie, Big Bill Broonzy, Tampa Red, T-Bone Walker, Clarence Gatemouth Brown, Bobby "Blue" Bland, and practically anybody with the last name of King, but especially Freddie, Albert, and B.B.

Defining early blues pieces were "Memphis Blues" and "St. Louis Blues," both by W.C. Handy, "Matchbox" by Blind Lemmon Jefferson, "Candy Man" by Mississippi John Hurt, "The Thrill is Gone" by B.B. King, and "Stormy Monday" by T-Bone Walker.

A large percentage of the blues masters are guitar players. Among the most legendary are Robert Johnson, Blind Lemmon Jefferson, John Lee Hooker, T-Bone Walker, Gatemouth Brown, and of course, the extraordinary B.B. King.

The rhythmic character of blues is based in common time. The harmonic structure tends to be major oriented, but the melodic material is usually minor, and pentatonic. What has come to be known as the "blues scale" utilizes the pentatonic minor with the addition of the flatted fifth degree. Color tones include the frequent contrasting of the third and the flatted third as well.

Blues lead playing is heavy on certain articulation techniques, most notably bends, vibratos, hammer-ons, pull-offs, vibratos and slides. A typical solo will sustain particular target notes as if to squeeze every last drop of feeling from them. Blues tends to have a slower, more easy going tempo, and when it is speeded up past a certain point, most people will perceive it as boogie-woogie or rock and roll. The older blues guitarists used their thumbs to sketch out a rhythm while they sang, and would play licks in between verses, choruses and phrases. The alternating bass version of this style as played by Mississippi John Hurt, was sometimes referred to as "Country Blues". Most modern blues guitarists use a pick, though. Another contrast between the older and more modern players was the use of amplification. For the earliest blues players, the electric guitar and its sonic advantages simply weren't available, so they relied on archtops and flattops usually strung with steel for volume.

Styles - Blues

An interesting development in the style which was made possible by the new technology has been attributed to T-Bone Walker. He would use his amplifier to sustain notes by means of controlled feedback when Hendrix was still in diapers.

Although it began as a more or less free form of expression, the format that this style has evolved to for guitarists of today is based on what is called "12 bar" blues. A typical 12 bar blues progression in the key of A is illustrated below.

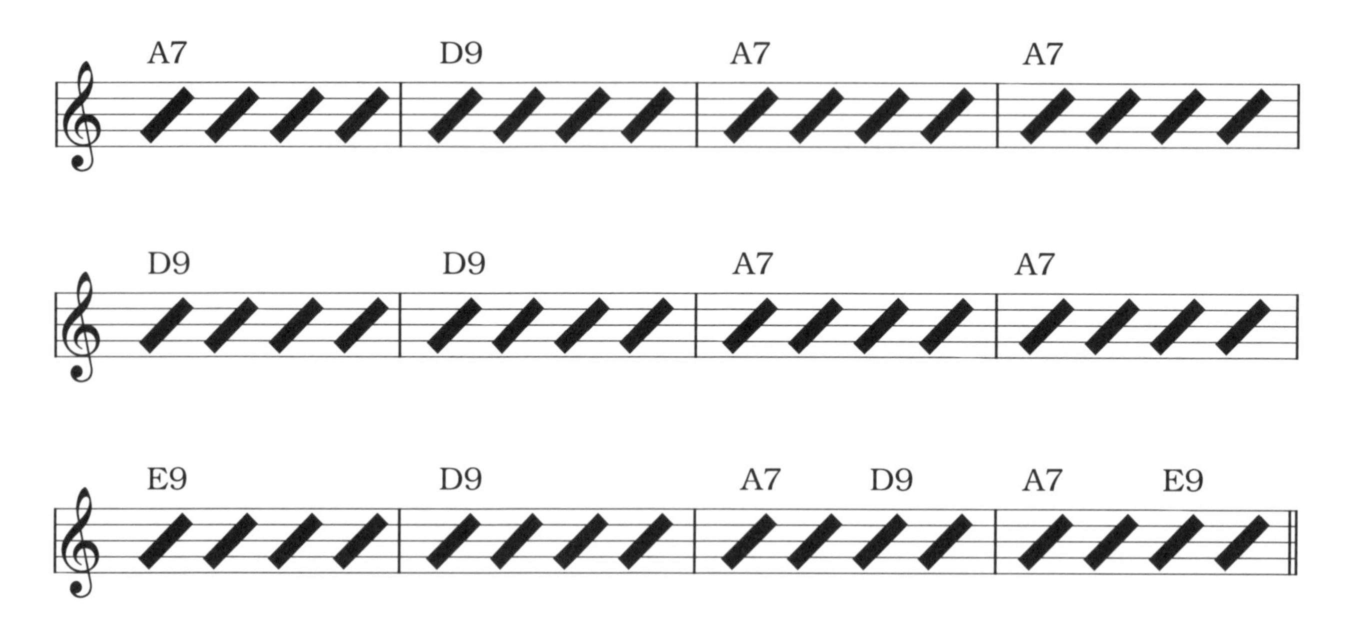

Continuing in the free form tradition, this basic background provides the blues instrumentalist with a solid, if somewhat predictable, harmonic structure upon which to base an improvised solo. There is little doubt when the changes are to occur and the blues guitarist can stretch out in 12 comfortable measures with no key changes. I've heard people can make a living doing this. Beats work.

If there are any guitarists who happened to have been abducted by aliens and still haven't heard the story of B.B. King's "Lucille," here's more or less how the story goes. Lucille, of course, is the name of his guitar. B.B and his band were playing a one-nighter during the winter in an old building that I think might have been a church. It was heated by nothing more than a 55 gallon drum with kerosene in the bottom. Suddenly in the middle of everything a fight broke out and of course the combatants knocked over the drum instantly setting the entire building ablaze. Everyone scrambled to safety including the Beale Street Blues Boy, who suddenly realized he'd left his only guitar in the burning building. Before anyone could reason with him, he ran back in to retrieve his instrument. Kids - don't try this at home. Just as he was making good his escape, guitar in hand, the roof caved in, and he was lucky to get out alive. So how did his guitar get named Lucille? That was the name of the woman the two men were fighting over.

Styles - Folk and Bluegrass

For guitar players, folk music can be divided into fingerpicked and flatpicked right hand styles. This area deals primarily with the flatpicking approach as typified in bluegrass guitar playing.

American folk music descended from from Irish, Scottish and English folk tunes that were played by people tucked away in rural mountain regions such as the Appalachians, Ozarks, Great Smokies, and Catskills. Here again, illiteracy played a part in this stylistic evolution. Since many hill people couldn't read or write, they would have to learn pieces by rote from one another. Like a rumor, when music is passed from one person to another, slight variations in interpretation eventually lead to considerable differences from the originals.

Among the noteworthy American folk and bluegrass musicians were Woodie Guthrie, Elizabeth Cotton, Pete Seeger, Mother Maybelle Carter and the Carter Family, Grandpa Jones, The Delmore Brothers, Gid Tanner and the Skillet Lickers, Bill Monroe and the Bluegrass Boys, The Stanleys, Flatt and Scruggs, Joan Baez and Peter Paul and Mary.

Famous songs include "This Land Is Your Land," "Freight Train," "Wildwood Flower," "Browns Ferry Blues," "Down Yonder," "Blue Moon of Kentucky," "Foggy Mountain Breakdown," " Will The Circle Be Unbroken," "Wabash Cannonball," "Billy In the Lowground," "Red Haired Boy," "Bill Cheatham," "Salt Creek" and "Black Mountain Rag." "Foggy Mountain Breakdown," you may recall, was the raucous banjo instrumental used as a getaway theme in the hit movie "Bonnie and Clyde".

Notable guitarists in this style include Lester Flatt, Doc Watson, Clarence White, Tony Rice, Dan Crary, and Norman Blake to name but a few.

Bluegrass music per se, can be traced directly back to Bill Monroe and his Bluegrass Boys band. It evolved from Kentucky hill country variations of both American folk music and its European predecessors. Bluegrass instrumentation centered around the fiddle, mandolin, banjo, acoustic guitar (steel stringed flattop) and double (upright) bass. For guitar players the style involved mostly rhythm playing, relying on the powerful bass notes and open chord forms of a D-28 to anchor the high tenor vocals and the melodic lead of the fiddle, banjo and mandolin.

Bluegrass and flatpicked folk guitar style evolved to a more melodic stature with the increasing recognition of a number of outstanding flatpickers such as Clarence White, Doc Watson, Tony Rice, Dan Crary, Norman Blake, and many others. The flatpickers took traditional folk music and fiddle tunes and adapted them to the guitar creating a fronting role where it had been pretty much a backup instrument before.

Styles - Rock and Roll

In early rock and roll, as pioneered by Ike Turner, Bill Haley, Chuck Berry, Carl Perkins, and Little Richard, the music featured the same 1 4 5 chords as you would find in blues, but played in a different order, at a faster tempo, and with a driving beat. If boogie woogie was fast, playful. blues, then rock and roll was hard driving boogie woogie on steroids, especially testosterone.

The roots of rock and roll are easily traced back to R&B, boogie woogie, blues, jazz, folk, country, and gospel in varying degrees depending on the artist. It was both a southern and southwestern phenomena, with major developments occurring in the Memphis and Cleveland areas due to airplay from a couple of ambitious radio stations.

Among the progenitors of this raucous style were Otis Blackwell, Elvis Presley, Bo Diddley, Jerry Lee Lewis, The Beatles, and The Rolling Stones. The song "Rocket 88" by Ike Turner, was about a car, had distorted guitar, and was #1 R&B hit in 1951. In retrospect, it is probably the first rock and roll song to get air time. By 1952, Bill Haley and company had produced "Rock The Joint," and the terms "rock" and "rock and roll" were well on their way into the mainstream American consciousness. "Rock Around The Clock," another hit by Haley and his Comets, was featured in the movie "Blackboard Jungle," The movie contained themes such as teenage rebellion, cars, violence, sexuality, crime, race, and alienation, all of which were to be reflected in the new music. In fact, rock and roll was the first truly biracial American music, as if white 1950's parents needed another reason to censor it. In a word, it was the first music style that celebrated youth and a denial of established values. It shared with blues more than just harmonic and melodic materials. Alienated teenagers could identify with the plight of the average black man and woman in an unquestionably racist period in American history.

In 1955, a young man named Chuck Berry released a song named "Maybellene" which was to become one of the first monster rock and roll hits, and the first of many by this savvy guitarist. Interestingly, "Maybellene" was an adaptation of a country/folk song named "Ida Red." Among the Berry hits to follow were "Johnny B. Goode," "Roll Over Beethoven," "Sweet Little Sixteen," and "My Ding-a-Ling," all of which helped to outline the defining boundaries of the new style. Berry's looks, songwriting, guitar playing, lyrics, and stage antics all contributed to his success, and the success of rock and roll as a style unto itself.

Other seminal rock and rollers were Otis Blackwell who wrote "Don't Be Cruel," "All Shook Up," and "Great Balls of Fire," and Carl Perkins who penned "Blue Suede Shoes," both contributing to the success of the more famous Elvis and Jerry Lee Lewis.

The guitar sound of most rock and roll had more of an edge - not pure distortion - but not really clean either, and was definitely louder and higher in the mix, often sharing a fronting role with vocals. The defining guitar part of the early rock and roll songs was chord and interval riffing, and single note lead playing. In terms of articulation techniques, anything was fair game including bends, pull-offs and hammer-ons, slides, trills, vibratos, tremolos, etc. The more outrageous, the better. The lyric themes usually centered around high school romance, parental interference, cars with their implied freedom, and alienation.

Styles - Rock and Roll

Rhythms were in common time, and the beats, backbeats, and tempos were designed to keep pace with the urban lifestyle of the American teen. Most rock and roll was major oriented in tonality, and like the blues, it tended to feature pentatonic minor and blues scale melodics with principle chords as a harmonic backing.

Most rock and roll guitar players strummed chords to a backbeat drum rhythm. **Backbeat** rhythm is when the accent is on the two and four counts of a measure. The tube amplifiers of the day would produce a warm kind of distortion that was more of an "edge" than what we know as saturated distortion nowadays. Semi-hollow body guitars such as the Gibson 335 were what Chuck Berry used (and still uses to this day), and when solid bodies became available, many rock and rollers turned to these as a means of controlling feedback at higher decibel levels. The traditional instrumentation of a rock and roll band has been guitar(s) bass and drums as the core unit, plus other instruments including keyboards, saxophones, etc. as added instrumentation.

Styles - Hard Rock and Metal

Rooted in a combination of alienation, blues, rock & roll, and technology, a new form of music with a definite edge to it came into existence. It was imported from England and home grown in urban America. The bands which typified the switch from light hearted fifties rock and roll to the harder edged sound, were a reflection of the sixties as an age of extremes in which as a teenager, you could find yourself in a free love rally in Central Park, or a free fire zone in Cambodia. Among the earlier groups were Cream, Led Zeppelin, Iron Butterfly, The Who, The Stones, Hendrix, The Doors, Black Sabbath, Deep Purple, and Alice Cooper. Later generations included Ozzy Osbourne, Aerosmith, Van Halen, Guns and Roses, Metallica, and Megadeath.

Among hard rock's defining compositions are "Whole Lotta Love," "Stairway To Heaven," "Inna Gadda Da Vida," "Iron Man," "Paranoid," "White Room," "Sunshine of Your Love," "Crossroads," "I'm Eighteen," "Welcome to My Nightmare," "Light My Fire," "This Is The End," "Smoke On The Water," "Highway Star," "Lazy," and "Welcome to the Jungle."

Hard rock split off from rock and roll with earlier groups like Cream, Iron Butterfly, and the Doors, but most definitively with the band Led Zeppelin. Iron Butterfly's name was in fact, was an intentional contrast of the elements of lightness and heaviness, but Led Zeppelin's music more convincingly contrasted the two extremes, culminating with the genre's anthem and FM radio's most requested song ever, "Stairway To Heaven." "Stairway" featured a lyrical arpeggiated introduction which developed into a driving rhythmic background for an classic electric guitar solo. As an apparent indication of extremes in textures, densities and weight, the term heavy metal was coined as a descriptive for the stylistic direction in which Led Zeppelin, perhaps more than any other band, was taking music. The band formed originally for the purpose of playing a type of British influenced electric blues. When this was explained to Keith Moon, the notorious drummer and hotel room decorator for the Who, he remarked something to the effect, "That'll go over big, just like a lead balloon." Hence the name.

Another term absorbed into the mainstream was first associated with audiences at Led Zeppelin concerts because the most fanatical front row fans would not just rock to the music, they'd actually bang their heads against the stage.

It is said that guitarist and songwriter Jimmy Page claimed to be in league with the devil, much the same as was thought of the great violin virtuoso, Niccolo Paganini, several generations ago. Both musicians seemed to have acquired an aura of mystique to the general public and any controversy which may have resulted probably had some promotional value anyway.

Paganini told a friend (J. Fetis the Belgian composer and critic) in a letter: "I had played the variations called "Le Streghe" (the Witches), and they produced some effect. One individual, who was represented to me as of a sallow complexion, melancholy air, and bright eye, affirmed that he saw nothing surprising in my performance, for he had distinctly seen, while I was playing my variations, the devil at my elbow directing my arm and guiding my bow. My resemblance to him was a proof of my origin. (Paganini was not pretty.) He was clothed in red - had horns on his head - and carried his tail between his legs." You know how it goes: that guy told a few people, and then they told a few people and before you know it, a legend was born. Groups like Cream, with their extended somewhat self-absorbed guitar solos, and Iron Butterfly with "Inna Gadda Da Vida," a song that took an entire album side, pointed the way for a new type of exploratory performance that set an introspective tone for their audiences, rather than the party atmosphere of the earlier rock and roll style. In a similar vein to Paganini, "Clapton Is God" was proclaimed in public restrooms and elsewhere throughout the land, only serving to underscore the important role music and performers played for people at certain periods in their development. It seems that the common denominator for the style is "extremeness." Whatever it is, rage, alienation, frustration or just plain volume levels, it must be done to extremes.

I think as people in certain parts of society became absorbed in the less enjoyable realities of life, the subject matter for artists in the genre became more nihilistic. No more driving around in cars trying to pick up girls. It was time to deaden the senses and talk openly about death. Rock and roll became metal, punk, thrash, and death metal. Musica in extremis.

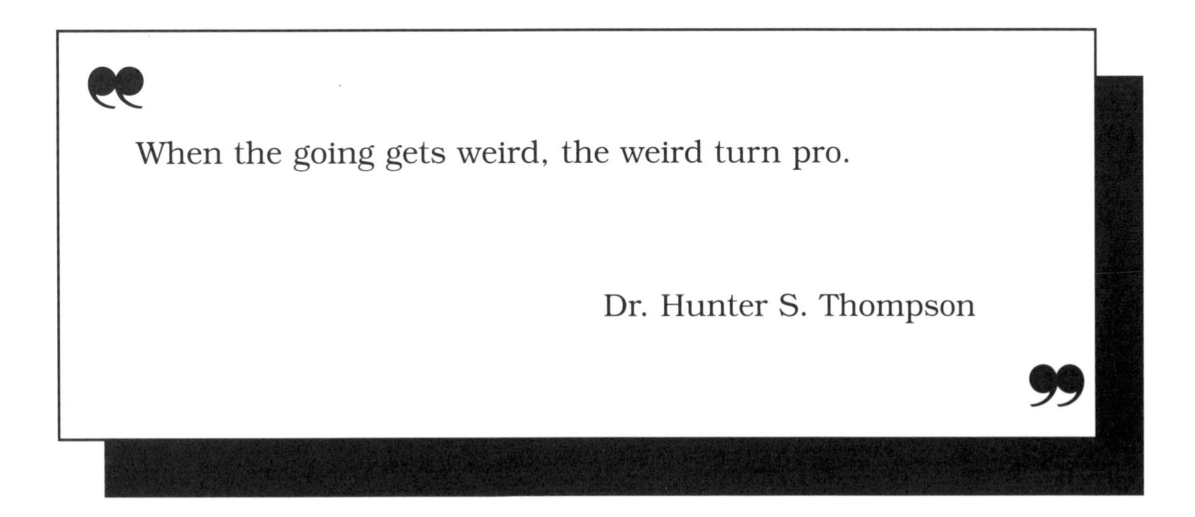

Guitar Arrangement

This section outlines briefly the most common ways guitar music can be arranged and under what circumstances. As a practical matter, you will either be playing someone else's music or your own compositions. If you're playing other people's music you have the option of faithfully replicating their arrangement or changing it to suit your own needs. Writing your own music gives you the freedom (or responsibility) to arrange the guitar parts any way you like, as the piece is being written.

The ways you can arrange music to be played on the guitar depends first on whether you perform as part of a group of musicians or as a solo artist. Here there are also advantages both ways. If the audiences attention is divided among members of a group, the arrangement needn't be as involved and you aren't under as much pressure to maintain such a high level of interest. For solo artists, The activity level of your playing must be considerably higher to keep up the interest level in your listeners, but your esteem in the eyes of the audience is commensurate also.

Within a group, a great deal of the guitar playing will involve riffs and rhythm "comping" (short for accompaniment), usually behind a singer's melody and lyrics, and solo lead playing and riffing in between vocal phrases and sections. If a song, by definition, consists of lyrics, melody and accompaniment, that means the singer is carrying two thirds of the song. If you are the singer and the guitarist, by definition you are carrying the band. Sort of a musician joke but not a funny one.

As a solo guitarist, you will have to provide both the harmonic and melodic materials of whatever you are performing. There are traditional approaches to voicing music for solo artist as well as what are termed chord melody and fingerpicked approaches to arrangement.

Voice leading is a term for the motion of the individual parts (traditionally soprano, alto, tenor, and bass) of a musical work. Traditional voice leading includes counterpoint, where secondary and tertiary melodic voices interweave the primary voice. The way these parts are arranged with respect to intervallic motion contributes greatly to the overall quality and character of the music.

Chord melody style is a type of arrangement where both the harmony and melody are represented, but without traditional voice leading or an alternating bass figure. As the name implies, in chord melody style you literally play a chord containing the a melodic tone, and follow it with (ordinarily) single melody notes or harmonic intervals.

The alternating bass of fingerpicking style provides a solid foundation for a type of solo arrangement associated with Merle Travis, Chet Atkins, and many others, where both the harmonic progression and the melody are represented within a repeating right hand figure.

Guitar Arrangement - Chord Melody

The term chord melody is used to describe an arrangement that uses primarily chords voiced such that the melody is in the highest voice, with (usually) single note melodic material added. There is no set format for the ratio of chords to single melody notes, and flow and taste seem to be the overall guide. Chord melody is a Jazz and Pop soloist's all purpose guitar format.

The following notation format is something I use for chord melody arrangements of music my students want to learn. It is a hybrid of tab and fretboard snapshots. The difference between this hybrid and the standard piano-vocal format is the precise form and position are used here whereas in traditional P-V any form of the chord will apparently suffice. Secondly, the rhythmic phrasing is left out simply because the students are already familiar with the pieces they want to learn, and this makes a cleaner presentation for them and a much shorter lead time to write the arrangement. Notice that below each graph the chord name, form and function are included for further comprehension. The following is an arrangement of a common opening turnaround of the music of the forties.

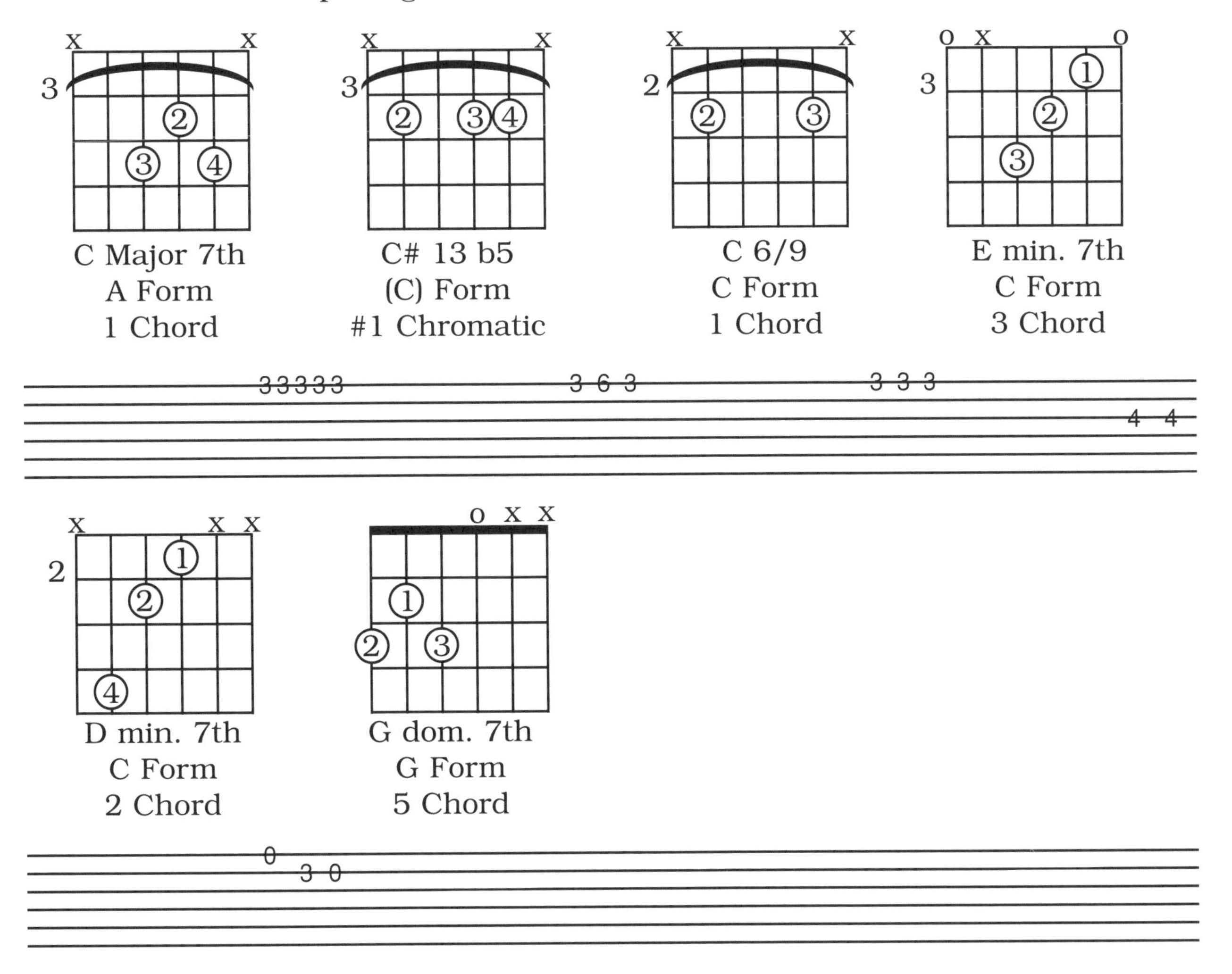

Guitar Arrangement - Fingerpicking

FingerPicking, a.k.a. Travis Picking after Merle Travis, is one of the easiest and most satisfying ways to play the guitar. To the average listener it sounds more complicated than it really is so as a player, you feel like you're getting away with something. There are thousands of pre-arranged songs and solos to play based on the same right hand figure. This figure is somewhat like Alberti bass in piano playing. Example 1 is the basic three-fingered right hand pattern that most fingerpicking styles are built around. It uses the thumb, index and middle fingers in a repeating pattern on four or more strings. If the tablature and notation are unfamiliar, you might want to refer to the section on notation formats first. The letters between the staves represent Thumb, Index and Middle fingers as well as Ring and Pinky of the right hand. The ⁒ symbol above the pattern specifies the number of repeats. The double vertical lines indicate the end of an example or section. The first few examples focus on the right hand only. To get the feel of things quicker, it sometimes helps to not look at your hand as you're playing.

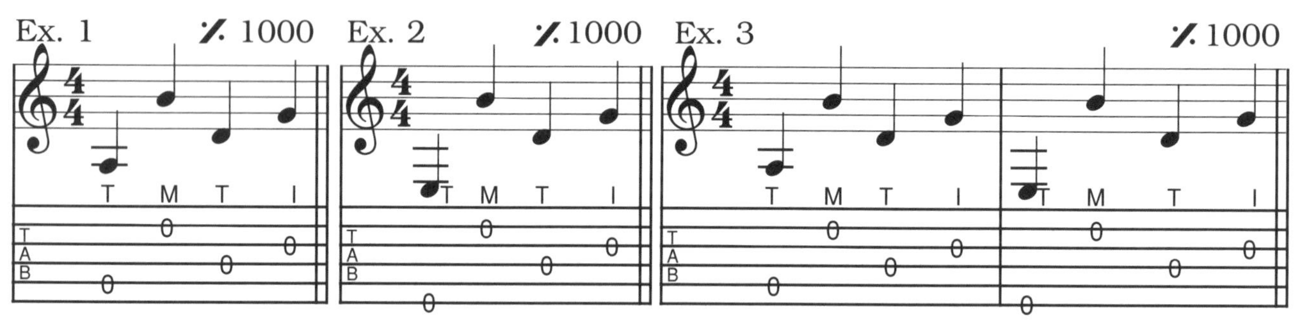

Since first impressions are usually the strongest ones, try to play the examples correctly the very first time. This is far easier than trying to unlearn a habit and then relearn again. It also promotes good long term learning habits. Play them slowly and deliberately until you get accustomed to the feel. Speed and fluidity will come after you have done several hundred (or thousand) slower ones. There is no shortcut for building up strength, coordination, and muscle memory. After enough repetition, the pattern will become automatic and you won't even have to think about it very much.

Example 2 is the same pattern with a sixth string bass note substituted so your thumb has to "hop" over the fifth string. Since the roots of chords are on various strings, the patterns will start on certain bass strings and will include certain treble strings as a rule. The root for the E and G forms is on the 6th string. The root for the A and C forms is on the 5th, and the D form root is on the 4th string. Example 3 combines the two previous ones using bass notes on the fifth and sixth strings.

> ♪ When fingerpicking, be sure your (plucking) thumb is extended well beyond the index and middle toward the headstock. This will cause your wrist to bend a little but the thumb won't keep bumping into the index. Try to make a right angle "V" between your thumb and index as seen from above. Play so your index and middle pull perpendicularly against the string. Tilting the guitar neck upward helps. ♪

Guitar Arrangement - Fingerpicking

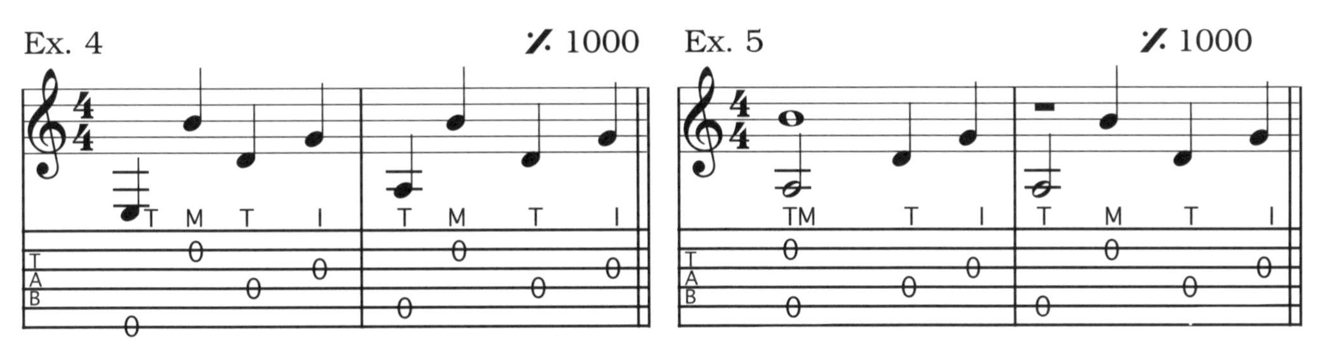

Example 4 is the same as Example 3, but with the bass notes reversed to accommodate, among other things, chords with the root on the sixth string. Example 5 introduces a melody note along with the bass and fill notes.

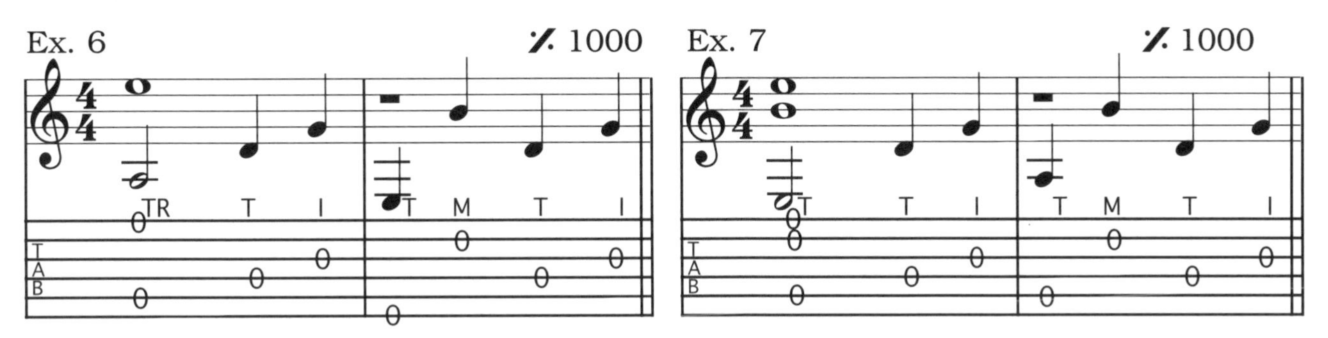

Example 6 introduces the ring finger playing a melody note and Ex. 7 has a chord being used as part of the overall pattern. At this point you can see that the variations on the basic right hand pattern are pretty much limitless. Next we'll apply these figures to some modest chord progressions and make them start to sound like something.

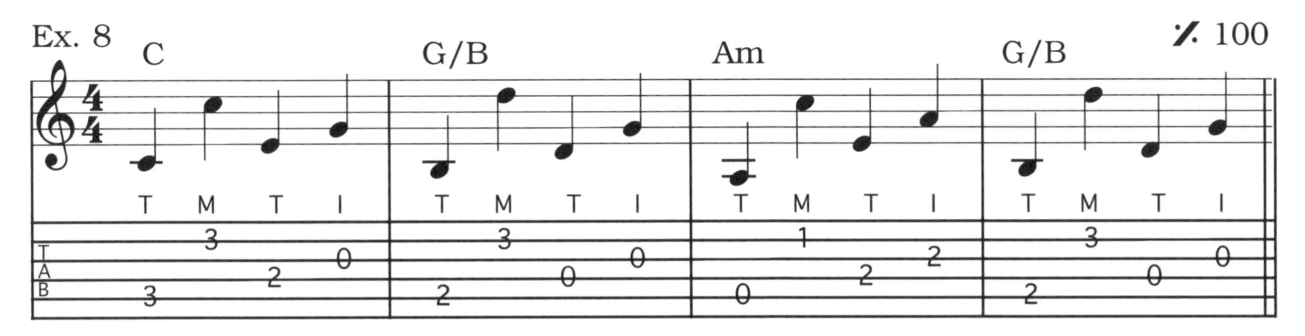

In the 8th example the most basic pattern is played through the C, G, and Am chords. The G has a B for its bass note (plus a D substituted for the B on the 2nd string) and is generally written as G/B. As the level of involvement progresses, the object will be to add more features to the basic right hand figure. Melody, bass lines and chord voicing are among the things to consider beyond the chord progression itself. In order to prevent the pattern from becoming stale and predictable, we'll also look for ways to make the right hand figure more rhythmically dynamic.

Guitar Arrangement - Fingerpicking

As you can tell, each example adds on another factor to be expected in the fingerpicking style. So far only two things in combination have been presented. Next we'll show three things in combination. In Example 9 below, the right hand figure featuring alternating bass is combined with both a chord progression and a melody. Naturally it builds on the progression presented in Ex. 8.

At this stage you are being required to rely on just the tablature and the notation to understand and play the music. The rhythmic nature of the exercise is going to be the most work, and if you are new to this, divide it into two parts. The bass line is almost static, using only eighth notes until the last two beats. The treble line can be divided into rhythmic units according to each beat as demonstrated in the chapter on rhythm. Combining these is a matter of working within the open chord forms, and keeping a steady beat with the thumb.

On the fourth beat of measure one, the B to C melody notes can also be played using a hammer-on although it isn't indicated.

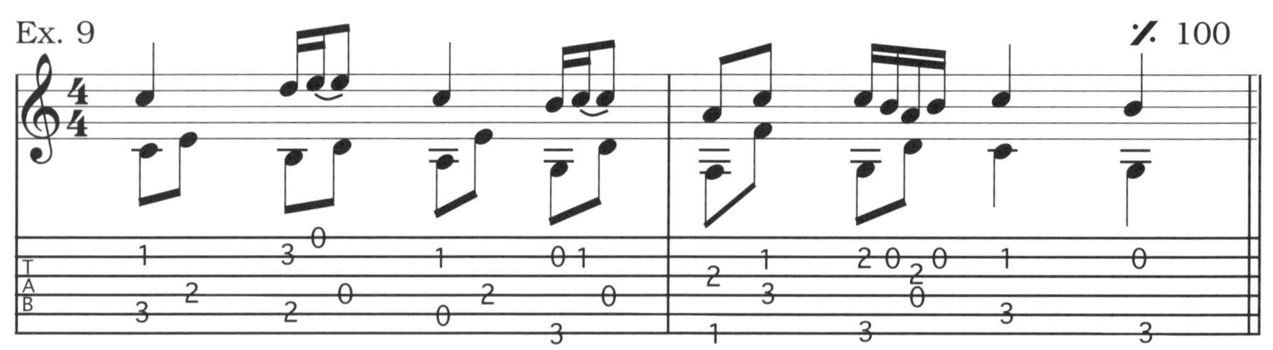

Next we'll add a more in the way of melodic and harmonic material, with secondary dominants in the form of a 5/5 and 5/6 that you should be able to recognize. It would be a good idea to go through the exercise and label each chord and its function within the key. It also has more rhythmic variety with tied and dotted notes.

It is useful to be able to identify the separate elements of every piece of music for a complete learning experience. Sure, its good just to learn new music, but better to understand it on all the different levels.

Example 10 is continued on the next page.

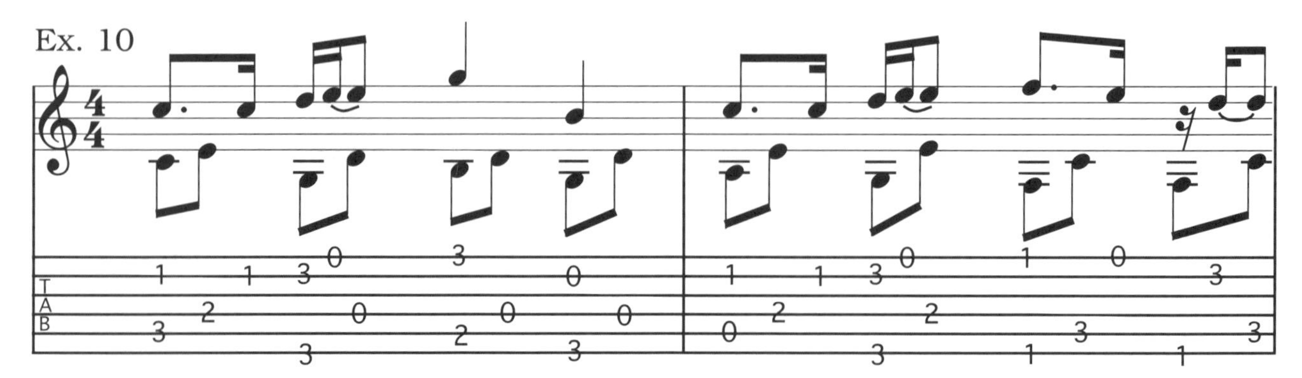

Guitar Arrangement - Fingerpicking

Each of the exercises were designed to develop some of the basic skills you will need to play in the fingerpicking style. The one common denominator of fingerpicking is the alternating bass played with the thumb. The terms alternating bass and fingerpicking have become synonymous. In contrast, classical music features strings plucked with fingers (and nails) but certainly isn't considered fingerpicking.

The alternating bass with its inherent rhythmic structure provides a background against which other music elements will stand out. It presents different difficulties for players with different goals. For beginning players, the biggest hurdle will be to keep the thumb going while the other fingers play chord tones. This boils down to first knowing which string the roots and fifths are on for the different chords and forms. For those who are interested in a fingerpicked accompaniment to vocals, it means being able to keep this going while chords progress without losing track of the lyrics and tune. For solo players, it means maintaining a steady bass while both chords and melodies progress.

The next study piece, "The River Song," is a fingerpicked instrumental and is presented on the following pages. It is also a featured etude in Video II on the subject of chords in progression.

The River Song

Bill Edwards

al fine
H
H

D.C. al 𝄋 fine
H

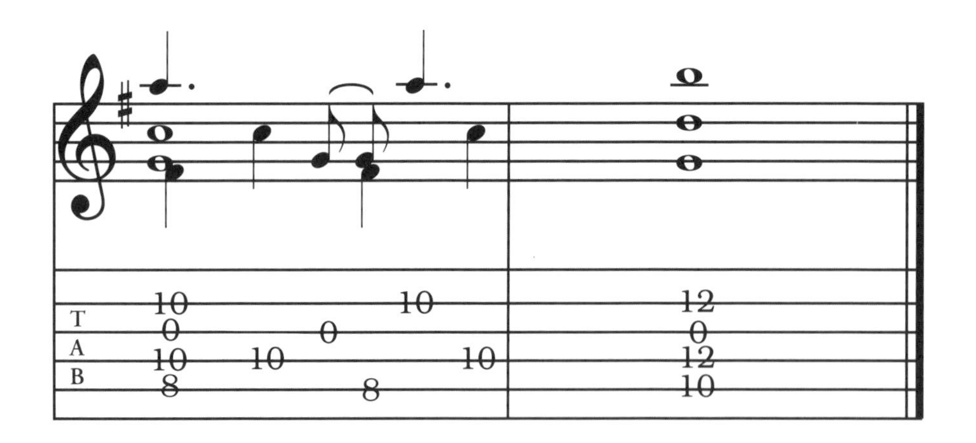
T
A
B
10
0
10
8
10
0
8
10
10
12
0
12
10

Only one who devotes himself to a cause with his whole strength and soul can be a true master. For this reason, mastery demands all of a person.

Albert Einstein

Sonics

This section is intended as a brief discussion on the characteristics and usage of common guitar effects or signal processors. For the record, guitar effects should be used to imbue a particular character or enhance the quality of a musical presentation.

Write down what you think is the most common guitar effect in use today. It is taken almost completely for granted, and if you guessed amplification, you are to be congratulated for an understanding of the basics of what we will term guitar sonics. The area of sonics is meant to deal with the non-guitaristic and non-musical aspects of what audiences hear when we as guitarists play. It is fortunate that we live in the era of the integrated circuit, because this stage of electronic evolution offers a wide range of capabilities to the modern guitarist the most basic of which is the ability to be heard by a large audience. The guitar's design from its inception has been a combination of mechanical and structural compromises which perform interrelated functions. The playing area of the instrument, the neck, is joined to the amplifying part, (the box or plank supporting the pickups), by the tone generators, the strings. This design is common to virtually all stringed instruments. Don't underestimate the importance of amplification. It is the way your audience hears you, and it can only help you one way, but it can hurt you two ways. The only way it can help you is if it enables your audience to hear you better. It can hurt you if it is not loud enough or too loud. Guess which one of those is the most common. It can also get in the way of the performance if it is not kept under strict control. Feedback is the biggest problem for amplified systems and occurs when the signal from the instrument (string/pickup) is fed directly back into the output devices (speakers). Feedback can be controlled by physically directing the speakers away from the instrument's pickups, or by isolating a resonant room frequency with an equalizer and eliminating that frequency from the mix.

Amplification for the performing guitarist is generally a two part affair. There is a stage level coming from the amp itself, and this is usually fed into the mixer for the house sound. As a practical matter, there are twice as many things to go wrong from the outset. The single most common bugaboo of performing musicians, is that they become attenuated to their own sound, and don't feel they are represented adequately in the mix. So guess what they do. And guess what that creates. And then what happens? Right, right and right. They turn themselves up, further unbalance both the stage and house sound, and then somebody else in the band does the same thing and starts the cycle over again ad infinitum. It becomes a loudness spiral. The reason for this is due in part to the long term effects of high decibel levels. On the psychological side, it has something to do with self promotion and at least to some extent, an overall sense of insecurity. If there is one area we as performing guitarists should be educated in, it is the area of amplification. One of the best ways to get a true picture of what your sound is like to the audience is to strap on a wireless and get as far away from the stage as your unit will permit. Standing outside of the building and hearing your band from a distance will give you a better sense of the overall band sound than standing on your side of the stage.

Right along with the amplification of a signal is the relative brightness or darkness of the overall sound which we refer to in an acoustical sense as tone. The two extremes of tone are treble and bass, and it is likely that early guitar makers became aware of this factor in terms of the material used for strings and the design of the tops of the resonating chambers. On amplified guitars, tone is controlled by either passive or active circuitry. In passive circuits, the bass is controlled by means of a low pass filter in the form of a capacitor, and variable resistance in the form of a potentiometer. It is significant that passive tone controls can only subtract from the overall signal. In active tone circuitry, aka equalization, you have the ability to not only add and subtract signal strength, but also to specify the bandwidths (frequency ranges) which are to be affected.

From a historical perspective, the next effect would perhaps be reverb and delay type effects. I'd bet that guitarists of ancient times would take their instruments out of the ale houses and into cathedrals for the sheer exhilaration of hearing the sound carry, maybe they believed, heavenward. There are three basic types of delay as perceived, and they are reverb, slapback and echo. The difference between these is the time between the original signal and the effected signal. Reverb occurs when the signal is delayed and combined within a range of approximately 30 milliseconds, slapback is in the range of (if I remember correctly) about 80 milliseconds, and echo is considered anything beyond slapback. Whereas reverb is a connecting and carrying of the instruments sound, slapback occurs at the moment that sound becomes disconnected from the original source. Slapback is easily produced with electronic delays, and the digital units are generally of higher quality than analog designs. Echo is usually associated with multiple repeats of the effected signal.

Most electronic signal processors were designed to reproduce effects that were the product of experimentation and evolution in the studio and on the stage. Distortion is an example of an effect that came into existence intentionally, after occurring unintentionally in real life playing situations. Legend has it that Ike Turner's amp fell off the car on the way to Memphis, and producer Sam Phillips stuffed the cones with paper just to get on with the recording session. When popular music started drawing larger audiences, musicians soon learned that the equipment that was adequate for most auditoriums of the day was insufficient for larger arenas and outdoor venues. If you get a chance to watch a Beatles retrospective, take a look at the equipment they used for the concert at Shea stadium, and you'll understand why all you could hear was screaming. (I think it was something like a four or six channel mixer pushing probably less than 100 watts, with about four speaker columns of the old Bogen or Shure type.) When this type of equipment was pushed to its limits, the weakest link in the chain, the speakers, would take the heat, literally. The signal sent to the speakers was greater than it could manage, and distortion, or clipping would result. Then, as the speakers attempted to dissipate greater amounts of energy, they would go into thermal overload and cause even more distortion until the lacquer suspending the coils melted. Eventually, this type of sound came to be associated with the success, style and direction of popular music, and a few guitarists would go so far as to slice up speaker cones with razor blades to enhance the distorted effect. Eventually the participants came to realize that there must be a way to achieve the effect without having to replace speakers so often. In essence, the signal to the speaker was being overdriven, or played beyond its practical limits. It was a logical next step to overdrive the signal fed to the speakers without the harmful result to the speakers themselves. This is when preamplification in the form of two stage guitar amps and "fuzz" boxes came into being. Instead of overdriving the speaker itself, the signal to the speaker was overdriven. Distortion or overdrive, as you know, eventually became associated with rock music and its stylistic descendants. Musicians and guitarists in particular seem to be afflicted with a strain of nostalgic egocentricity where their equipment and their sound is concerned. To this day you hear guitarists proclaim that they don't make amplifiers that sound as good as the ones made in the good old days. Naturally, they just happen to own one of these fine collectables and for the right price...

The flange effect similarly evolved from a studio trick that is attributed to John Lennon. Did you ever wonder where the term flanging derives from? I understand that he used to experiment with the recording and the mixdown machines in the studio. In this particular instance, he'd put his thumb on the flange of the mixdown machine's take up reel, and de-sync the signal in an unusual way. The effect we know as the flanger came about because an electronics whiz tried to imitate the way it sounded. Phase, flange and chorus are electronic effects based on the ability to split a signal, modify it, and reintroduce it into the circuit path later.

The chorus effect has become the most popular of the three lately, and it gets its sound from slightly detuning the split off signal and cycling the variations against the unprocessed signal. In a way, this is similar to the 12 string guitar and the piano effect. Each string is slightly out of tune with the other and this produces a lush harmonic quality that is very rich sounding. The phase effect is what the name implies. The signal is reintroduced into the circuit path out of phase with the original. This makes a cycled whooshing sound that was the rage in the seventies. Eighties, if you were a country player.

Compression is a means of electronically fattening up a signal such that it not only sustains better, but also evens out the peaks and valleys. When compression and overdrive are combined, a "saturated" distortion is produced that can sustain for long periods. Ask Carlos Santana how this works.

The tremolo (literal meaning) was standard equipment on many amplifiers during the sixties and seventies, also. This effect was a cycled alternation in volume that could be set for speed. It was used in a lot of guitar music of the sixties and early seventies. Vibrato was also seen on amps, and it was an effect that cycled changes in pitch. To some extent these older analog effects have been phased out by digital effects such as harmonizers where a signal could be duplicated simultaneously by another a set interval apart. If you've studied intervals, you know that playing the same one over and over gets redundant quickly, so this type of effect loses its value in a fairly short amount of time. The octave effect is an early form of this where the primary signal was matched by two secondary signals, one, an octave below, and the other two octaves below, permitting a three note bass kind of sound. Octave pedals could also be set on the lowest signal only, in order to imitate a bass guitar.

So far, the effects mentioned have been static in terms of how they function. In other words, set em and forget em. The dynamic, or interactive effects are the wah-wah, the volume pedal, and the vibrato bar (tremolo bar) The wah-wah and the volume pedal are foot operated. The wah is a variable tone control that could produce effects that often came across as crying sounds. The tremolo bar gained a resurgence in popularity with the development of designs that actually stayed in tune. Coupled with an interest in dive bomb, chain-saw, Harley hog, and similar sound effects, the tremolo had risen to the top of the heap by the mid eighties. Guitarists are always on the lookout for technology that will give them a sonic edge over the competition, or at least enable them to keep up with current trends. The range and quality of equipment the player has available to him nowadays is an embarrassment of riches. The temptation is to let our sound take control of our music. A great many professional guitarists have pretty much the same over-processed sound.

If you want to get noticed, you'll have to stand out from the crowd. Maybe when it comes to sound effects, less is more. When Hendrix experimented with all those effects, he was on the cutting edge, but nowadays modern signal processing is within the reach of everyone, so our attitude tends toward getting our money's worth out of them. Do all your songs sound the same because you use your one best sound for everything? Vary your setup. Try to step away from your personal preferences and ask yourself if it really helps the quality of the music it is supposed to enhance or is it a way to mask weakness in other more essential areas.

?

Q: How do you get a guitarist to:

1) Turn up? A: Put a volume control on his guitar.
2) Turn down? A: Put a chart in front of him.

?

Guitar Tuning

By this point you are more than a little familiar with the concept of a pattern organization on the fretboard that is as important as any other aspect of learning to play the guitar. This section deals with the physics, mathematics, mechanics and history underlying that tuning system by examining: 1) the science of acoustics upon which musical experience is founded, 2) our present system of temperament, and its evolution, and 3) the history and evolution of the guitar's tuning system.

When Fretboard Logic was first published, yours truly would eagerly promote the book to other guitar players with a short description to the effect that it would help them because it explained the reasoning behind the guitar's tuning. Before I could get another word out they would quickly assure me that they already knew how to tune their guitars and were looking for a book to help them learn how to play it better or something to that effect. Although I managed to create a lot of wrong first impressions, there is, in fact, a great deal worth discussing about tuning systems per se, from a historical perspective to present day common usage.

Something many players don't realize but might have suspected all along is that when a guitar is correctly tuned, it does not produce acoustically correct intervals and so is not capable of producing perfect chords even under optimal circumstances. One of my favorite guitarisms on this subject is from the guy who said, "If I ever get this danged thing in tune, I'm gonna weld it in place." The first section deals with coming to grips with the necessary compromises that were adopted long ago but still continue to promote misconceptions that plague musicians and guitarists in particular. Our present system came into popular usage around J.S. Bach's time and like the guitar's own tuning system, is difficult if not impossible to improve upon because of its sheer versatility and practicality. The third section deals with the evolution of the guitar which led to the system in use today. It should be noted that this area was researched as much for my own interest than out of any sense of obligation teachingwise, but as with most endeavors of this sort, it was well worth the effort. Also, it seemed fitting that the last chapter of the last book should end at the beginning - with an explanation of a tuning system.

Before we go any further, I want to state that I am of the belief that most guitar players subscribe to a type of thinking that would be characterized as right brain oriented, left brain being the more ordered and analytical type of thinking. If differential calculus books were crib toys for you, then you're a left brainer. Us right brainers are supposed to be more, uh, creative and stuff. So, knowing how most guitar brains are, it is with trepidation that I utter the "M" word. Without some math there is no way to discuss why tuning can be so hard especially, and ironically, for people who have good pitch recognition. By the way, pitch recognition is simply a matter of concentration and practice. It can be compared to the ability to visually distinguish subtle differences in colors. Please don't confuse this remark with the numerous attempts dating back to the 19th century, to establish an association between the seven colors of the spectrum and the seven pitches in a diatonic scale. Such associations are purely subjective and by a simple comparison of the numerous attempts at this, it can be shown there has never been any consistency or relevance from one to another. Other than they make money for the folks that sell them, they are an exercise in "bogusity," as a friend would say.

Guitar Tuning

From the outset, the difference between perfect and relative pitch are undifferentiated. Any musician has relative pitch, and a musician with perfect pitch would call it anything but a gift. Pitch recognition is a knack easier for some to acquire than others, but there's nothing extraordinary or even all that special about it. Lately it has become so oversold that I have to be physically restrained whenever some twit announces that he has "perfect pitch." Math, on the other hand is everywhere. Even if you aren't a left brainer you might eventually appreciate that numbers can always be reduced to their most fundamental relationships with little, if any, of the ambiguity of words.

Acoustics and Tuning

The foundation of almost all musical experience is the vibration of elastic matter within the range of human hearing. Elasticity appears in many forms such as stretched materials, *columns* of air, rigid materials, etc. The vibrational properties are realized in musical instrument design from the crudest to the most technologically advanced.

Acoustically, all vibrations can be characterized by two primary properties: amplitude and frequency. **Amplitude** pertains to a vibration's relative loudness or softness and **frequency** to its relative highness or lowness. Amplitude means the same as loudness and frequency the same as pitch (for now). On a guitar, you can actually see a string's amplitude by plucking it harder or softer and watching how wide it oscillates. Frequency can also be seen by shortening the length of the string and watching it speed up, but it is much more difficult unless special equipment is used. Pitches are determined by an arithmetic number in terms of its cycles per second. Loudness is determined on a geometric basis in terms of how it is perceived. Pitch is specific and loudness much more relative.

A discussion on tuning has to begin with a naturally occurring acoustical phenomenon called the overtone series or harmonics. The overtone series is the tones other than the fundamental, the lowest and most easily perceived tone, that make up every note played. The number and intensity of an instrument's harmonics determine the timbre, or quality of the tone. Richer sounds, like notes from a bowed violin or an acoustic guitar, have more overtones; purer sounds, like notes played on a flute or an (unmodified) electric guitar, have fewer. Everyone has produced tones on their guitar by lightly touching but not fretting the string just over certain frets and then plucking the string near the bridge. These are harmonics or partials. Each and every partial or harmonic contributes to the overall timbre or quality of an instruments sound. The relative strength of each partial, given the instruments design, gives its tone what could be considered an "acoustical fingerprint" by which we distinguish one from another. Even timbres similar in character can be easily distinguished by subtle cues from the harmonics. The pure tone of an (uneffected) electric guitar is easily distinguished from the pure tone of a flute. Another term comes into play here: intonation, or pitch accuracy. The reason a guitar has frets is to provide the player with easy, accurate intonation. (The idea of frets is a clever and lasting invention many hundreds of years old, and here again, it is hard to know who gets the credit.) The placement of the frets is not a simple matter and is a compromise corresponding to the even tempered tuning system. Tuning problems arise because there are necessary compensations made for the overtone series that create an imperfect pitch relationship on the fretboard. We will demonstrate mathematically that when you tune by matching the harmonics on the seventh and fifth frets of adjacent string pairs, you get the guitar dog's biggest flea, and that is playing noticeably out of tune. Nothing makes you sound more like an amateur than playing noticeably out of tune. And don't bother asking me how I know. Lets take a closer look at the overtone series. A scientific definition for the overtone series is: a series of tones consisting of the fundamental tone and the overtones produced by it, whose frequencies are *consecutive integral multiples* of the frequency of the fundamental. (You might want to read that last sentence over again about forty-six times.) It boils down to the consecutive integral multiples part. Simply put, consecutive integral (integer) multiples is "mathese" for taking a number and multiplying it first by 1, then by 2, then by 3, then by 4 and so on. For example, consecutive integral multiples of the number 3 are: 3, 6, 9, 12, and so on. No problemo. Now let's attach a more useful musical number to it and do it again. Let's use 440 Hz as in "A-440" which is the standard reference for tuning 12 tone instruments all over the world.

By the way, just to cover the bases, Hz is an abbreviation for Hertz, an award term for cycles per second. For those new to this term, acoustical frequencies, or those that are able to be heard by humans, are normally designated in Hertz (Hz) and Kilohertz (Khz) or thousands of cycles per second for ease of use. The highest and lowest limits of human hearing are usually given at 20 Hz to 20 Khz.

Consecutive multiples and the overtone series in cycles per second of A 440 are: 440, 880, 1320, 1760 and so on. An important result of the consecutive integral multiple process is that it produces a consistent series of intervals, or two-note groupings and ratios to be discussed momentarily. Watch how the math (frequencies in cycles per second) and the music (the order of intervals) line up in the overtone series on the fretboard:

Frequency		C.I.M.		Interval		Note	Where on Guitar
440 Hz	=	440 x 1	=	Unison	=	A	1st string 5th fret
880 Hz	=	440 x 2	=	Octave	=	A	1st string 17th fret
1320 Hz	=	440 x 3	=	Fifth	=	E	1st string 24th fret

So far so good. Now lets apply this relationship in detail to a more guitar oriented frequency: 110 Hz. 110 Hz is the frequency of the open A string as you might have known. This is a good starting point because the multiples are easy to see and you are able to play the harmonics and hear the results on your guitar.

Frequency		C.I.M.		Interval		Note	Where on Guitar
110 Hz	=	110 x 1	=	Unison	=	A	5th String Open
220 Hz	=	110 x 2	=	Octave	=	A	5th String 12th fret harmonic
330 Hz	=	110 x 3	=	Fifth	=	E	5th String 7th fret harmonic
440 Hz	=	110 x 4	=	Fourth	=	A	5th String 5th fret harmonic
550 Hz	=	110 x 5	=	Maj. Third	=	C#	5th String 4th fret harmonic
660 Hz	=	110 x 6	=	Min. Third	=	E	5th String 3rd fret harmonic

Guitar Tuning

The order of intervals resulting from the consecutive integer multiples is also a constant. The intervals in order are: Unison, Octave, Fifth, Fourth, Major 3rd, Minor 3rd, Minor 3rd, Major 2nd, Major 2nd, Major 2nd, Major 2nd, Minor 2nd, Major 2nd, Minor second, Minor 2nd, Major 2nd. The consecutive integer multiples of the naturally occurring overtone series produce a series of intervals which, given the twelve tone system, can be reduced to a series of notes where each note has an exact pitch. The C.I.M.s produce another constant in the form of a ratio between intervals as discovered by Greek philosopher and mathematician Phythagoras. This is how it works. If the frequency of a given tone is 1, then its octave will be 2 according to the C.I.M. This makes the ratio of the octave to the fundamental 2:1. Since the C.I.M. principle says the next multiple is 3, then the ratio of the next interval to the last one is 3:2 and the interval is a 5th. The next C.I.M. is 4 so the next ratio is 4:3 and the interval is a 4th and so on. Below is another chart to show the relationships between the ratios and the resulting intervals of the overtone series.

Interval	Ratio
Unison	1:1
Octave	2:1
Fifth	3:2
Fourth	4:3
Major 3rd	5:4

Temperament

Throughout history, there have been various schemes for tuning the intervals of the twelve tone system, or temperament, and as attitudes and technologies evolved, tuning systems evolved right along. **Temperament** is the general term for the systems of tuning in which the intervals are compensated, or deviated from acoustical correctness according to the mathematical precepts of Pythagoras. These adjustments have always been necessary since tuning systems based on the pure intervals are very limited minimizing the availability of keys and harmonic progression.

The **Pythagorean scale** is a scale in which all the frequencies are derived from the interval of the fifth and the ratio of 3:2 by multiplying upwards and dividing downwards. It was devised to closely follow the overtone series and produce acoustically pure intervals. The third of C, for example, is derived as the fourth consecutive fifth (C-G, G-D, D-A, A-E), and the ratios are 3/2 x 3/2 x 3/2 x 3/2 = 81/16. Reduced downward two octaves (divided) = 81/64. This third is slightly higher (8 cents) than that of equal temperament, and much higher, 22 cents (almost a quarter of a semitone) than that of just intonation. The term cent means one hundredth (1/100) of a semitone. In intervallic terms the **cent** is the standard of measure just as Hz is in pitch measurement.

Just intonation is a theoretical system of tuning in which the third as well as the fifth are acoustically correct, and in which all the other intervals are derived from these two in the manner described above, dividing downward and multiplying upward. This system of tuning results in even greater limitations than the

Pythagorean, and is included here for completeness only.

The **mean-tone system** was in vogue prior to our present day system of tuning. The mean-tone system featured pure 3rds and almost pure 5ths in the simple keys, or those with few accidentals, but was virtually unusable otherwise. Keys with more than a few sharps or flats were fairly uncommon from the 14th to 16th centuries, and it is likely for that very reason.

All of which brings us to our present day system of temperament originally termed well tempering, but now called equal. The "equal" in equal temperament pertains to the result of each key being equal to the next regardless of the number of accidentals, for the purpose of transposition, modulation, etc. This comes about as a result of making the octaves pure and compensating the other intervals. **Equal temperament** is based on the division of the octave into 12 equal parts (the 12th root of 2), each part representing a semitone. This fairly modern system makes it possible for the first time to play in all keys with no side effects such as would occur when accidentals were used with other tuning systems.

The theory behind equal temperament was known as far back as the 16th century, but it did not gain wide acceptance until J.S. Bach's lifetime. Bach produced a work of historical significance called "The Well-Tempered Clavier" which featured keyboard pieces in every key possible using the system. From that point on, equal temperament has become the standard because although the intervals are not perfect, the ability to make a smooth transition from key area to key area makes it the most practical by far.

In equal tempering the fifths are flatted so the octaves come out true doubles. Remember that the violin family of instruments are tuned in fifths and have no frets meaning that every note must be manually intonated. When the strings are matched for perfect fifths (tuning is traditionally done by aligning or justifying the adjacent strings), the tuning is just oriented. Because there are no frets, the players of this family of instruments are constantly adjusting for note accuracy or correct intonation by sliding, rolling, vibrato etc. Pianos have three strings per note in the middle range, and the strings are tuned slightly out of sync with each other to produce a richer tone.

The following is the formula for calculating exact frequencies in the even tempering system of tuning: $\mathbf{F = r\,(2^{1/12})^N}$ Where:

F= Freq.
r = reference pitch (110, 220, 440, 880, etc.)
$\mathbf{2^{1/12}}$ = 1.0594630943593
N = Number of 1/2 tones from known pitch to desired pitch non-inclusive

or: $\mathbf{F = r * (1.0594630943593)^N}$

Example: To find C above A 440:

$440\,(1.0594630943593)^3 =$
440 (1.1892071150027) =
523.25113060119 =
523.25

Example: To find D above A 440:
$440\ (1.0594630943593)^5 =$
$440\ (1.3348398541701) =$
$587.32953583484 =$
587.34

To find F (4th Stg, 3rd fret):
$110\ (1.0594630943593)^8 =$
$110\ (1.5874010519683) =$
$174.61411571651 =$
174.61

Below are the open string's freqs.

To find (open 6th string) E:
$55\ (1.0594630943593)^7 =$
$55\ (1.4983070768767) =$
$82.406889228219 =$
82.41

Open A: **110** (Reference pitch)

To find (open) D:
$110\ (1.0594630943593)^5 =$
$220\ (1.3348398541701) =$
$146.83238395871 =$
146.83

To find (open) G:
$110\ (1.0594630943593)^{10} =$
$110\ (1.7817974362808) =$
$195.99771799089 =$
196.00

To find (open) B:
$220\ (1.0594630943593)^2 =$
$220\ (1.1224620483094) =$
$246.94165062807 =$
246.94

To find (open 1st string) E:
$220\ (1.0594630943593)^7 =$
$220\ (1.4983070768767) =$
$329.62755691287 =$
329.63

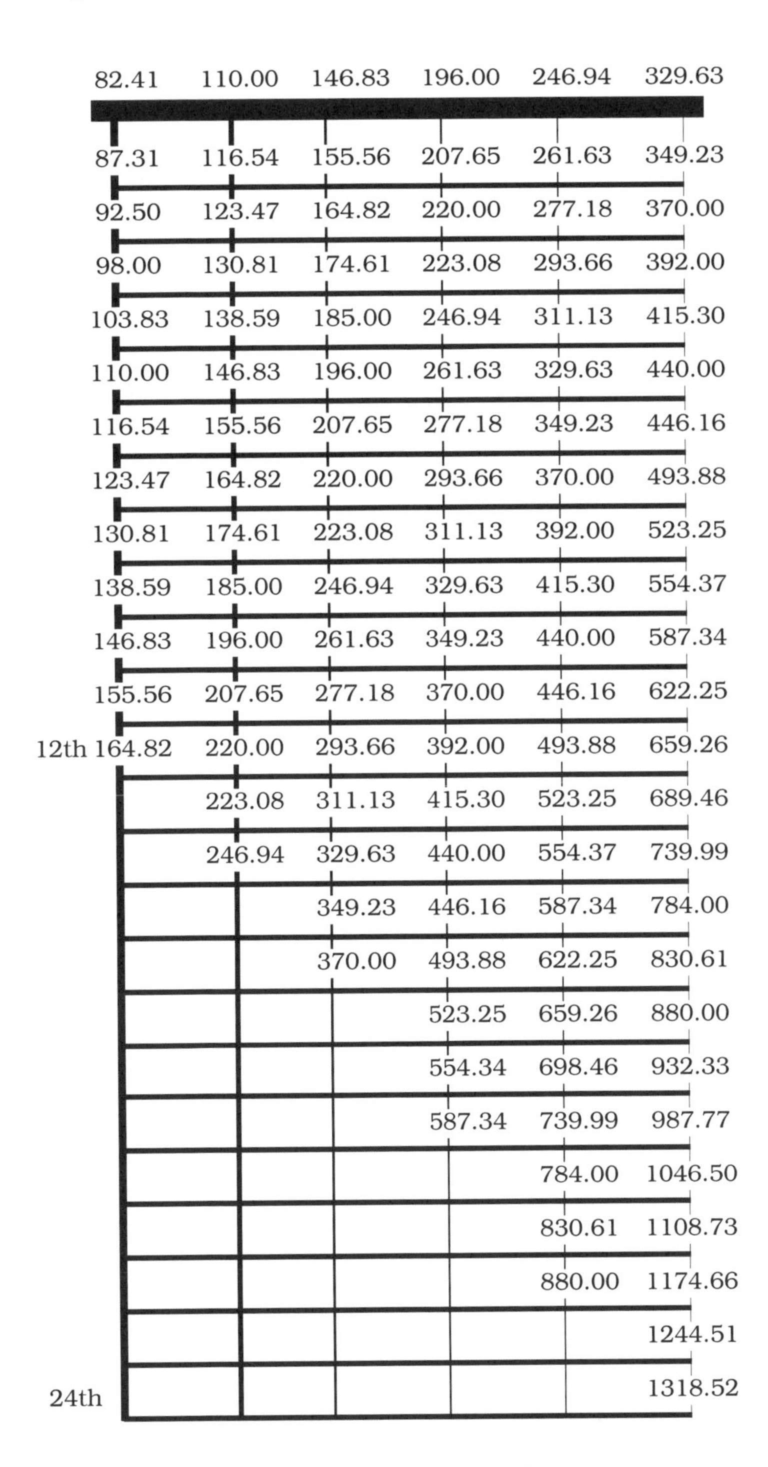

Equal Tempered Fretboard Frequencies
(Rounded to two decimal places.)

Guitar Tuning

Using the methods discussed, we can compare the frequencies that occur when playing the harmonics against the even tempered frequencies. We've established the reference of A-440 plus its multiples and divisions as a basis for comparison. Using open A-110 as our starting point, the Pythagorean method for determining the frequency of the E harmonic (the 5th of A) is as follows: 110 x 3/2 = 330/2= **165**. Don't forget that the 3/2 figure came from the ratio of the consecutive integral multiples for the fifth. The equal tempered frequency as calculated on the previous page using the 12√2 is **164.81**. Not off by much but check out the difference in Hz between one A at 164.81 and A# at 174.61. The difference is 9.8 Hz. At these frequencies, a mere 1 Hz is about a ten percent discrepancy or 10 cents off. Thus the .19 Hz difference in this one frequency represents about a couple of cents. Not that noticeable per se, but take a look at how much variation is occurs in some of the frequencies below.

What follows is a chart of pitches on the A string as calculated using the Pythagorean system as compared to Equal Temperament.

Note	Pythagorean	Equal Tempered
A	110.00	110.00
A#	117.47	116.54
B	123.75	123.47
C	132.15	130.81
C#	139.22	138.59
D	148.67	146.83
D#	156.62	155.56
E	165.00	164.81
F	176.20	174.61
F#	185.63	185.00
G	198.22	196.00
G#	208.83	207.65
A	223.00	220.00

One or two other things should also be mentioned concerning the process of tuning. Whenever a carpenter is marking consecutive pieces of wood to be cut the same length, he has the option of using each successive piece as the guide for the next mark, or using just one piece to make the mark for each successive piece to be cut. Which one is more accurate and why? If you answered to use just one piece to make all the marks, you are correct. Using only one as a guide avoids the gremlin of accumulated error. **Accumulated error** is a term for when unnoticeable imperfections are multiplied until they are noticeable. (You would accumulate less error if you were to use the first string as the sole reference pitch for the others.) Add accumulated error to the method of tuning by harmonics and you have a formula for being noticeably out of tune. Postscript. If you just want to get in tune, use an electronic tuner, and be sure that the strings are not hung up in any of the intrument's mechanisms, slots, etc. When using an electronic tuner, if you are below the target, tighten almost to the "zero" point on the meter and pluck the string hard and it will jump the last few cents. If you are above the target, tug the string the rest of the way to the zero instead of moving the machine heads. These tactics serve to "settle" the string into place and take up any latent slack that may still be in the system. Guitars with tremolos are especially sensitive and require more time and patience. A comparison of low and high frequencies as illustrated on the fretboard graphic a couple pages back, shows that the half step's value in Hz is constantly increasing. Its value in cents is constant, however. The unit of intervallic measure being the cent, we can get a feel for this value by comparing it to something we are naturally familiar with as guitarists: bends. As guitar players we are used to bending in whole tones, half tones and microtones (quarter tones and less). If a half tone is 100 cents, then a quarter tone, or a half fret bend, is 50 cents. An eighth tone is 25 cents and a sixteenth tone is 17.5 cents, and so on.

Evolution of the Guitar and its Tuning System

The last section is devoted to a discussion on the evolution of the guitar and its tuning system. The guitar's ancestry can be traced significantly back to the lute. The lute is of Arab descent, and artwork as early as the 13th century depicts four string versions of this predecessor to the guitar. Manuscripts show it to have been tuned in straight fourths. Within the 14th century the strings evolved into pairs or **courses** and tunings included the interval of a 3rd between outer 4ths. It should be apparent at this point that the guitar's tuning system was an evolutionary process spanning centuries, and not the achievement of any one person, as has been suggested. The instruction books of the day recommended tightening the highest string almost to the breaking point and tuning the others from that reference point. There is little doubt that this was to permit the maximum level of volume the delicate instrument was capable of producing. Less taut strings weren't as prone to breakage, but they were slower to recover for rapidly played passages. The next step in the evolution was the addition of two more courses bringing the total to six, with the standard tuning 4th, 4th 3rd, 4th, & 4th. Although surprisingly close to modern guitar tuning, it fails to achieve the same results with respect to pattern organization. During the 17th century, new combinations of intervals and numbers of strings were experimented with including nine course versions; the intervals 4th, 4th, 3rd, 3rd, & 3rd; and 4th, 3rd, 3rd, 4th, & 3rd.

The lute during this period of history was far and away the most popular choice for the virtuoso performer. The design of the instrument was refined to a point of near perfection (within existing technologies) and the guitar's more immediate relatives only succeeded in gaining an edge to an extent due to ruggedness of design and construction. Notable among these predecessors is the vihuela, a Spanish instrument more guitar-like than lute-like. Also worth mentioning are the cittern, the pandora and the English guitar. The cittern featured a **re-entrant tuning,** meaning the fourth course was an octave higher than the third as with the modern ukelele. The cittern also featured wire strings which, again, were louder and brighter than either the gut or silk strings of the day. More variations in construction produced the gittern, and the guitarra, but none of these featured the tuning system now in use. The closest was a 16th century five course instrument dubbed the Spanish guitar, with the intervals 4th, 4th, 3rd, & 4th. Now we're getting close. During this period, a sixth course was added (a 4th in the bass), and the courses were replaced by single strings. This was the instrument known to Paganini, Schubert, Sor, and other notables. And this was the tuning system which may one day find its rightful place in the history of the instrument, as clearly the optimal combination of number of strings and intervallic spacing for four fretting fingers.

Guitar Tuning - Postscript

A friend of mine who happens to be a guitar brain and a history professor, has a pet theory about the evolution of guitar design. He makes a pretty good case that the only consistency in guitar design has been in the direction of loudness. His arguments are more than a little plausible considering the following revisions in the tone production capabilities of the instrument. From the earliest known ancestors, it was given more strings and the size of its resonating chamber steadily increased. Steel strings were substituted for gut and fiber, and the box was reinforced. The construction grew sturdier and more robust until a solid plank was implemented and the volume was derived from a separate source. Once electronic pickups and amplification were implemented, the combination enabled the instrument to produce so much volume that now you can't come away from a concert without your ears ringing from the sound pressure levels. But the evolution of the instrument has enabled performers to reach the sized audiences that the master lutenists of the 14th century could only dream of. What began as a delicate parlour instrument has evolved into a sonic sledge hammer that has practically no limitations on volume.

1) An analog tone generator.

2) Six drift-prone monophonic oscillators on a plank of wood.

Hartley Peavey and
Craig Anderton -
upon being asked to define a guitar.

Coda

The three volumes of the Fretboard Logic series have each been developed with certain objectives in mind. In Vol. I, the pattern organization resulting from the tuning system was presented as a wholly guitaristic issue, separate from the ordinary musical requirements and not universally appreciated. In Vol. II, the primary tonal groupings used in music of all types were presented in the context of this pattern organization in order to provide the player with a means to construct the musical entities known as chords, scales, and arpeggios without the necessity for the rote memorization of large amounts of seemingly unrelated information. In Vol. III, the focus widened to encompass as many of the issues facing the practicing guitarist as practical. The overall goal has been to offer a familiar and comfortable place to work (the patterns of the fretboard), the tools with which to do the work (the tone groupings) and the methods and practices with which the work is best understood and accomplished (the guitar player's menu).

In the years since the first book was published, among the most common responses to the method has been something to the effect that the readers wished they could have had it years and years ago. As a result, a conscious effort was made in Vol. III to include the things the author himself wished he could have had years and years ago.

Although every effort has been made to produce the books accurately, and without error, a certain amount of errata is to be expected, and the author throws himself at the mercy of his readers on this account. He is eternally grateful to those who send corrections although he kicks over his garbage can and swears in Technicolor® every time another mistake is discovered.

Recommended Reading

This section is intended to serve as both a general bibliography and recommendation for further study, amusement, and enlightenment.

The Rolling Stone History of Rock and Roll, Miller
Making Music, George Martin
The Schillinger System of Musical Composition, Schillinger
The Musicians Business and Legal Guide, Mark Halloran
Harmony, Walter Piston
The Guitar Book, Tom Wheeler
Fundamentals of Musical Acoustics, Arthur Benade
Clive, Inside the Record Business, Clive Davis
Hitmen, Frederick Dannen
Rock Hardware, Tony Bacon
Complete Guitar Repair, H. Kamimoto
The Beatles Recording Sessions, Lewisjohn
Guitar Electronics, Donald Brosnac
Home Recording for Musicians, Craig Anderton
The Ultimate Guitar Book, Tony Bacon
American Guitars, Tom Wheeler
The Harvard Brief Dictionary of Music, W. Apel
Psychotic Reactions and Carburetor Dung, Lester Bangs
This Business of Music, Shemel and Krasilovsky
A Whack On The Side Of The Head, Roger von Oech
The Guitar And Other Fretted Instruments, Albert Birch
Treatise On Harmony, Rameau
Sensations Of Tone, Hemholtz
The Craft Of Musical Composition, Hindemith
The Book of Musical Anecdotes, Norman Lebrecht
Hammer of The Gods
Star Making Machinery
World Book Encyclopedia
The Rolling Stone Interviews

Glossary

A tempo - return to previous tempo

Accelerando - Gradually increase tempo

Accent - Emphasis added to a tone or group of tones usually occurring on the first beat of a measure. Emphasis added to normally weak beats is termed syncopation.

Accidentals - 1. The symbols which increment notes by half steps. They are the sharp, flat, natural, double sharp and double flat. 2. Notes that are in a key "by accident".

Accumulated error - a term for when unnoticeable imperfections are multiplied until they become noticeable. Describes a little known problem concerning methods of tuning in which each successive string is used as a reference pitch.

Acoustics - The branch of physics dealing with sound therefore providing the scientific basis for all musical phenomena.

Action (guitar) - the distance from the top of frets to the bottom of the strings. This distance the string must travel to reach the fret.

AKA - abbv. for also known as.

Alteration - Changing a tone in half step increments. See accidentals.

Analysis - The separation of a whole into its constituent parts, and the determining of the proportions of those parts.]

Arpeggio - A chord played like a scale. Chord tones played in succession.

Articulation Techniques - the various non-standard methods of activating the strings such as hammer ons, pull offs, etc.

Attenuation - a reduction in strength, weakening. Pertains to sound as it is managed and perceived.

Beat - The repetitive temporal unit of rhythm.

Backbeat - A common time rhythm in which the accent is on the 2 and 4 counts as opposed to the 1 and 3.

Bar, barre- The use of the index finger to fret multiple strings for the purpose of playing forms in various positions.

Glossary

Bar lines - In notation, the vertical lines that separate one measure from another.

CAGED Sequence - The arrangement of chord and scale forms as they occur naturally on a guitar fretboard.

Cent - 1/100 of a semitone. This is the unit of measurement of intervals. There are 1200 cents in an octave, and the chromatic scale is 0, 100, 200, 300, 400, etc., cents. Compare to frequency.

Changes - Term used to describe the motion from one guitar chord to another.

Chord - A group of three or more (different) tones sounded simultaneously. On a guitar, chords are perceived as forms in positions.

Chord Form - A fretboard pattern which results from the combination of the guitar's tuning system and the twelve tone system of music indicating notes to be played simultaneously. There are five basic chord forms.

Clef - In standard notation, the symbol at the beginning of a composition which determine the relative pitches of the lines and spaces.

Comping - a corruption of the term accompaniment. For guitarists is generally strumming rhythmically to a progression.

Course - in stringed instrument design, a pair of strings played as one.

Crossover - A change of position on the fretboard such that the left hand passes over its previous position.

D.C. al Coda - Da Capo al Coda - return to the beginning of the piece and continue to the Coda sign, then jump to the Coda.

D.C. al Fine - return to the beginning of the piece and play to the Fine.

D.S. al Fine - return to the Segno (sign), play to the Fine (end).

D.S. al Coda - return to the Segno, and continue to the Coda sign, then jump to the Coda.

Degree - A numerical value ascribed to notes in a key for the purpose of equating them in any key.

Diatonic Scale - A scale with seven tones. Aka heptatonic.

Glossary

Dot - A mark placed after a note indicating to increase its duration by one half.

Downbeat - Refers to the downward motion of a conductor's baton. The downbeat is the strong, usually first, count of a measure.

Duration - The length of time a note is held or tone sounded.

Enharmonic - Acoustically equivalent. Same tone but with different names.

Equal Temperament - A method of tuning the pitches of the twelve tone system whereby the octaves are favored as true, meaning exact frequency doubles, and the other intervals are adjusted in relation to them. Equal temperament imperfectly corresponds with the overtone series since the intervals other than the octaves are not true. The system makes each key is the equivalent of the next, and harmonic activity involving multiple key areas practical.

Etude - A composition usually intended to improve a certain technique.

Extension - A finger reach out of the normal playing area.

Fine - Marks the end of the music

FingerPicking - Aka Travis Picking. Right hand guitar style featuring a repeating pattern. Associated with Merle Travis and Elizabeth Cotten.

Five Basic Forms - The five chord and scale patterns which result from the guitar's tuning.

Form (guitar)- A distinct fretboard pattern resulting from the instrument's tuning system in combination with musical systems. Contrast with chord, scale, etc.

Formula (chord)- The combination of odd numbered degrees of a key and alterations which define each type of chord.

Frequency - The number of occurrences of a specified event within a given interval. The rate of repetitions of a tone. In music it is more or less synonymous with pitch and pertains to the perceived highness or lowness of a tone.

Frets - The metal strips precisely located on the playing area of the guitar enabling easy and accurate intonation.

Function - In harmony the characterization of a chord's tendency to progress to a chord with another function. The three primary chord functions are tonic, sub-dominant, and dominant.

Fusion - when characteristics of more than one style are combined to produce a type of music that is distinct from either of the original styles.

Group (Guitar) - In lead patterns relating each to a chord form for the purpose of naming the scale via form and position. Ex. C group, G group.

Harmony - A simultaneous sounding of tones of a musical nature. In general, the vertical structure of music. Contrast with melody.

Heptatonic - Seven toned.

Hertz - A term used to denote cycles per second. Abbv. Hz.

Interface - The common boundary between adjacent regions. In guitar this pertains to the operational aspects of the instrument as a pattern organization between the player and the music.

Interval - Any two notes sounded either simultaneously or in succession. The distance in pitch between two notes.

Intonation - 1. The accuracy of pitch in producing music. Adherence to correct pitch. 2. (Guitar) - setting - The positioning of the string saddles to permit highest possible accuracy of pitch.

Inversion - In music when the order of the notes of a chord are changed such that a note other than the root is the lowest tone.

Iteration - Repetitions and layers of repetitions.

Key - a group of notes derived from the twelve tone system.

Keynote - The first and central note in a key. Aka tonic.

Key Signature - The sharps or flats at the beginning of a composition specifying the notes to be altered, and indicating the key.

Lead Pattern - A fretboard pattern resulting from the combination of the guitar's tuning system and the twelve tone system of music indicating notes to be played in succession. There are two basic lead patterns and they differ from scale forms in that they are regular patterns in various positions. Contrast with scale form.

Glossary

Learning - The process by which changes in behavior result from experience or practice. Most forms fall into four categories: classical conditioning, instrumental conditioning, multiple response learning, and insight learning.

Lyrics - The words to a song.

M.M. - Malzel's Metronome or metronome marking.

Mathematics - the study of number, form, arrangement, and their relationships.

Mean-tone tempering - A system of tuning favoring perfect thirds and almost perfect fifths. Inaccurate beyond keys with more than three accidentals.

Measure - A subgroup of beats the first of which is accented. Measures are delineated by bar lines. A measure is a subunit of a musical works meter.

Mechanics (Musical) - The design, construction , operation, application and properties of sound producing devices.

Melody - A succession of tones of a musical nature where each tone possesses the characteristics of pitch and duration. Each successive pitch has direction (motion) relative to the previous one. Each successive duration has rhythm relative to the previous one. The horizontal structure of music. Contrast with harmony.

Meter - The basic organization of beats and accents measure by measure as specified by the time signature.

Metronome - A device that produces a steady beat at a desired tempo.

Mode - A specific tonal orientation. A group of tones with a specified center.

Modulation - The process of changing keys in a composition.

Music - Organized sound. Contrast with noise.

Name, naming - In music the letter and accidental designation of notes, chords, scales, etc. Contrast with type and function.

Noise- Non-musical sounds of a disorganized nature.

Notation - A system of symbols for recording music in written form.

Note - A musical concept denoting specific pitch and duration values. Ex. the G# note; half-note etc. 2. The written symbol itself. Contrast with tone. Generally, the note is what you see, the tone is what you hear.

Nucleus - In guitar, a form in which the degrees occur in succession from string to string starting from the root. In other instruments, this is termed "root position".

Octave - A pitch and its double. The term octave in music pertains to the eighth alphabet letter.

Glossary

Open (Guitar)- Unfretted.

Open Position - Chords, scales, etc. played from the lowest possible point on the fretboard and including unfretted notes.

Pentatonic - Five toned.

Phrase - A musical statement.

Physics - The science of matter and energy and their interactions. Branches of physics include acoustics, mechanics, optics, thermodynamics, electromagnetism, etc.

Pitch - The relative highness or lowness of a tone.

Power Chords - Common name for intervals of a fifth played with heavy distortion. Often includes octave as root, fifth, root.

Position - The number of the fret by which a form is referenced, usually by the index finger.

Progression - A sequence of chords.

Pythagorean Scale - A scale attributed to the Greek philosopher and mathematician whereby all tones are derived from the interval of the fifth and the ratio of 3:2 thereby matching the naturally occurring overtone series. See temperament, equal temperament.

Quatrad - A four note chord, aka seventh chord.

Rasgado- Sweeping the strings with the thumb or successive fingers to produce a rapid arpeggiation of the strings.

Re-entrant tuning - a tuning system whereby certain strings which would be low ordinarily, are tuned higher, usually by an octave, or vice versa.

Resolution - A period of repose or harmonic inactivity following tension such as a consonant tone, interval, or chord following a dissonant one.

Rest - A temporary cessation of tonal activity of a specific duration.

Ritardando - Gradually decrease tempo

Rhythm - In a general sense, anything that pertains to the durational characteristics of music. Rhythm is normally metric in nature in that its values are multiples of a temporal unit known as a beat. Beats are grouped into units termed measures (of time). In a more specific sense, rhythm is the patterns formed by the arrangement of note (duration) values.

Root - The first and lowest degree of an interval, chord, scale or arpeggio and note which specifies its name.

Rubato - "Robbed time" where strict adherence to timing is disregarded.

Scale - A group of notes sounded in succession.

Scale Form - A fretboard pattern which results from the combination of the guitar's tuning system and the twelve tone system of music indicating notes to be played in succession. Scale forms differ from lead patterns in that they are irregular patterns in only one position. Contrast with Lead Pattern.

Sequence - 1. A succession of events, forms, notes etc. 2. Musical and non-musical data stored in digital form.

Seventh Chord - A four note chord, aka quatrad. The seventh chords are Major seventh, minor seventh diminished seventh, augmented seventh, dominant seventh, and minor seventh flat five.

Song - Music form consisting of lyrics, melody and harmony.

Sound - Low frequency vibration normally within the range of human hearing of 20-20K Hz. With the exception of electronic oscillation, musical sound occurs when an elastic body is caused to vibrate. The two primary characteristics of musical sound are frequency and amplitude.

Staff - The five lines of standard notation on which pitches are placed.

Style - Pertains to the types of music as distinguished by cultural, historical, geographic, ethnic, religious, socioeconomic, and demographic considerations.

Sweep - Term used to describe arpeggios played with a chordal right hand technique.

Symmetrical Chords - Chords whose lower and upper intervals are the same.

Syncopation - In rhythm when an accent is on a weak beat creating an unusual metric result. Off beat.

Tablature - A system of notation esp. for the guitar specifying the strings and frets to be played.

Target note - The final note in a phrase.

Technique - The physical aspects of playing.

Tempo - Relative speed at which a piece or section is played.

Tempo 1 - Return to original tempo.

Temperament - Various systems of tuning the pitches of the twelve tone system such that certain intervals are 'tempered' or deviated against the acoustically correct pitches of the Pythagorean scale. Systems using acoustically perfect intervals place a practical limit on the number of keys and harmonic material possible.

Tension - A physiological effect of notes, intervals and chords on the listener. Pertains to the dissonance of certain combined tones and suspense created in a musical composition.

Theory - The study of pitch and time relationships in music.

Tie - A curved line from one note to another indicating to sustain duration for the value of both notes.

Timbre - sound quality as determined by the relative strength of a sound's over-tones. That which distinguishes tones of equal frequency and amplitude from one another.

Time Signature - The two numbers at the beginning of a musical composition specifying its meter. The number on top determines how many beats per measure; the number on the bottom determines what type of note gets a beat.

Tone - An audible frequency with the qualities of pitch, duration, intensity, and timbre. Contrast with note. In common usage, the tone is what we hear, whereas the note is what we see when written.

Tonic - The first and central note in a key. Aka keynote.

Triad - A three note chord. The four types of triads are Major, minor, diminished and augmented.

Tuning System - In a stringed instrument, the combination of a specific number of strings or courses, with a specific intervallic spacing. Refers specifically to the modern guitar's six open strings tuned in intervals of 4th, 4th, 4th, 3rd, & 4th, the result of which is an integral pattern organization of chord forms, scale forms and lead patterns.

Twelve Tone System - A system of divisions of a pitch and its double ($12\sqrt{2}$) such that there are twelve pitches (semitones) of equivalent value between them (inclusive).

Type - Pertains to an interval's, chord's, scale's, etc. musical character, such as a "minor" chord or a "Major" scale. Contrast with name and function.

Upbeat - Refers to the upward motion of a conductor's baton. Upbeats are the weak beats in a measure.

Voice - An individual part of a chord or esp. a choral composition.

The Last Word

There are different ways to learn the truth about music. This is how I learned it. Our band used to practice at night in an office building owned by the singer's parents. One day her brother, Johnny, who has Downs Syndrome (actually PDD-NOS), came along to watch us play. The deal was he'd get to sit in with us pros if he behaved himself and didn't disturb us while we practiced. Throughout the rehearsal he sat quietly with his hands folded in his lap fiercely determined not to bother us while we polished our playlist for what must have seemed like an eternity to him. At the end of the rehearsal, he joined in on the one song he knew, "Johnny B. Goode" and there came a transformation you had to see to believe. It is not possible to adequately describe the sheer unrestrained intensity with which he threw himself into that song. His face turned beet red, the veins popped out of his neck, and his shirt was soaked with sweat. His eyes rolled around in his head while he screamed at the top of his lungs, his body a writhing, twisted, Gumby-thing. Ok, he got the words wrong, he got the chords wrong, and he got the melody wrong, but he got the important part right. He got "it" right. He reached down and grabbed hold of the essence of some unnameable force that makes music transcendent. I realized later that the passion, intensity, and raw emotion that he put into "Johnny B. Goode" made the rest of us look like frauds. That's how I learned the truth about music.

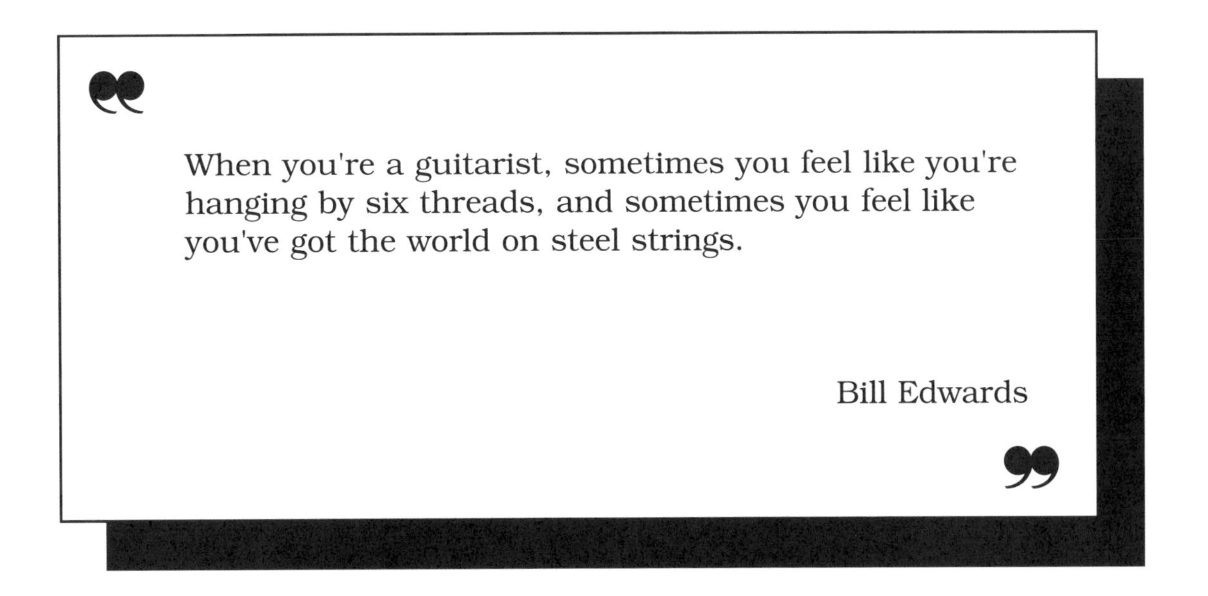